More Critical Acclaim for *Cracking Eastern Europe ...*

" ... a treasure trove of valuable information for those interested in investing and trading in those Eastern European countries in transition."

> *John P. Hardt*
> Associate Director
> Congressional Research Service,
> U.S. Congress

"Country-by-country, detail-by-detail, a truly comprehensive guide to trading with the world's newest emerging and fastest growing markets — a valuable reference for doing business in the global marketplace."

> *Janet Harris-Lange*
> President
> National Association of Women
> Business Owners

" ... should be required reading for business executives planning to do business in the new and expanding markets of Eastern and Central Europe. This excellent book gathers comprehensive information and puts it into an extremely 'user-friendly' format...saves time, energy and frustration, while providing an extra competitive edge in a very aggressive business environment."

> *Lew W. Cramer*
> Assistant Vice President
> US West, Inc.

" ... helps the interested business person focus his investment research."

> *Judith D. O'Neill, Esq.*
> International Telecoms Partner
> Steptoe & Johnson

CRACKING EASTERN EUROPE

EVERYTHING

MARKETERS

MUST KNOW

TO SELL

INTO THE

WORLD'S

NEWEST

EMERGING

MARKETS

**ENDERLYN
DZIGGEL**

PROBUS PUBLISHING COMPANY
Chicago, Illinois
Cambridge, England

This publication is designed to present, as simply and accurately as possible, general information on the subject. It should be noted that the information presented is not all inclusive. Processes may have altered due to rapid changes in the industry. This publication should not be used as a substitute for referring to appropriate experts and is sold with the understanding that the publisher is not engaged in rendering legal, accounting, or other personalized professional service. If legal or other expert assistance is required, the services of a competent professional should be sought.

ISBN   1-55738-254-9

Printed in the United States of America

BB

2   3   4   5   6   7   8   9   0

DEDICATION

This book is dedicated to those corporations with vision who are accepting their role as leaders, and as powerful resources of human energy and money, to effect social change and raise the quality of lives in countries around the world. Their decisions, based on an awareness of global ethical responsibility, can positively affect our basic problems of hunger and poverty, the environment, and the lives of children.

TABLE OF CONTENTS

LIST OF FIGURES

APPENDIX

LIST OF TABLES

ALBANIA

BULGARIA

HUNGARY

POLAND

ROMANIA

YUGOSLAVIA

APPENDIX

PREFACE

This book has been written to assist Western firms and individual entrepreneurs crack the virgin marketplace in Eastern Europe. In addition to Albania, Bulgaria, Czechoslovakia, Hungary, Poland, Romania, and Yugoslavia, the territory of the former East Germany is also covered, since in most respects it is still on a par with its Eastern brethren — and hence, still a very attractive business opportunity.

The Introduction provides a regional overview. It compares and contrasts the individual country situations and highlights a few of the common themes to be encountered.

In the chapters that follow, each country is profiled separately. The same basic topical outline is covered for each country: historic and geographical contexts; socioeconomic and market demographics; politics and finance; policies to attract business; and important contacts and statistics. A map and key points are also included for each country.

Each chapter concludes with a listing of key business contacts for the region, including U.S. government and multilateral resources. A comprehensive listing of key resources and trade shows follows. Finally, an exhaustive compendium of useful statistics is provided in the Appendix.

ACKNOWLEDGEMENTS

The authors wish to thank Margaret Engle, Mike Frischkorn, Eric Nelson, Dr. Elizabeth Robinson, Eleanor Enderlin, Taba, and our family, friends, colleagues, and all the people at Probus Publishing Company who were so supportive during the creation of this book.

We are especially grateful for the assistance of the many people of the emerging democracies of Eastern Europe, the Baltics and the Commonwealth of Independent States, whom we have met and worked with throughout our travels.

INTRODUCTION

METAMORPHOSIS

Within a year of the liquidation of the Iron Curtain, which divided its artistocratic boulevards and symbolized the harsh Cold War posture of East versus West, Berlin has become *the* most desirable city to locate corporate offices in all of Europe. At least two international magazines reported the results of site selection surveys and analyses which ranked Berlin well above such traditional business hubs as Brussels, Paris, and London. Welcome to the 1990s!

The reason is quite simple. Berlin, which existed as an island outpost of capitalism surrounded by the former German Democratic Republic (East Germany) for four decades, is today fully integrated with the whole of Germany. This integration brings with it an arsenal of benefits. The benefits from the East include abundant skilled labor at relatively low wages (initially one-tenth that of West Germany), prime real estate for development, and the most technologically advanced economy in all of what once was the East Bloc. From the West comes a staggering influx of fresh capital (for example, well over 50 billion deutsche marks will be spent on the modernization of the telephone network in the former East Germany) and access to the more than 320 million consumers in the European Community (EC).

The integration of the two Germany's foreshadows the scope and pace of the Pan-European economic integration which will be firmly underway by the year 2000. According to United Nations population projections, the European region will have 576 million inhabitants by then, approximately one-quarter in the territory once defined as Eastern Europe. As a first important step in this integration, Poland,

Hungary, and Czechoslovakia reached agreement with the EC in October 1991 to become full EC members as soon as economically viable. Most observers believe that this could occur early in the next decade. The metamorphosis of Eastern Europe has begun.

A NEW PLAYING FIELD

The term East Bloc has always been a deliberate misnomer. While correctly characterizing the Soviet post-war hegemony of the region, it also conveyed the false impression of unity and union. In reality, the geopolitical boundaries which defined many of the states in Central-Eastern Europe were quite artificial and potentially volatile. The armed hostilities in Yugoslavia are clearly indicative of this.

Despite the existence of a free trade zone among the members of COMECON and CMEA (similar to the EC and EFTA), which theoretically integrated the economies of Eastern Europe with the Soviet Union and the Baltic states, in practice entire industrial sectors (such as consumer electronics and computers) were hermetically sealed compartments that were responsive solely to the command economist-planners in Moscow. There was very little "spin-off" value in the domestic economy and far less value in the neighboring countries. Obviously, without pricing mechanisms and the free flow of goods, capital, and labor, misallocation of resources was the rule rather than the exception.

Today, the political barriers to regional cooperation and trade have been eliminated. In most of the capitals of Eastern Europe, democratically-elected governments have been empowered to implement free-market reforms. In some countries, for example Poland, the leadership has moved swiftly by enacting "flash cut" price decontrol and privatization of assets. Yugoslavia's changes, for example, were purely cosmetic.

The barriers still remaining will be overcome slowly with time and massive amounts of technology transfer and capital. Basic principles of market economics and business management are still understood at only the rudimentary level by the vast majority of the population. Massive environmental cleanup must be undertaken. This is conservatively estimated at over $100 billion over five years. Power plants and factories must be refurbished or replaced with current technology. Most of the technology is comparable to Western technology in the 1940s.

Basic infrastructure such as roads, telephones, and energy are woefully inadequate to meet Western expectations of efficiency in commerce. For example, the roads connecting most of the capitals and industrial centers in the region are poorly maintained two-lane highways. Travel is slowed further by long delays in border check-points — not to mention herds of sheep or ox-drawn carts blocking roads along the way in Romania and Bulgaria.

Perhaps more important for today's information-driven society, communications links are unreliable. Even in the capitals and major cities, call-block-rates are in excess of 50%. This means that only every other call attempt even gets a dial-tone. Lately, international connections to the West from hotels in the East have made great progress (spurred by hard currency incentives), but communications among the countries of the region are still crippled. There are no immediate incentives to improve, as payments in East currencies are abhorrent.

What all of this means to the astute Western business person is a virgin market with enormous potential for growth. With some of the countries already firmly politically committed to ascendancy to the EC, economic transformation to meet tough EC conditionality (not to mention International Monetary Fund and World Bank standards for loans) is certain to continue at a brisk pace. Already, EC technical standards and specifications are routinely employed in procurement tenders ranging from automobile safety to telephone systems to pharmaceuticals.

The aspirations of several of these countries to regain their pre-war positions as economic powerhouses and cultural centers must not be underestimated. For example, the leadership of the Czech & Slovak Federal Republic (CSFR) has often invoked the notion of rivaling Germany as the industrial center of Continental Europe. They assert the unverified claim that Czechoslovakia's per capita income was the third highest in the world in the 1930s and 1940s. Is this realistic? Most Westerners would be surprised to learn that Czechoslovakia ranked number 21 in Gross National Product (GNP) in 1989, the year of its "velvet revolution," behind Belgium, but ahead of Austria.

General economic conditions in the region are good, particularly in those countries that have implemented concrete price and ownership reforms. Poland is in the lead, with Hungary and Czechoslovakia closely tied for second. Inflation, which was in the high double-digits for much of 1989 to 1990, has held steady between 4%-7% in these three countries. Certainly, the political risk exposure is far less than in many Latin American and African countries, and the up-side potential is far greater.

Deriving hard currency (or free, unrestricted convertibility on the world's financial markets) from business operations is still a challenge, but much has been accomplished since the fall of 1989. Many countries have solid laws governing ownership, trade, and commerce and a healthy crop of Western attorneys, accountants, and business facilitators have sprung up throughout the region. Certain sectors, particularly those catering to Western customers (hotels and cellular telephone providers) and export-oriented businesses are doing quite well.

In addition, European multilateral and bilateral aid is swamping Eastern Europe on all fronts, including technical assistance grants, structural assistance loans, and funding of large infrastructure projects, such as construction of power plants and roads. The United States has earmarked $720.5 million in SEED money (Support for East European Democracy) for the period of fiscal year 1990 to fiscal year 1992, while Non-U.S. multilateral aid (including the World Bank and the European Bank for Reconstruction & Development, based in London) totaled $8.5 billion in commitments as of May 1990, reaching $11 billion by October 1991.

CULT OF ENTREPRENEURSHIP

A Westerner arriving for the first time in Warsaw, Budapest, Prague, or Sofia today will be met with a remarkable hustle-bustle of small-scale entrepreneurial activity. In each city, several square blocks are set aside as pedestrian-only, fostering a wide assortment of street vendors not unlike those found throughout Western Europe. Wares may range from "exotic" fruits (bananas, for example) to prerecorded music cassettes featuring Madonna and Aerosmith to furs and caviar.

Some of these vendors are displaced workers who were dismissed as inefficient factories and shops were closed or privatized. But most are likely to have been labeled "black marketers" under the previous regimes. Even under martial-law conditions prevalent in much of the region for decades, intuitive entrepreneurs have prospered and are now free to ply their trade in the open.

Moving up the socioeconomic ladder, there has been widespread privatization of small shops and service organizations, now run largely by "mom and pop" owners. In some cases, these are families who emigrated during the communist regimes and have now repatriated to join friends and families. The restructuring of this important "middle class" has gone relatively swiftly and without much incident in most of the countries.

The privatization and restructuring of the large-scale megaenterprises has been far less successful, although clearly the process is far from over. The Soviet style of production was characterized by large conglomerates mandated to produce massive quantities of wares without regard to quality, cost, or demand. Consequently, the plants were notoriously inefficient and environmentally devastating. As a general rule, most products produced in Eastern Europe were produced for consumption in the Soviet Union and "sold" at unrealistically low prices in order to receive energy from the Soviet Union, also at vastly subsidized prices. With the collapse of the Soviet market, most of the industrial sector is struggling. Despite wage rates less than one-tenth that in the poorest EC member state, much of the industrial sector will require substantial retooling to be competitive with the West.

There were, nonetheless, a few gems among the rubble. General Electric acquired Tungsram of Hungary, which produced world-class lighting fixtures and equipment. The transaction price was around $150 million in 1989. Several Western automobile manufacturers have likewise acquired plants and assembly facilities in the East for handsome sums.

But many of the large "properties" suffered from stalled negotiations or unenforceable contracts. In the early days of the new republics, it was unclear who "owned" these facilities. Was it the Communist party, the workers, the management, or the local city council? In many cases, there were competing claims.

This meant that "parallel negotiations" were often necessary to achieve some degree of legitimacy of the stake. Unfortunately, the Western deal-makers were not the only ones employing this strategy — quite a number of deals stalled when it was revealed that contracts were nonexclusive (meaning that the identical "exclusive concession" was in fact assigned to numerous parties). The successful deals were those which ensured that all interested parties or claimants walked away with something.

Initially, "sour grapes" also played a significant role in the sabotage of some of these deals. Former Communist party bosses saw an end to the gratuitous lining of their pockets and actively interceded to spoil the perception that democracy and free market reforms would benefit the masses. Some obviously believed — and certainly hoped — that the "glasnost" experiment would invariably collapse within a short period of time. Their goal was to see the demise happen sooner rather than later. Others merely rode with the wave, reluctantly changing their Communist affiliation to fit the fashion, in an attempt of preserving their own jobs.

THE SEARCH FOR "GREEN PASTURES"

Based on the lessons learned from the initial rounds of deal-making, many companies abandoned the search for "gems" and concentrated on "green pasture" opportunities. Several factors made this strategy inherently more attractive. First, in many cases, "green pastures" literally meant that nothing had been built or developed on that site, and thus there were few if any competing claims of ownership. It also indicated that the risk of environmental liability was considerably less than in situations where a plant had been in full operation for decades without environmental controls or documentation. Second, building from scratch meant that one could be perceived as the "good guy" — creating jobs and not eliminating them. Third, it was far easier and made more business sense to assemble good in-country business partners, rather than partners who were merely being "bought off" to make the deal work. Finally, there actually were some real gems. For example, a prime piece of real estate was found in Bratislava, Czechoslovakia (which sits on the Danube River directly across from Vienna). Hundreds of prime riverfront acres were found to be in the hands of a single family — no construction was permitted for the past 40 years, since the site formed the "no-man's-land" of the Iron Curtain between Czechoslovakia and Austria. (Mine removal may be necessary, of course!)

GIVING NEW MEANING TO "BANKING RELATIONSHIPS"

While Eastern Europe has made great progress in a very short time, many wrinkles still need to be worked out. There is still a critical gap in the service sector, especially service which does not require "greased palms" for routine transactions (this definitely still includes the bureaucracy). For example, a major Western airline with offices throughout the region employs locals on a full-time basis simply to maintain a "personal relationship" with their banks. It found that if their employees were not physically on the premises of the bank, routine transactions simply were "set aside."

Westerners who are used to jumping in their cars to conduct business will find that this can only be accomplished with careful logistical planning, especially on cross-border trips. Gasoline/service stations are still relatively sparse, rarely carry lead-free gasoline or are often sold out. Romania still requires Westerners to purchase gasoline with coupons, at four times the local rate. Parking is universally a problem throughout the region and there are few parking lots or garages. Driving Western cars, especially with Western license plates, invariably invites "citations" regardless of the circumstances. Fortunately, most citations are inexpensive by Western standards (for example, $5 to $10 for traveling 160 km/hr in a 60 km/hr zone). Lastly, most Western car rental firms restrict cross-border travel for fear of theft.

For cross-border travel, railroads are an equally poor choice. Besides lengthy delays at the border, most trains make local stops every few minutes, thus lengthening the duration of a trip considerably. Service onboard is poor but getting better.

Air travel is relatively easy between the capitals throughout the region and especially to major hub cities in the West (Frankfurt and Zurich are especially superb). Soviet Aeroflot used to provide regular connections between most of the major cities in the East, as well as connections to the Baltics, the Soviet Union, and selected points abroad (such as Cuba). As of the dissolution of the Soviet Union, however, most service has been canceled and will likely be unreliable in the future.

Most countries have their own national airline. Malev Hungarian Airlines probably offers the best onboard service, followed by LOT Polish Airlines. The Czechoslovak Airlines are known by their insignia "OK" and are generally just that. The planes are only marginally more comfortable than a freighter. The other carriers primarily link only with major international destinations such as Moscow, Frankfurt, and New York.

English is the primary business language throughout the region, closely followed (often grudgingly) by German. French is spoken among officialdom and some parts of Romania. Most Westerners will have difficulty orienting themselves in Bulgaria and the Serbian region of Yugoslavia, as the Cyrillic alphabet is used (derived from the Greek). The Cable News Network (CNN) is readily available at most Western hotels throughout the region, as are the major entertainment channels from Western Europe via satellite. MTV and American rock and roll have made a solid impression among the youth, even in the most remote villages of Romania and Albania.

Office space is extremely hard to find throughout the region and is expensive. In January 1992, prices ranged from 25 to 50 deutsche marks per square meter per month in the major capitals; prices are generally quoted in deutsche marks. The realtor/agent market is in its infancy, and in fact, most businesses locate space through classified newspaper advertising or personal contacts.

As a general rule, the best method of market entry is through a local partner. Besides the obvious benefits of language capability, potential business contacts, and market insights, many organizations can also offer sorely needed office space and other amenities. In this context, the former foreign trade organizations (FTOs) are surprisingly good partners.

Under the Communist regimes, these FTOs often held the monopoly rights for the import and export of virtually all commodities and had vast networks of contacts worldwide. With the collapse of the Soviet market, the FTOs are shrinking dramatically, and thus offer superb access to surplus space and human resources. For example, one highly successful FTO in Czechoslovakia has seen its annual revenues halved in the period from 1989 to 1991, with a commensurate reduction in force (its revenues nonetheless exceed $700 million annually). Since it owns large modern office buildings throughout Czechoslovakia, including one in the center of the most lucrative district in Prague, they make for a potentially attractive partner.

As elsewhere in the world, gaining a solid understanding of the market and establishing a local presence are fundamental elements of establishing a successful business in Eastern Europe. Such efforts in Eastern Europe will be richly rewarding in the decades to come.

CRACKING EASTERN EUROPE

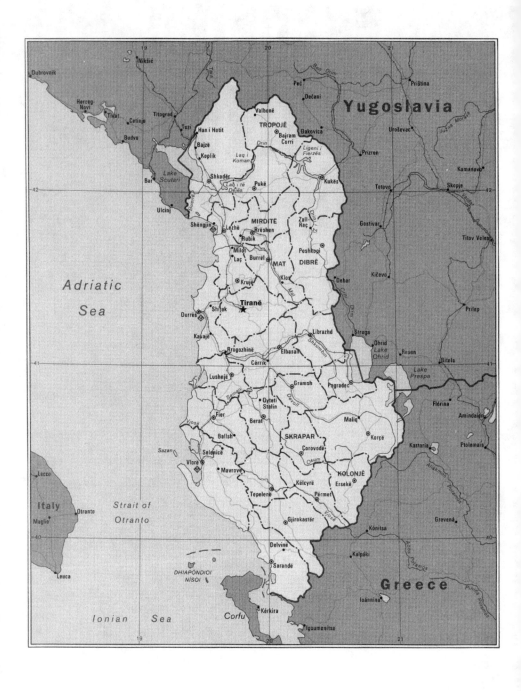

ALBANIA

ALBANIA
In a Nutshell

		Urban Population
Population (1992)	3,200,000	34%

Main Urban Areas		Percentage of Total
Tirana (Capital)	225,700	7.05
Durres	78,700	2.45
Elbassen	78,300	2.44
Shkodra	76,300	2.38
Vlore	67,600	2.11
Korca	61,500	1.92

Land Area   11,099 square miles
27,400 square kilometers

Comparable European State   Slightly smaller than Belgium
Comparable U.S. State   Slightly larger than Maryland

Language   Albanian (dialects: Gheg, Tosk)

Common Business Language   None

Currency   Lek (= 100 Quindarkeas)

Best European Air Connection   Frankfurt (Lufthansa)

Best Ground Connection   Athens (500 kilometers)

Best Hotel   None

CHAPTER CONTENTS

INTRODUCTION AND REGIONAL ORIENTATION

Geographical and Historical Background

Slightly larger than the state of Maryland, Albania is wedged between Yugoslavia and Greece, situated at the entrance to the Adriatic, across from Italy. The terrain is approximately three-fourths mountainous and one-fourth fertile river valleys and coastal lowlands. The climate is mediterranean along the coast; temperatures inland vary.

Albania came into existence as a principality in 1913. It became independent after World War I in 1920 and was ruled by the increasingly authoritarian regime of King Zog. After a decade of attempts by Yugoslavia, Greece, and Italy to wield influence and dismember it, Albania became dominated by Italy in 1930. Albania was occupied by 1939 and throughout the war by Italian and German troops.

After the war, Enver Hoxha and his communist resistance movement became one of the few indigenous communist movements to come to power in Eastern Europe, possibly giving more legitimacy to its government and less need to rely on the Soviets. The small state was then able to pursue more independent policies than elsewhere in the bloc.

In 1948, Hoxha sided with the Soviet Union against Albania's traditional threat, Tito, in Yugoslavia. This alliance was only temporary, however, and Hoxha broke with the Soviet Union sensing a better opportunity with the newly emerging power China. Albania formally left the Warsaw Pact in 1968, probably prompted by the Prague Spring and crackdown in Czechoslovakia. Albania split with China in 1978, and has been unique in its isolationist policy since then.

Albania under Hoxha has often been referred to as more Stalinist than Stalin himself, due to its reputation for repressive policies and centralized control over politics, economics, and society. Since Hoxha's death in 1985, his successor Ramiz Alia has initiated a series of reforms, mostly geared toward improving economic conditions, which are deteriorating. In December 1990, several opposition political parties were legalized. Both political and economic policies are currently being approached pragmatically.

Albania has been determined to improve relations with the West. One of its goals has been to join the Conference on Security and Cooperation in Europe (CSCE). It was granted observer status in mid-1990. Alia continues to push for full membership, but until Albania's human rights record is improved, such status is unlikely. Efforts to improve relations with the West can even be traced before Hoxha's death, as early as 1983 with increased contacts between Albania and Italian diplomats and business people. The Federal Republic of Germany, France, and Greece also agreed to diplomatic relations in the 1980s.

Alia's regime has also pledged to address Western concerns over human rights issues. These issues were the obstacle to opening relations with the United States, but after holding parliamentary elections on March 31, 1991, the first free elections since 1944, the two countries formalized relations. The two countries have not had formal diplomatic relations since prior to World War II. The State Department has said that the United States hopes to open an embassy in Albania by early 1992. The former U.S. embassy in Tirana is currently being leased by the Italians, so it is not yet available. Two U.S. diplomats were posted to Tirana in November of 1990.

Demographics

Albania is officially an atheist state. Before Hoxha proclaimed it to be an atheist state in 1967, the population was approximately 70% Muslim, 20% Albanian Orthodox, and 10% Catholic. The population of Albania was 3.21 million in July 1990.

The language is Albanian. English has recently become the most widely known second language, especially for business; French and Italian may also be spoken.

Socioeconomic Indicators and Conditions

Spurred by a stagnating centralized economy, the government of Albania has been implementing reforms in the economic system, as well as in political and social spheres. A "New Economic Mechanism" was implemented in 1991 with the goal of replacing the centrally planned economy. However, the new system is not clearly defined; emphasis appears to be on attracting foreign investment, decentralizing industries, and limited privatization. According to U.S. Department of Commerce reports, the per capita gross national product for 1990 was $US 930 (using purchasing power methodology). The population growth rate, approximately 2.1% per year in 1990, is one of the highest in the world. Consequently, the population is quite young, with approximately 50% under 26 years old.

Albania's infrastructure and social programs, especially in medicine and education, are in need of reform. There is a lack of modern medical equipment and technology reported.

Since the relaxation of border controls in 1989, Albanian refugees have been pouring into neighboring Greece and Italy. These refugees occupy the grounds of foreign embassies in the hopes of emigrating. Over 500 Albanians, many part of Albania's large Greek minority or Jews, streamed over the Greek border in late December 1990, causing friction between the warming relations between Greece and Albania. Reports that Albanian border guards were shooting those who attempted to flee across the border also damaged relations. A similar disaster occurred at Durres when many refugees nearly sank ferry boats trying to get to Italy.

Approximately 18,000 refugees were in Brindisi, Italy, in March 1991. Many believe that the refugees are fleeing economic conditions.

Social controls have been relaxed, and Albanians are now allowed to openly practice religion. The first public Christian services were held in December 1990.

Albania has a number of natural resources, including gas, oil, coal, chromium, copper, iron, and nickel. Agricultural products include wheat, corn, potatoes, sugar beets, cotton, and tobacco. Industry is concentrated in textiles, timber, construction materials, fuels, and semiprocessed minerals.

Despite those resources and products, the recent economic prognosis is grim (Table 1-1). According to the State Department, agricultural output has fallen by 35% to 50%, in 1991, and manufacturing lost 11% to 13% of its output in 1990. Albania is facing energy shortages, and its inflation rate is estimated to be 30% per year and rising out of control. The gross national product is estimated to fall below $500 per capita for 1991. The New Economic Mechanism has recently been abandoned, and the government has made an appeal for international aid. Industries are reported to be poorly organized and there is inadequate technology. Other problems include shortages of staple goods.

Table 1-1: Domestic Economy

	1986	1987	1988	1989
GNP ($B)	N/A	N/A	N/A	N/A
GNP Growth (percentage)	1.6*	1.8*	N/A	N/A
GNP per Capita ($)	930*	940*	N/A	N/A
Assets w/BIS Banks ($M)	15	100	139	268**
Liabilities w/BIS ($M)	42	83	113	261**
Exchange Rate ($US 1=leks)	6.66	6.17	5.69	6.00*

* Estimate
** End June 1990

Source: U.S. Department of Commerce. International Trade Administration. 1991. *Foreign Economic Trends and Their Implications for the United States—Albania*. Washington, D.C.: Government Printing Office.

Political/Institutional Infrastructure

The political and institutional framework in Albania, like that in most East European states, appears to be undergoing a process of change. Most importantly, the "leading role" of the Communist party has been reduced, albeit only slightly, since opposition parties have been allowed to form, free elections have been held, and the top leadership has called for bureaucratic changes. President Ramiz Alia, for example, recently resigned from all his posts in the Communist party, which included the party's first secretary and memberships on the Central Committee and the Politburo, in order to comply with new constitutional requirements. Alia has also been critical of the inefficiency of the bureaucracy and has called for a stronger rule of law in speeches.

The legislative body in Albania is made up of a multiparty, 250-seat Parliament.

Political Organization

The Albanian government is communist, based on the constitution of 1976. The executive branch is lead by the Chairman of the Presidium of the People's Assembly, Chairman of the Council of Ministers. The unicameral People's Assembly is the legislative branch. The Supreme Court, regional, and district courts comprise the judicial branch. There is universal and compulsory suffrage for those over age eighteen.

The Albanian Party of Labor (communist) still holds most of the power in Albania. Opposition parties were legal only as of late 1990, the main one being the Democratic party. Sali Berisha is one of the key opposition leaders. Other parties include the Republican party and the Ecology party.

In 1991, the Albanian Party of Labor committed itself to attracting foreign investment, purchasing new technology, and developing public services. A proposed revised constitution would allow citizens to participate in foreign investment and travel abroad, but the centralized economy would be maintained. On the other side, the Democratic party supports radical economic reform and the transition to a market-based system.

President Ramiz Alia of the Labor Party is the Head of State. He formerly held all key party positions, but he resigned them in May 1991 in order to comply with new constitutional requirements. In February 1991, Alia named a new government, including the appointment of Fatos Nano to the post of premier. Nano, an economist, is reputed to be more reform-minded than his predecessor Adil Carcani. The new government did not include any members of the opposition parties.

The Council of Ministers is the executive body. The head of government is Prime Minister Fatos Nano.

Political Party

In the March 1991 elections, the Labor party received 168 seats (out of 250). The main opposition party, the Democrats, won 75. The Labor party's strength was in the rural areas, while the Democrats took the urban areas. The Democrats boycotted Parliament in April 1991, however, in response to the shooting of four party members protesting against alleged vote fraud.

Federal/Regional/Municipal Organizations

Albania is divided into 26 districts.

Trade Flows

Top 10 Import/Export Trade Partners

Albania's main trade partners are Yugoslavia, Italy, Romania, West Germany, Hungary, Czechoslovakia, and Greece. Yugoslavia accounted for approximately 12.5% of Albania's total trade in 1984, according to the U.S. Department of State. Trade with CMEA members for that year was approximately 42% of total trade, and trade with the West and developing countries was approximately 45% (Table 1-2). Trade with China was only approximately 1% of the total. Albania has refused to trade with the Soviet Union in the past. Trade with the United States was conducted through intermediaries in third countries.

Table 1-2: Trade Statistics

	1986	1987	1988	1989
Global Exports ($M)	147	170	185	230*
Global Imports ($M)	78	100	165	245*
Global Trade Balance ($M)	69	70	20	(15)
U.S. Exports (FAS $M)	4.5	3.3	7.2	5.3
U.S. Imports (CIF $M)	3.1	2.1	2.4	2.8
U.S. Trade Balance ($M)	1.4	1.2	4.8	2.5

* Estimate

Source: U.S. Department of Commerce. International Trade Administration. 1991. *Foreign Economic Trends and Their Implications for the United States—Albania*. Washington, D.C.: Government Printing Office.

Top 10 Import/Export Commodities

Albania has emphasized increasing its exports of raw materials, especially in minerals (such as barite, fluorite, albitophyre), refractory clays, and decorative stones. Its manufactured goods are not considered competitive in world markets, which may account for the fact that less than 36% of Albania's foreign trade is with industrialized countries. Major exports in 1984 were in electricity, metal ores, copper, petroleum, coal, tobacco, and textiles. Imports were concentrated in machinery and equipment.

Principal U.S. exports include coal, spare parts, hoods, measuring instruments, microscopes and plastics. U.S. imports include medicinal plants, nutmeg, foliage, metal coins and printed matter.

The U.S. Department of Commerce has identified the best investment potential to be capital goods and raw materials needed for production. Albania has noted needs to import cotton, rubber, leather, plastics, industrial oils, coal, oil, cast-iron, processed aluminum, synthetic threads and fibers, livestock fodder, and pharmaceuticals in 1991. Electricity and foodstuffs will also be necessary. Finally, there has been some interest by Albania in importing consumer goods, such as televisions and VCRs, refrigerators, washers, radios and cassette players, sewing machines, clothing irons, watches, and hair dryers.

Policies to Attract New Business

The Albanian government passed the country's first law on foreign investment in July 1990; the law's emphasis is on investments that will increase exports, create jobs, and improve technology transfers. German, French, Italian, Chinese, and Bulgarian firms have made notable investments. Albania has concluded trade agreements with Yugoslavia, Greece, France, Belgium, and Germany.

Preferred Foreign Investment Projects

Albania seeks investment and assistance in renovating or constructing bottling plants, food processing industries, mining and refining centers, and cigarette plants. Other assistance is needed in capital goods, raw materials, and consumer goods.

Tourism is also a sector in which foreign investment may prove viable. Albania offers 217 miles of coastline, similar to that of Yugoslavia and Greece. The number of tourists in 1990 (30,000) increased by approximately 10,000 more than the number in 1989, indicating the potential market. Business opportunities include: sales of hotel and restaurant equipment, hotel management contracts, and construction contracts to upgrade, renovate, and build new hotels. Joint ventures in hotels and coastal or ski resorts are also possible.

Investment Incentives and Privileges

Foreign investments receive national treatment, according to the Foreign Investment law. Authorization for an investment is to be obtained from the Council of Ministers. Investments in the banking sector must also seek approval of the Albanian National Bank.

The application for authorization requires the name of the enterprise, the center of activity, data on foreigners involved, nature and organization of the enterprise, and a study of the enterprise's work, including a technical and economic analysis. Authorizations may be issued for up to ten years, and applications for extensions of authorizations must be made one year prior to the expiration of initial authorization.

Trade transactions may be done independently or in cooperation with the Albanian foreign trade organizations. Financing is possible using the lek or foreign currency. Foreign currency accounts must be obtained at the Albanian National Bank; accounts at foreign banks need separate approval. Foreign investors may obtain credit in foreign currency from the bank.

Tax Incentives

Taxes will be determined by the Ministry of Finance, and enterprises must turn in the firm's balance sheets at the end of the year. Materials or equipment imported for the production of exports or for reinvestment are exempt from customs duty.

APPROACHING THE MARKET

Foreign Trade and Investment Decision-Making Infrastructure

Although Albania may prove to be a long-term, high-return investment, the risks are also high. The state has a monopoly on trade, so the investment decision-making structure is highly centralized and bureaucratic, thus a possible detriment to potential investors.In addition, not only is there significant foreign debt (estimated to be $US 500 million in 1990 and to exceed $US 1 billion by the end of 1991) but the political situation is extremely volatile. The State Department predicts that the authority will collapse, and the transition will not be peaceful.

Setting Up Business Operations

A license is necessary for all imports into Albania. Applications should be filed with the Ministry of Foreign Trade. The Albanian State Bank must also approve international transactions. The Albanian Foreign Trade Organization importing the goods is responsible for getting the necessary approvals.

Shipping must include commercial invoice and bill of lading. Sanitary and inspection certificates will be specified in the contract when required. Insurance should be obtained from the Albanian State Bank for Savings and Insurance.

In May 1991, the U.S. Department of Commerce reported that no information is available on Albanian customs duties.

Agents and Distributors

The state monopoly on foreign trade has been retained. Foreign firms must work with one of the state trade organizations that make purchasing decisions to negotiate contracts and oversee details of the transaction.

Setting Up Offices, Retail Stores, and Service Facilities

Foreign ownership of real estate is prohibited. Property must be leased from the government.

Transportation and Freight (Air/Sea)

About one-quarter of Albania's 3,100 miles of roads are paved. Trucks and buses run, but traffic is light. Stagecoaches are still used, but primary means of transportation for Albanians are bicycles or walking. Donkeys are used to haul cargo. The Albanian government signed a contract with Greek construction firms to construct a 124-mile highway from the Greek border to Durres.

Railways include 317 miles, mostly of standard gauge, but none are electrified. In 1986, Shokder and Titograd, Yugoslavia, were connected by rail. Inside Albania, main lines run from Shokder (north) to Vlore (south) and from Durres (west) to Pogradec (east). New rail lines to mining sites and the coast are reportedly planned. Approximately one-third of freight traffic is currently on the railways.

Of Albania's four seaports — Durres, Vlore, Shengjin, and Sarande — Durres handles most of the foreign trade.

Only Rinas Airport, 25 kilometers from Tirana, handles international flights. A new air traffic control service was established in October 1990; Albanian officials are working with representatives from the European Air Traffic Control Organization and Italian authorities to allow flights from Italy, Yugoslavia, and Greece to pass over Albanian air space.

INVESTMENT CLIMATE

Privatization, Investment Protection, and Dispute Settlement

Albania, like most of the other East European countries, has taken steps toward the privatization of state-run enterprises. In January 1991, the government announced plans to allow people not related to each other to form small-scale private enterprises. This expanded the initial decree of July 1990 that legalized such businesses as long as ownership was restricted to a single family.

Law suits and arbitration may be used to settle disputes over the expropriation of an investment. Labor disputes are resolved by Albanian courts. Disputes involving foreign workers should be resolved according to terms specified in the employment contract.

Joint Ventures and Wholly Owned Subsidiaries

There have been no U.S. joint ventures reported so far.

FINANCING AND CAPITAL MARKETS

Banking and Other Financial Institutions

The State Bank of Albania, the central bank, regulates the money supply, finances enterprises, and manages foreign exchange transactions and international banking relations.

The opening of Illiria Bank, the first bank in Albania with foreign capital, is indicative of the government's commitment to attracting foreign investment and development assistance. Formed by the Swiss company Illiria Holding SA and the Albanian National Bank in December 1990, the bank began trading in January 1991. A priority of the bank is attracting foreign capital and investment to Albania, especially to the trade, light industry, tourism, construction, and food markets.

The Albanian Central Bank is Banka e Shtetit Shqiptar, Tirana, Albania. Tel: (355) (42) 24-35, 21-54. Telex: 2153, 2133, 2118.

Payment Modalities

Currency

The lek is Albania's currency. It is not convertible. In January 1991, the official exchange rate was 10 leks = $US 1. The black market rate was reportedly 25 times that. Albania maintains strict controls over foreign exchange.

Foreign investors have the right to repatriate part of their earnings under Article 25 of Decree 7407. According to the U.S. Department of Commerce, this provision had not been tested as of May 1991, so it is unclear whether repatriation of local currency profits will be allowed.

Countertrade and Buybacks

Countertrade is frequently used to finance transactions using exports such as bauxite, copper, aluminum oxide, cement, chromium, oriental tobacco, sunflower oil, herbs, Persian carpets, petroleum and its products, iron nickel ore, marble, nickel silicate ore, pig iron, fur hats, gloves and coats, urea fertilizer, and handicrafts.Some of the difficulties a firm may encounter in countertrade deals include low quality products and untimely fulfillment of contracts.

Tapping International Aid Institutions

Albania has modified its New Economic Mechanism and appealed for international assistance to help alleviate the impending collapse of the country's economy. The Italian government has provided a $US 900 million credit line, promising an additional $US 750 million to be invested in the transportation infrastructure. Albania has applied for membership in the World Bank and the International Monetary Fund (IMF), and its application may be accelerated by the World Bank, but the IMF and European Community (EC) are pushing for radical economic and political reforms before approving aid. Albania is a member of the United Nations and specialized organizations, including International Atomic Energy Agency, International Telecommunications Union, World Health Organization, Food and Agriculture Organization, Universal Postal Union, and World Meteorological Organization.

LICENSING, PATENTS, AND TRADEMARKS

Trademark, Patent, and Copyright Protection

Patents and inventors certificates are the forms of legal protection for patents. Although a patent gives the inventor legal ownership, the invention can be licensed only to a state enterprise. Patents are valid for 15 years from the date of application. Inventors' certificates provide recognition for the inventor, but the state maintains ownership of the invention. In these cases, the inventor is compensated for the use of the invention. Certain items, such as chemicals and medical and biological inventions, are not patentable; only inventors' certificates are available.

Trademarks, conferring exclusive rights to the owner, are entitled to be registered by the first applicant, according to Decree Number 2490 of July 22, 1957, as amended on June 1, 1967. The registered trademark is enforceable. Foreign citizens may register trademarks only if a reciprocal agreement exists between the citizen's country and Albania and if a proof of registration in the home country can be provided. As of May 1991, no agreement exists between the United States and Albania. Trademark registrations are valid for ten years from the date of application and may be renewed for additional ten-year periods. Foreign trademark registration may not exceed the period of registration in the country of origin. There are 34 classes of goods for registration. If the trademark is not used within three years of its registration, the exclusive right expires.

Copyright protection is provided to literary, artistic, and scientific materials under Decree Number 538 on Copyrights of September 24, 1947, as amended in 1951. Foreign works are protected only if published for the first time in Albania. Copyright protection is for the life of the author. After the author's death, the copyright shall be given to the spouse until death or remarriage, or to the author's children until they are 25 years old.

VISITING AND LOCATING

General Travel Checklist

The United States reestablished diplomatic relations with Albania in Spring 1991. However, there is still no American embassy, and consular assistance is newly installed (November 1991). The State Department has also issued travel advisories urging caution when traveling in Albania because of political unrest and demonstrations. Most travel to Albania is restricted to participation on group tours.

Visas

Visas, necessary for business and tourist travelers, may be processed through any Albanian embassy. There is not yet an Embassy in the United States, so it is recommended that Americans use the Paris Embassy. Business travelers who plan to travel outside of Tirana must complete additional documents as well as the standard visa. Visa requests may be faxed to: Krenar Haderi, First Secretary, Embassy of the Republic of Albania, Paris. Fax: (33) (1) 45-53-89-38, Tel: (33) (1) 45-53-51-32. Requests will be forwarded from there to Tirana for approval.

A request should include a cover letter outlining the purpose of the visit; any travel information available, including proposed dates of travel and where the visa will be picked up (Rome, Belgrade, Athens, Paris embassy); name, date of birth, place of birth, father's name, job title (for business travelers); passport number; and brief proposed itinerary. Visa requests should be made well in advance, since they may take a while to approve.

Information may also be obtained through the Permanent Mission of the People's Socialist Republic of Albania, 320 East 79th Street, New York, New York, 10021. Tel: 212-249-2059.

Currency

The currency is the lek. It is illegal to exchange money outside of authorized banks and to export leks. Black market transactions are not recommended. It should be kept in mind that it is difficult to exchange unused leks for hard currency.

Getting Around

The easiest method is probably by tour bus, which are relatively new and comfortable. Travel may be slow, however, due to carts and animals on the roads. Tourists may also want to be aware of the Albanian custom of nodding to mean "no" and shaking the head to mean "yes."

Accommodations and Housing

Foreign visitors usually stay in the Hotel Tirana on Skanderbeg Square or the Hotel Dajti on Martyrs of the Nation Boulevard, the two government hotels. Both accept Mastercard and Eurocard, as does a hotel in Durres and a shop at Rinas Airport. It is recommended that you drink bottled water, not tap water.

Electricity Supply

Eighty percent of the electricity is from hydropower. Recent drought conditions have forced Albania to import electricity. Coal is also a source of electricity.

Telecom, Postal, and Courier Services

Telephone service between the United States and Albania was established in May 1990, and direct dial has been possible since fall 1990. The country code for Albania is 355. The Tirana city code is 42.

Albania operates 14 AM radio stations and four FM stations. There are nine television stations. International broadcasts are received from Yugoslavian and Italian television. There are approximately 50,000 televisions and 210,000 radios in Albania.

Business Hours

Holidays in Albania include the following: New Year's Day, January 1; Republic Day, January 11; Labor Day, May 1; Revolution Day, November 7; Independence Day, November 28; and Liberation Day, November 29.

There is a six-day work week. Many stores close between noon and 4:00 p.m. Banks are open from 7:30 a.m. to 11:30 a.m.

Tipping

Albanians are not legally allowed to accept tips in hard currency. It is frequently done anyway, but you are urged to be discrete in giving tips.

What to Wear

One travel writer warns that men with long hair or beards may find them clipped by immigration authorities, although this was not supported by the writer's experience. Jeans are allowed, but conservative attire is suggested.

Health Care

Sanitary conditions are reported to be significantly below Western standards. Travelers are advised to bring toilet paper, wet wipes, or similar products.

Availability of Foreign Products

Such items will be available only at hard currency shops, usually found in hotels. There are some souvenirs, as well as products like soft drinks and juices.

Shopping

Shops may be open only sporadically. Carrying small bills and coins is advised, because most transactions will take place in hard currency stores that may not have the correct change for larger bills or may provide change only in lek.

Dining Out

Hotels serve preset menus.

Sightseeing and Tourist Information

Group travel is the recommended way to see Albania. Information may be obtained from: Albturist, Deshmoret e Kombit Bul., 6 Tirana, Albania. Tel: (355) (42) 38-60, 48-53. Telex: 2148 HODAJT AB.

The embassies in France and Italy also have sightseeing and tourist information. In Greece, contact Albturist-Pianitis, 3 Akadernias, Athens 10671. Several travel agencies in Great Britain also handle tours. They include:

- Regent Holidays, 13 Small Street, Bristol BS 1DE. Tel: 2722 11711.
- Voyages Jules Verne, 10 Glenkworth Street, London NW1 5PG. Tel: 011 44 71 486 8080 or 486 8084. Fax: 011 44 71 486 8571. Some Americans have not been allowed into Albania from Britain, but this policy is under discussion with Albanian officials.
- Exotik Tours, 1117 St. Catherine St. West, Suite 806, Montreal, Quebec, H3B 1H9. Tel: 514/284-3324; 800/361-1007. Fax: 514/843-5493.
- Pecum Tours, 2002 Colfax Avenue South, Minneapolis, MN 55405. Tel: 612/871-8171. 800/231-4313 for bookings. Fax: 612/871-8502.
- Delta Reizen, Hardewikerstraat 3, 9712 GR Groningen, Postbox 1577, 9701 BN Groningen. Tel: 011 31 50 146200. Fax: 011 31 50 138740.
- Kontakt International, Prins Hendrikkade 104, 1011 AJ Amsterdam. Tel: 011 31 20 323 4771. Fax: 011 31 20 3258057.
- International Cruise Center, 250 Old Country Road, Mineola, New York 11501. Tel: 516/747-8880. 800/221-3254. Fax: 516/747-8367.

The Short-Term Business Visitor

Airlines Serving

Airlines that fly into Rinas Airport, 25 kilometers from Tirana, include: Swissair, Lufthansa, Air France, Alitalia, Olimpik (Greek), Tarom (Romanian), and Malev (Hungarian).

The Expatriate

In addition to the information needed by the short-term visitor, the expatriate needs to know how to set up bank accounts; how to find housing and where to live; the nature of the school system for expatriates; and holidays observed.

Hourly/Annual Mean Wages

Wages for foreign workers are stipulated by labor contracts. Wages and social security provisions for Albanians must meet requirements set by Albanian law. New wage rates went into effect on October 1, 1990, raising the monthly salary to approximately 570 leks ($US 57) and the minimum monthly income to 450 leks ($US 45). The average wage is 6,000 leks per year (approximately $US 600), according to U.S. Department of Commerce statistics. Wages for employees of private businesses will not be fixed.

Labor Force

The labor force is predominantly rural. More than half are thought to be farm workers.

Employment and labor relations.   The labor union declared itself independent from the Communist party in 1990 and vowed to fight for better working conditions and higher wages.

By January 1991, miners were on strike demanding wage increases and better working conditions. Initially, the state warned that it could offer no better than increasing wages up to 50%, lowering the retirement age from 55 to 50, and providing free transportation to and from work. Before the miners returned to work, however, the state was forced to concede a pay increase of up to 60%, as well as promising improved working conditions. The Communist party's acknowledgement of the strike, the first-ever since it came to power, indicates the relaxation of Stalinist control.

Conditions of work.   The regular work week is six days. Opposition political parties have included a change to a five-day work week as part of their platform.

ALBANIA

KEY CONTACTS FOR BUSINESS

Albanian Commercial Office
1131 University Boulevard #1122
Silver Spring, MD 20902
   Tel: 301/649-4562
Contact: Sazan Bejo, Charge D'Affairs

Albanian-American Trade Association
1010 Vermont Avenue, NW #512
Washington, DC 20005
   Tel: 202/737-0213
   Fax: 202/347-0625
President: James V. Elias
Executive Director: Robert C. Gordon
(Publishes *Albanian-American Trade Advisory* for members)

Albanian-American Civic Association
   Tel: 202/547-7580 (Washington metro)
   Tel: 914/472-6872 (New York metro)
Director: Former U.S. Congressman Joe Diogurdi

UNIREX Center
205 Import Circle
Huntsville, AL 35806
   Tel: 205/852-8888
   Fax: 205/851-7384
Contact: S. Bego Cason
(Formed to act as clearinghouse for major Albanian project solicitations/tenders)

U.S. Department of Commerce
ITA/East European Division
14th & Constitution, NW Room 3413
Washington, DC 20230
   Tel: 202/377-4915
Albanian Desk Officer: Lynn Fabrizio (January 1992)

Chamber of Commerce of the People's Republic of Albania
Konferenca e Pezes Street
6 Tirana
    Tel: 355-42-7997 or 4226 or 2934
    Telex: 2179 DHOMA AB

Albanian Central Bank
BANKA E SHTETIT SHQIPTAR (The State Bank of Albania)
Tirana
    Tel: 355-42-2435 or 2154
    Telex: 2153 or 2133 or 2118

Government Officials (December 1991)

President (Head of State):   Ramiz Alia

Council of Ministers

Chairman (Prime Minister, Head of Government):   Vilson Ahmeti
Deputy Chairman & Minister of Mining & Energy Resources: Abdyl Xhaja
Deputy Chairman & Minister of Agriculture: Zydi Pepa
Minister of Foreign Affairs: Ilir Bocka
Minister of Economy: Gjergji Kondo
Minister of Defense: Alfred Moisiu
Minister of Public Order: Vladimir Hysi
Minister of Justice: Kudret Cela
Minister of Finance: Robert Ceku
Minister of Food & Light Industries: Iliaz Mehmeti
Minister of Foreign Economic Relations: Ylli Cabiri
Minister of Home Trade & Tourism: Robert Gjini
Minister of Construction: Luigji Aleksi
Minister of Transportation: Ilir Mataj
Minister of Education: Alfred Pema
Minister of Culture, Youth & Sports: Vath Korreshi
Minister of Health: Kristo Pano
Chairman of State Control Commission: Ylli Memisha
Chairman of Committee of Science & Technology: Petrit Skende

Albanian Commercial Offices in Europe & Mexico

AUSTRIA

Embassy of the People's Socialist Republic of Albania
Jacquingasse 41
A-1030 Vienna
Tel: 43-222-783-795
Telex: 133248

BULGARIA

Embassy of the People's Socialist Republic of Albania
bu. Asparouh 8
BG-1000 Sofia
Tel: 359-2-521-467 or 522-414

CZECHOSLOVAKIA

Embassy of the People's Socialist Republic of Albania
22 Pod Kochtany
CS-12520 Prague 6-Bubenec
Tel: 42-2-379-329

FRANCE

Embassy of the People's Socialist Republic of Albania
Rue de la Pompe 131
F-75116 Paris
Tel: 33-1-553-5132
Telex: 611534

GREECE

Embassy of the People's Socialist Republic of Albania
Colonakis rue Caracristou 1
Athens
Tel: 30-1-723-4412
Telex: 210351

HUNGARY

Embassy of the People's Socialist Republic of Albania
1063 Munkacsy Mihaly utja 6
Budapest 6
Tel: 36-1-229-278

ITALY

Embassy of the People's Socialist Republic of Albania
Via Asmara 9
1-00199 Roma
Tel: 39-6-838-0725
Telex: 614169

MEXICO

Embassy of the People's Socialist Republic of Albania
Solon 337, Polanco 5
CP 11560
Telex: 1771391

ROMANIA

Embassy of the People's Socialist Republic of Albania
Aleea Stefan Gheorghiu 4
Bucharest
Tel: 40-0-793-180

SWEDEN

Embassy of the People's Socialist Republic of Albania
Tyrgatan 3-A
S-11427 Stockholm
Tel: 46-8-219-145

TURKEY

Embassy of the People's Socialist Republic of Albania
Nene Hatum Cad. 89
Gazi Osman Pasa
Ankara
Tel: 90-4-274-929

TURKEY

Consulate General of the People's Socialist Republic of Albania
Tesvitiye omer Rustu Pasa
Sokak 3
Istanbul
    Tel: 90-1-466-470
    Telex: 26042

YUGOSLAVIA

Embassy of the People's Socialist Republic of Albania
Kneza Milosa 56
Belgrad
    Tel: 38-11-646-864

Albanian Foreign Trade Organizations

AGROEKSPORT
4 Shkurti Street
6 Tirana
    Tel: 355-42-5227 or 5229 or 3128 or 4179
    Telex: 2137 AGREKS AB
Services: Imports and exports agricultural products, livestock, and seafood.

INDUSTRIALIMPEKS
4 Shkurti Street
6 Tirana
    Tel: 355-42-4540 or 4051 or 5490 or 6123 or 2711
    Telex: 2140 INDEKS AB or 2112 IMP AB
Services: Imports and exports artistic handmade articles, chemical, textiles and apparel, and consumer goods.

MINERALIMPEKS
4 Shkurti Street
6 Tirana
    Tel: 355-42-3370 or 5832 or 3848 or 4667 or 5832
    Telex: 2123 MINEKS AB or 2116 METIMP AB
Services: Imports and exports minerals, metals, and decorative stones.

MAKINAIMPORT
4 Shkurti Street
6 Tirana
    Tel: 355-42-5220 or 5221 or 5224 or 5225 or 3267
    Telex: 2127 or 2128 MAKIMP AB
Services: Imports agricultural equipment, appliances, medical equipment, drilling equipment, transportation equipment, telecom equipment, computers and electronics, and machine tools. Exports explosives.

ALBKOOP
4 Shkurti Street
6 Tirana
    Tel: 355-42-4179
    Telex: 2187 ALBKOP
Services: Imports and exports textiles and apparel.

TRANSSHQIP
4 Shkurti Street
6 Tirana
    Tel: 355-42-3076 or 4659 or 7429
    Telex: 2131 TRANSH AB
    Cable: TRANSSHQUIP - Tirana (Albania)
Services: Enterprise responsible for transporting Albanian exports and imports internationally by sea, road, and rail.

ALBKONTROLL
Bul. E. Hoxha
45 Durres
    Tel: 355-42-2354 or 3377
    Telex: 2181 ALBKON AB
Services: Enterprise responsible for the inspection of imports and exports regarding quality, packing, marking, labeling, classification and division of goods, control of the storage facilities, suitability of the transport method, and loading and unloading of the goods. Either party in a trade transaction may request ALBKONTROLL's services.

ALBTRANSPORT
Rinas Airport
Services: Enterprise that provides services related to the air transportation of passengers and cargo, including aeronautical services and airport ground handling services. Its services are authorized by bilateral agreements signed between the Albanian government and the civil aviation authorities of foreign governments.

ALBTURIST
Deshmoret e Kombit Bul.
6 Tirana
    Tel: 355-42-3860 or 4853
    Telex: 2148 HODAJT AB
Services: Enterprise responsible for operating all facilities and services related to tourism within Albania.

NDERMARRJA E PERHAPJES SE LIBRIT
Konferenca e Pezes Street
Tirana
    Tel: 355-42-3323
Services: Imports and exports books, newspapers, magazines, and other publications.

BULGARIA

BULGARIA
In a Nutshell

		Urban Population
Population (1992)	9,065,000	67%

Main Urban Areas		Percentage of Total
Sofia (Capital)	1,128,859	12.45
Plovdiv	356,596	3.93
Varna	305,891	3.37
Burgas	197,555	2.17
Ruse	190,450	2.10
Stara Zagora	156,441	1.73
Pleven	133,737	1.47
Tolbukhin	111,037	1.22

Land Area	42,823 square miles
	110,550 square kilometers
Comparable European State	Moderately smaller than Greece
Comparable U.S. State	Slightly larger than Tennessee
Language	Bulgarian (Cyrillic alphabet)
Common Business Language	English
Currency	Lev (= 100 Stotinki)
Best European Air Connection	Frankfurt (Lufthansa, Delta)
Best Ground Connection	Athens (500 kilometers)
Best Hotel	Sheraton Balkan Sofia
	($225 per night as of 1/92)

CHAPTER CONTENTS

INTRODUCTION AND REGIONAL ORIENTATION

Geographical and Historical Background

Bulgaria, located in Southeast Europe on the east side of the Balkan Peninsula, measures 110,910 square kilometers of total area. It is bordered by Romania on the north, Greece and Turkey on the south, Yugoslavia on the west, and the Black Sea on the east. Although much of the terrain is mountainous and hilly, there are also vast plains. In 1989, of the total population of 8.97 million, 1,137,000 lived in the capital city, Sofia. Other heavily populated cities include Bourgas (200,000), Rousse (91,000), and Varna (306,000). The overall climate is best described as moderate continental, but temperatures vary between extremes in the mountains and mild weather in regions near the Black Sea.

Bulgaria was founded as a Slav-Bulgarian state under the leadership of Khan Asparouh in 681. For nearly a century and a half, it came under the rule of the Byzantine Empire. After a brief period of independence in the 12th century, the Ottoman Empire gained control and ruled from 1396-1878. Bulgaria became an independent state in 1878 following the Russo-Turkish Liberation War. During the interwar period, Bulgaria initially leaned toward parliamentary and social democracy, but a fascist coup in 1923 brought authoritarian rule to the state.

During World War II, Bulgaria joined the Axis Pact. By 1944, however, it became clear that Germany was losing. Seeking to cut its losses, Bulgaria switched sides after the government was overthrown in a coup. With assistance from the Soviet Red Army, a communist movement called the Fatherland Front took over the state. The communists consolidated their power over the next few years, and Bulgaria was declared a republic in 1946 after a national referendum.

Bulgaria was a hard-line communist state until November 1989, when, following the events in other East European states, communist leader Todor Zhivkov was removed from power after 35 years of rule. Unlike many of the other East European revolutions, however, the ouster amounted to an internal party coup, rather than the replacement of the government by a former opposition group. The Communist party quickly renamed itself the Socialist party and retained its grip on the country by winning the majority of seats (211 of 400) in the legislative elections of 1990, becoming the only communist party to do so in the East European revolutions of 1989. Despite those election results, the Socialist party is far from having a solid grasp on the future of Bulgaria.

The new government, led by Prime Minister Andrei Lukhanov, faced rapidly deteriorating socioeconomic conditions and was unable to successfully initiate economic and political reform. This was primarily due to the inability of the Socialist party to form a coalition with opposition parties, particularly the Union of Democratic Forces. In November 1990, mass demonstrations and strikes forced the resignation of Lukhanov. The protests can be viewed as evidence of the population's increasing intolerance of the communists, as well as increased public input into the system.

The new Prime Minister, Dimitar Popov, who does not belong to any political party, formed a coalition government in early December 1990, but political, social, and economic conditions remain unstable. Political intolerance may be the most difficult barrier for the Popov government to overcome, and there is always the possibility of the coalition's collapse and a reactionary backlash by the opposition.

The situation, however, is not bleak on all fronts. The mere fact that such demonstrations have been permitted in what has traditionally been one of the most Stalinist states indicates the degree to which social and political controls have been relaxed. In addition, Bulgaria has restored or improved foreign relations with a number of states in the West and the Vatican. For example, a clear indication was the government's announcement that it would allow researchers access to state archives to determine any possible Bulgarian involvement in the 1981 Pope assassination attempt.

Demographics

Of the total 1989 population of 8.97 million, approximately 85.3% are Bulgarian. Significant minority groups include Turkish, 8.5%; Gypsy, 2.6%; Macedonian, 2.5%; Armenian, 0.3%; and Russian, 0.2%. As in most East European countries, ethnic tensions are resurfacing and beginning to play a major role in politics. Bulgarian-Turkish relations are particularly difficult, because the relaxation of social controls has prompted a Turkish movement as a reaction against the 1984-1986 Turkish Assimilation campaign.

Bulgarian Orthodox is the dominant religion, comprising 85% of the population. Other religions include Muslim, 13%; Jewish, 0.8%; Roman Catholic, 0.5%; and Protestant, 0.5%. The official language is Bulgarian.[1]

Socioeconomic Indicators and Conditions

Despite earnest attempts at economic and political reform, Bulgaria has been paralyzed by chronic food and consumer goods shortages, a lack of energy and fuel supplies, and a worsening financial crisis. The international embargo with Iraq and reductions in oil obtained from the former Soviet Union have further strained domestic economic conditions. For example, in some parts of the country electricity is available only 12 hours per day, and foodstuffs and gasoline are rationed. Local shops are frequently empty. Frustration with living conditions led to mass protests in Sofia, resulting in former Prime Minister Andrei Lukhanov's resignation.

At the same time, 1990 saw a major drop in production and little growth of the Bulgarian economy (Table 2-1). This can be attributed to political uncertainty, as well as to the drastic economic reforms instituted in January 1989. Despite the official removal of the government's legal monopoly on foreign trade organizations, the Bulgarian Socialist party has been slow to reduce its control over economic affairs. Also, the failures of previous reform efforts has done little to inspire enthusiasm for the reform process. Lingering doubts persist about its effectiveness and whether it will be fully implemented. There is some reason for optimism, however. Politicians signed an agreement in January 1991 aimed to promote a peaceful transition to democracy. The accord set general elections for May 1991 and local elections for February or March 1991.

Even in difficult years, Bulgaria has traditionally been a net exporter of food, primarily fruit, vegetables, meat, poultry, and wine, so the prospects of a food shortage are particularly indicative of Bulgaria's problems. The underlying reality is not so much an actual shortage of produce, but a shortage of product being put on the market. Both peasants and suppliers are hoarding produce in the hope that policy debates will be resolved in their favor. Peasants are pushing for land reform measures and suppliers want higher prices.

Table 2-1: Key Indicators for Domestic Economy

	1986	1987	1988	1989
GNP (1985 $B)	60.7	61.1	64.2	66.2
GNP Growth (percentage)	5.0	0.7	5.0	3.2
GNP per Capita ($)	6,767	6,812	7,157	7,380
Gross Dept ($B)	5.1	6.3	7.8	8.9
Net Debt ($B)	3.70	5.26	6.03	6.97

Source: U.S. Department of Commerce. International Trade Administration. 1991. *Foreign Economic Trends and their Implications for the United States—Bulgaria.* Washington, D.C.: Government Printing Office.

Political/Institutional Infrastructure

Political Organization

The Dimitrov Constitution of 1947, which formed a People's Republic, was revised in 1971, establishing the state council, the highest executive body, as the supreme body of state power. A new constitution is proposed for 1992.

The national legislature is a unicameral Parliament, a national assembly, with 400 seats. The last elections were on June 10 and June 17, 1990. Parliament is elected to two-year terms.

President Zhelyn Zhelev, elected August 1990, is the head of state. Other key officials that make up the national government include Prime Minister Dimitar Popov, Minister of Foreign Affairs Victor Valkov, Minister of Foreign Economic Relations Atanos Paparizov, and Minister of Finance Ivan Kostov.

Political Parties

The majority of the 400 seats in Parliament are held by the Bulgarian Socialist party (formerly the Communist party), which won 211 seats and took 47% of the votes in the 1990 election. Other main political parties with representation in Parliament include Union of the Democratic Forces (the main opposition party), holding 144 seats with 36% of the vote; Bulgarian Agricultural National Union, with 16 seats and 8% of the vote; and Movement for Rights and Freedom (comprised primarily of ethnic Turks), with 23 seats and 6% of the vote (Table 2-2).

Table 2-2: Major Parties with Representation in Parliament after 1990 Election

Party	Percentage of Votes	Seats
Bulgarian Socialist Party	47	211
Union of the Democratic Forces	36	144
Bulgarian Agricultural National Union	8	16
Movement for Rights and Freedom	6	23
Other	3	6

Source: U.S. Department of Commerce. International Trade Administration. 1991. *Foreign Economic Trends and their Implications for the United States—Bulgaria*. Washington, D.C.: Government Printing Office.

Federal/Regional/Municipal Organization

Bulgaria is divided into 29 provinces called okrug.

Trade Flows

Top 10 Import/Export Trade Partners

Bulgaria's leading trade partners for 1989-1990 were U.S.S.R., GDR, Czechoslovakia, Poland, FRG, and Romania. The U.S. trade balance with Bulgaria in 1989 was $123.4 million (Table 2-3).

Table 2-3: Trade Statistics

Bulgarian-Global Trade (in $M)	1986	1987	1988	1989
Global Exports	14,203	16,049	17,293	16,674
Global Imports	15,269	16,357	16,650	15,496
Global Trade Balance	-1,066	-308	643	1,278

U.S.-Bulgarian Trade (in $M)	1986	1987	1988	1989
Imports	55	43	55	57
Exports	106	98	147	181
Balance	51	55	92	124

Source: U.S. Department of Commerce. International Trade Administration. 1991. *Foreign Economic Trends and their Implications for the United States—Bulgaria.* Washington, D.C.: Government Printing Office.

Top 10 Import/Export Commodities

Bulgaria's main imports include machinery and equipment, fuels, minerals, raw materials, metals, chemical fertilizers, rubber, and textiles. Primary exports include machinery and equipment, foods, textiles, fuels, raw materials and metals, chemical products, fertilizers, and rubber. Table 2-4 lists major products traded. Imports from the United States include tobacco, petroleum oils, mixtures of urea and ammonium nitrate, urea, and wine. Exports to the United States include corn, soybeans, polyvinyl chloride, tobacco extracts and essences, and chemical wood pulp.

The best export prospects, as identified by the U.S. Department of Commerce in 1991, include computers and software, electronics, process controls, measuring instruments, chemicals, and plastics.

Table 2-4: Major Products Traded (1989)

Exports	Percentage
Machinery and equipment	59.8
Processed food products	11.8
Industrial food products	11.2
Fuels, mineral raw materials, and metals	7.0
Chemical products, fertilizers, and rubber	3.5

Imports	Percentage
Machinery and equipment	43.3
Fuels, mineral raw materials, and metals	34.6
Other raw materials	5.2
Industrial consumer goods	5.1
Chemical products	5.0

Source: U.S. Department of Commerce. International Trade Administration. 1991. *Foreign Economic Trends and their Implications for the United States—Bulgaria*. Washington, D.C.: Government Printing Office.

Finance and Investment Policies

The primary legislation regulating foreign investment in Bulgaria is Decree 56, passed on January 9, 1989. Foreign investors can establish wholly owned branches or subsidiaries, and limited foreign ownership (over 50%) is permitted, but foreign ownership participation in excess of a 49% stake requires state permission. The decree also stipulates that profits from products of enterprises in the free trade zone are tax-exempt for the first five years. Firms may retain 50% of convertible currency earnings to use in importing inputs or for sale to other firms; repatriation is not guaranteed and must be from export earnings. Wages may be paid in foreign exchange. The decree also allows 100% equity, 70-year leases, and 30%-40% profit terms.

The signing of the U.S.-Bulgarian Bilateral Trade Agreement on April 22, 1991 should help to improve conditions for investors and expand economic and trade relations between the countries. In addition to providing for most-favored-nation status to both states, the agreement provides for American firms in Bulgaria to receive national treatment in establishing bank accounts, as well as the ability to immediately repatriate hard currency earnings. Other benefits that will make doing business in Bulgaria easier include permission to advertise, the ability to contact end-users directly, and the ability to engage local contractors and distributors. Other provisions commit Bulgaria to strengthen its intellectual property legislation and to introduce new legislation on proprietary information and integrated circuit layout designs. Both countries agreed that they will not mandate the use of barter or countertrade in transactions.

The Economic Community (EC)-Bulgarian Trade Agreement, signed April 4, 1990, liberalizes trade, promotes EC investment, and includes a ten-year pact that will ease EC restrictions on Bulgarian imports. The pact also promotes cooperation in agriculture, science, and technology.

Bulgaria has been a member of the International Monetary Fund and the International Bank for Reconstruction and Development since September 25, 1990. It has had observer status to General Agreement on Tariffs and Trade (GATT) since 1967. It is eligible for Support for East European Democracies (SEED) funds, although a Bulgarian Enterprise Fund has not been formed comparable to Poland, Czechoslovakia, or Hungary. It is not formally eligible for Generalized System of Preferences (GSP), although it may be possible under the Jackson-Vanik waiver.

Policies to Attract New Business

Preferred Foreign Investment Projects

Priority sectors include agriculture and agribusiness, infrastructure development, energy, environmental protection, telecommunications, and transportation, especially the airport and roads. The financial sector is also a target area. Tourism was also recognized as a target area for both the United States and Bulgaria in the U.S.-Bulgarian Trade Agreement, which includes rules on the establishment and operation of tourism promotion offices and commercial tourism enterprises in both countries.

Investment Incentives and Privileges

Bulgaria is preparing a Foreign Investment Encouragement Bill. The draft provides protection and security for foreign investments in Bulgaria. The Agency for the Encouragement of Foreign Investment (AEFI) will be responsible for issuing permits to foreign investors. Certain types of enterprises and income, such as those in key sectors like agriculture, may be tax-exempt or taxed at a lower rate.

Tax Incentives

Profits from products with enterprises in the free trade zone are tax-exempt for the first five years.

Free Trade Zones/Special Economic Zones

A free enterprise zone has been set up near Varna. The Rousse International Free Zone provides services to companies operating within this zone (ul. Blagoev 5, BG-7000 Rousse, POB 107. Tel: (359 82) 722 47. Fax: (359 82) 700 84. Telex: (865) 62285).

APPROACHING THE MARKET

Foreign Trade and Investment Decision-Making Infrastructure

Investment permits are obtained and approved, as necessary, by the Agency for the Encouragement of Foreign Investment (AEFI). Foreign investors may still encounter bureaucratic red tape, but most difficulties should be reduced because only joint ventures with foreign investment share in excess of 49% must complete the process. Certain enterprises and partnerships may register through a domestic partner.

State and Private Services

Market Research

Market research and consulting firms include the following:

- Bulgarkonsult (130 Tsar Boris, BG-1000 Sofia. Tel: (395 2) 884 820; 872 355; 802 729. Telex: (865) 23201) for technical assistance and urban planning.
- Club Economic Alternative (Chervena zvzda 165 3a, BG-1390 Sofia. Tel: (359 2) 8451. Telex: (865) 22429; 22349; 22657).
- Eckopt-Escort (ul. Alabin 34, BG-1000 Sofia. Tel: (359 2) 803 558. Fax: (359 2) 881 311. Telex: (865) 23960).
- INFORMA - Information Center for Technology Transfer (ul. A. Chapaev 55a, BG-1574 Sofia. Tel: (359 2) 700 281; 719 003; 718 153. Fax: (359 2) 704 145. Telex: (865) 23178).
- Institut za Prouchavane i Vuzdeystvie na Pazara (Bl. Dondukov 41, BG-1000 Sofia. Tel: (359 2) 878 449).
- Vangelia-A (bul. A. Vitosha 62, BG-1463 Sofia. Fax: (359 2) 800 102).

The Foreign Trade & International Markets Center is the applied research and information services for the Ministry of Foreign Economic Relations (ul. Kaloyan 8, BG-1000 Sofia. Tel: (359 2) 851 31. Telex: (865) 22271).

Incorporation/Registration

For incorporation/registration, U.S. commercial representatives register with the government of Bulgaria in accordance with a simple procedure, codified in the U.S.-Bulgaria Bilateral Trade Agreement.

Twelve Bulgarian state representative agencies are headquartered in the Interpred building in Sofia. Each acts as an individual enterprise, with its own property, bank account, and authority to enter into contracts with Western firms. Agencies are not supposed to represent firms with competing interests, but in reality this is sometimes difficult. A number of specialized agencies not under the Interpred system have developed.

Permission is not required to conclude an agreement with an agency for representation work, but the agency must register the agreement with the Ministry of Foreign Economic Relations within seven days of the signing. There is no limit on the number of years for which agency agreements can be negotiated.

Legal Services

Legal representation, protection, consulting, and other assistance for foreign nationals in Bulgaria and for Bulgarian nationals abroad is available through the Law Office for Foreign Legal Matters (ul. Alabin 31, BG-1000 Sofia, Bulgaria. Tel: (359 2) 877 782; 870 316. Fax: (359 2) 890 581. Telex: (865) 22104).

Setting Up Business Operations

Forms of Business Organization

The Agency for the Encouragement of Foreign Investment (AEFI) will issue permits and regulate foreign investment. Types of investment include the purchasing of stock in existing businesses, setting up joint ventures, or foreign ownership of joint-stock companies and subsidiaries. Investments must contribute to the economy but not become a monopoly, and they must obey all Bulgarian regulations. Joint stock companies with less than 49% of foreign capital do not need permission; applicants should present the application to the proper civil court and the court's ruling to AEFI not later than two weeks after the date the court made the ruling.

AEFI will issue a permit for ventures with over 50% foreign equity. If foreign capital does not exceed $US 3 million, the permit will be issued within 20 days. Otherwise, the permit will be issued within 30 days.

Limited liability company. The principal fund must be at least 50,000 leva. Foreign participation that exceeds 49% must receive permission from the state authority.

Sales Promotion, Fairs, Conferences, and Advertising

The U.S.-Bulgarian Bilateral Trade Agreement provides firms with the right to advertise. Bulgarreklama Agency is the national advertising agency of Bulgaria and arranges official exhibitions (ul. Parchevich 42, BG-1040 Sofia. Tel: (359 2) 85 151 Telex: (865) 22318).

Agents and Distributors

Foreign business people are allowed to hire local consultants and distributors, according to the U.S.-Bulgarian Bilateral Trade Agreement.

Setting Up Offices, Retail Stores, and Service Facilities

Sofcommerce conducts services including commercial and financial operations, engineering and leasing operations, import-export of machinery, equipment and consumer goods, renting offices and sales against foreign exchange, advertising and tourist services (ul. Moskovska 41, BG-1000 Sofia. Tel: (359 2) 393 339. Telex: (865) 22670).

Real estate. Companies with foreign participation or subsidiaries are not allowed to own land. They may obtain fixed-term leases for property and construction.

Transportation and Freight (Air/Sea)

The rail network is 4,033 kilometers, of which 1,994 are electrified. The road network is 32,839 kilometers, of which 2,923 are main roads and 197 are express-ways. Balkan, the Bulgarian airline, provides freight service on domestic and foreign flights. Maritime transport can be obtained through Bulfracht (ul. Gurke 5, BG-1000 Sofia. Tel: (359 2) 875 581. Telex: (865) 22161). Despred provides international forwarding of exports via rail, air, road and water (ul. Slavyanska 2. Tel: (359 2) 876 016. Telex: (865) 22306). Another international transport firm is Mezdoun-arodni Prevozi (Gorublene 438, BG-1000 Sofia. Tel: (359 2) 781 121. Telex: (865) 22356; 22380).

INVESTMENT CLIMATE

Privatization, Investment Protection, and Dispute Settlement

A Privatization Act was passed in March 1991. There are plans to privatize between 15 to 20 companies in the near future. As of April 1991, seven companies have already taken steps toward privatization.

Joint Ventures and Wholly Owned Subsidiaries

Bulgaria has passed relatively liberal joint venture legislation, but the number of joint ventures and the amount of capital involved in joint ventures has been extremely low compared with other Central and East European states. Only 70 joint ventures were registered in 1990. Officials estimated the amount of total joint venture investment in 1990 to be $25 million, with the West's share making up approximately $10 million.

Subsidiaries are more popular to establish because the Bulgarian law is liberal in this respect. The decree provides for low capital requirements and significant tax advantages.

Cooperation Agreements, Leasing, and Franchising

Items subject to leasing include land, plantations or perennial plants, animals, agricultural objects such as dairy or stock-breeding farms, hotels, commercial establishments, public catering and services, construction and means of transport, equipments, and factories. Details regarding the executing of a leasing contract can be found in Chapter Six, Articles 128-138 of the Regulations for the Application of Decree No. 56 on Economic Activity.

Taxation and Regulatory Conditions

Several tax laws are pending. Bulgaria and the United States have agreed on bilateral application of GATT principles, including national treatment on internal taxation and regulations affecting treatment of imported goods.

Joint-stock companies with foreign capital must pay income tax, value-added tax, duties, and excise tax at the rates and fees according to Bulgarian law. Exempt from taxation are licensing fees, income used to buy bonds, fees for technical services related to providing equipment, and income from a company with foreign capital in a free trade zone. Raw materials and equipment to be used in an export-oriented company are also exempt from import duty.

Company Tax

The profits of companies with foreign participation and subsidiaries of foreign businesses are taxed at 30%. The profits of a foreign business undertaking independent activity are taxed at 40%. Profits from goods and activity within free trade zones are exempt from taxes for the first five years and then will be taxed at 20%. Companies with foreign participation of greater than 49% and a value of more than L 5 million in convertible currency, functioning with state approval, are tax-exempt for five years from the date of registration if they act in certain high technology in agricultural and food industries, to be determined by the Council of Ministers.

Personal Income Tax

Personal income, including dividends, shares, interests, royalties from licenses and authorship, remuneration for technical services, and rents are taxed at 15%. The following are exempt from taxes:

- dividends received on the condition that they will be used to purchase stocks and bonds within Bulgaria
- interest on certain loans
- license fees received for items of key industrial importance, as sanctioned by the Council of Ministers
- remunerations for technical services given with the delivery of fully equipped facilities or certain trade equipment

Insurance

The state insurance agency is Bulstrad (ul. Dunav 5, BG-1000 Sofia. Tel: (359 2) 851 91. Telex: (865) 22564).

FINANCING AND CAPITAL MARKETS

Banking and Other Financial Institutions

There are three main Bulgarian banks, in addition to several newly created commercial banks. The Bulgarian National Bank pursues the state banking policy and is the main money-issuing bank. It makes settlements between banks and organizes payments with foreign banks.

The State Savings Bank accepts savings deposits by the public in leva and foreign currency. Although it is primarily for the public, it does also work with some firms. It also issues credits to individuals for the purchase or construction of housing and for their businesses.

The Bulgarian Foreign Trade Bank works primarily in foreign exchange and on account management for companies that hold foreign currencies.

Commercial banks provide credit in leva and foreign currency, acting with their own assets. They also perform most other banking operations. The commercial banks available include: The Agricultural and Cooperative Bank; Bank for Agricultural Credits; Biochim; The Construction Bank; The Economic Bank; Elekronika; Mineralbank; The Transport, Agricultural and Building Equipment Bank; and The Transport Bank.

As of January 1991, the foreign banks in Bulgaria were Banco di Napoli and Societe Generale.

Either most-favored-nation status or national treatment, whichever is better, will be used in maintaining bank accounts; transferring funds between Bulgaria, the United States and third countries; exchange rates; and the use and receipt of local currency. The regulations are detailed in the U.S.-Bulgaria Bilateral Trade Agreement.

Payment Modalities

Currency

Along with the rest of the former CMEA members, Bulgaria began trading on a hard currency basis on January 1, 1991. The official rate in December of 1991 was 15:1. The black market exchange is still flourishing and is approximately double the official rate at 30:1. U.S. enterprises will be able to repatriate hard currency earnings from trade.

Tapping International Aid Institutions

Bulgaria was accepted as a member of the International Monetary Fund and the International Bank for Reconstruction and Development on September 25, 1990.

LICENSING, PATENTS, AND TRADEMARKS

Licensing Policy, Procedures, and Payments

The Patent & Trademark Bureau of the Bulgarian Chamber of Commerce and Industry (bul. Al. Stamboliyski 11a, BG-1040 Sofia) represents foreign nationals in patenting inventions and registering trademarks. Bulgarians registering patents and trademarks abroad also use its services (Tel: (359 3) 872 631. Telex: (865) 22374). Copyrights are registered by Jusauthor Copyright Agency, (Slaveikow Sq. 11, POB 872. Tel: (359 2) 879 111).

Trademark, Patent, and Copyright Protection

Both Bulgaria and the United States adhere to the same multilateral intellectual property conventions. The U.S.-Bulgarian Bilateral Trade Agreement signed on April 22, 1991 obligates Bulgaria to strengthen legislation in trademark, patent, and copyright protection. New legislation on proprietary information and integrated circuit layout designs is also to be introduced.

VISITING AND LOCATING

General Travel Checklist

Visas

Visas are now readily available from Bulgarian embassies around the world, as well as at border checkpoints.

Currency

The Bulgarian currency is the lev. In 1990, US $1 = 0.82 lev. Banknote denominations are 1, 2, 5, 10, and 20 leva. Coins include 1, 2 and 5 leva, and 1, 2, 5, 10, 20, and 50 stotinki (1 leva = 100 stotinki).

Getting Around

Rental cars are available through the Tourist Service and Information Office. Chauffeur-driven rentals and taxi service are also available.

Accommodations and Housing

Balkantourist, through the Interhotels chain, provides accommodations throughout the country. Private lodgings may also be rented. Detailed information, hotel ratings, and price listings can be found in the Balkantourist tariff directory and hotel directory. For reservations, contact: Balkantourist, Sofia, 1 Vitosha Blvd., Telephone: 43 331. Telex: 22567 and 22568. The Bulgarian Association of Tourism and Recreation, in various U.S. cities, can also book housing.

Electricity Supply

Electric outlets provide currency at 220 volts.

Shopping

CORECOM are duty-free shops, which sell Bulgarian and imported goods in convertible currencies. Regular Bulgarian shops are likely to be empty, as suppliers withhold goods in hopes of higher prices.

Dining Out

Folk-style "Mehanas" in Sofia serve traditional Bulgarian cuisine, and some also feature folk song and dance. Restaurants serving Hungarian, Vietnamese, Czech, Russian, and other European cuisines are also available.

Sightseeing and Tourist Information

Balkantourist can provide information and arrange for tours in Bulgaria. Tickets for the numerous cultural and sporting events may also be purchased through Balkantourist.

Recreational Opportunities

Most hotels offer swimming pools and saunas, and some also have tennis courts.

The Short-Term Business Visitor

Airlines Serving

Balkan is the Bulgarian national airline. It services passenger flights and freight on domestic and international flights. In July 1991, Balkan Air began offering non-stop flights from New York JFK to Sofia for $699 (United States dollars) for standard coach fair, with first/business class for only $100 more on a first-come first-serve basis. (These prices are certain to change — consult your travel agent.)

The Expatriate

In addition to the information needed by the short-term visitor, the expatriate needs to know how to set up bank accounts; how to find housing and where to live; the nature of the school system for expatriates; and holidays observed.

Hourly/Annual Mean Wages

Bulgarian law freezes wages in the public sector, which should encourage workers to move into the private sector. Wages may be paid in foreign exchange.

Labor Force

The majority of the labor force, estimated at 4,300,000, work in industry (33%) and agriculture (20%).

Employment and labor relations. Direct hiring practices were legalized in the U.S.-Bulgarian Bilateral Agreement. Parties may negotiate employment contracts. Labor disputes involving Bulgarian citizens will be settled in Bulgarian courts.

A right-wing labor union, Podkrepa, grew in political power in 1990. Nation-wide strikes, initiated by Podkrepa, gained support through a confederation of trade unions, and eventually led to the replacement of Socialist Prime Minister Andrei Lukhanov. The new Prime Minister, Dimitar Popov, is not affiliated with any political party. The strikes were called to protest deteriorating social and economic conditions, especially chronic food and energy shortages.

Employment and medical insurance. Employees must be insured against temporary or permanent disability under Bulgarian insurance legislation.

ENDNOTES

1   U.S. Department of Commerce. International Trade Administration, 1991. *Foreign Economic Trends and Their Implications for the United States—Bulgaria*. Washington, D.C.: Government Printing Office.

BULGARIA

KEY CONTACTS FOR BUSINESS

Federal Ministries (March 1991)

Prime Minister: Dimitar Popov
bul. Dondukov 1
BG-1000 Sofia
    Tel: 359-2-8691 or 8501
    Telex: (865) 22272

Ministry of Agriculture & Food Industry
bul. Khristo Botev 55
BG-1000 Sofia
    Tel: 359-2-8531
    Telex: (865) 22325 or 22326
Minister: Boris Spirov

Ministry of Construction, Architecture & Public Works
ul. Kiril i Metodiy 17
BG-1000 Sofia
    Tel: 359-2-838-41
    Telex: (865) 22182 or 22183
Minister: Ivan Krustev

Ministry of Culture
bul. Al. Staboliiski 17
BG-1000 Sofia
    Tel: 359-2-861-11
    Telex: (865) 22652 or 22715
Minister: Dimo Dimov

Ministry of Economy & Planning
bul. Dondukov 21
BG-1000 Sofia
    Tel: 359-2-8601
    Fax: 359-2-878-324
    Telex: (865) 22933
Minister: Naiden Naidenov

Ministry of Employment & Social Affairs
ul. Trijadiza 12
BG-1000 Sofia
　　Tel: 359-2-8601
　　Telex: (865) 23173
Minister: Emiliya Maslarova

Ministry of Environment
ul. V. Poptomov 67
BG-1000 Sofia
　　Tel: 359-2-876-151
　　Fax: 359-2-521-634
　　Telex: (865) 22145
Minister: Dimitar Vodenicharov

Ministry of Finance
ul. Rakovski 102
BG-1000 Sofia
　　Tel: 359-2-8491
　　Telex: (865) 22727
Minister: Ivan Kostov

Ministry of Foreign Affairs
ul. Al. Zhendov 2
BG-1000 Sofia
　　Tel: 359-2-714-31
　　Telex: (865) 22529
Minister: Victor Valkov

Ministry of Foreign Economic Relations
12, Sofiiska Komuna St.
BG-1000 Sofia
　　Tel: 359-2-882-011 or 872-041
　　Fax: 359-2-803-968
　　Telex: (865) 22024 or 22025
Minister: Atanas Paprizov

Ministry of Industry & Technologies
ul. Slavyanska 8
BG-1000 Sofia
　　Tel: 359-2-870-741
　　Telex: (865) 23490 or 23499
Minister: Ivan Pushkarov

Ministry of Justice
bul. Dondoukov 2
BG-1000 Sofia
Tel: 359-2-8601
Telex: (865) 22933
Minister: Pencho Penev

Ministry of Education
bul. Al. Stamboliyski 18
BG-1000 Sofia
Tel: 359-2-8481
Telex: (865) 22384
Minister: Matey Mateer

Ministry of Public Health
5, Lenin Square
BG-1000 Sofia
Tel: 359-2-8631
Telex: (865) 23654
Minister: Ivan Chernozemski

Ministry for Science & Higher Education
ul. Chapaev 55a
BG-1574 Sofia
Tel: 359-2-735-41
Minister: Gueorgui Fotev

Ministry of Transport & Communications
ul. Vasil Levski 9/11
BG-1000 Sofia
Tel: 359-2-317-121 or 871-081
Telex: (865) 23200 or 22553
Minister: Vasselin Pavlov

Central Government Organizations (March 1991)

Bulgarian Academy of Sciences
ul. 7-mi Novembri 1
BG-1000 Sofia
Tel: 359-2-841-41

Bulgarian Telegraph Agency
bul. Lenin 49
BG-1504 Sofia
Tel: 359-2-8561
Telex: (865) 22587

Central Statistical Office
ul. 6-ti Septembri 10
BG-1000 Sofia
Tel: 359-2-883-607
Telex: (865) 22001

Committee of Communications & Informatics
ul. Gurko 6
BG-1000 Sofia
Tel: 359-2-882-095
Fax: 359-2-802-580
Telex: (865) 22515
President: Atanas Popov

Bulgarian Posts & Telecoms
ul. Gourko 6
BG-1000 Sofia
Tel: 359-2-870-893
Fax: 359-2-802-580
President: Nikola Krekmanski

Committee on Energy
ul. Triyaditsa 8
BG-1000 Sofia
Tel: 359-2-861-91
Telex: (865) 22708
Chairman: Nikola Todoriev

Committee for Environmental Protection, Council of Ministers
ul. Vl. Poptomov 67
BG-1000 Sofia
Tel: 359-2-876-151
Telex: (865) 22145

Committee for Geology
bul. G. Dimitrov 22
BG-1000 Sofia
Tel: 359-2-838-51
Telex: (865) 22337

Committee for Material Supply, Council of Ministers
ul. Anguel Knuchev 2
BG-1000 Sofia
Tel: 359-2-8561
Telex: (865) 22436

Committee on Quality
ul. 6-ti Septembri 21
BG-1000 Sofia
    Tel: 359-2-8591
    Telex: (865) 22570

Committee for Radio
ul. Dragan Zankov 4
BG-1000 Sofia
    Tel: 359-2-8541
    Telex: (865) 22557 or 22558

Committee for Television
ul. San Stefan 29
BG-1104 Sofia
    Tel: 359-2-43-481
    Telex: (865) 22305

Trade and Investment Facilitation Services

Bulgarian Chamber of Commerce & Industry
bul. Stamboliiski 11a
BG-1040 Sofia
    Tel: 359-2-872-631
    Fax: 359-2-873-209
    Telex: (865) 22374
President: Vladimir Lambrev
International Relations Contact: Maria Petunova

Bulgarian Industrial Association
ul. Ekzarkh Yossif 37
BG-1000 Sofia
    Tel: 359-2-878-417
    Fax: 359-2-872-604
    Telex: (865) 23523 or 23607
International Contact: Bojidar Danev
    Tel: 359-2-545-0066

Private Producers Union
ul. T. Kableshkov 2
BG-1000 Sofia
    Tel: 359-2-550-016

Scientific Institute for International Cooperation & Foreign Economy
j.k. Chervena zvezda 165 N3A
BG-1000 Sofia
    Tel: 359-2-714-81
    Fax: 359-2-222-71
    Telex: (865) 705154
International Contact: Dmitri Stojanov

Union for Citizens' Economic Initiatives
bul. Stamboliiski 2a
BG-1000 Sofia
    Tel: 359-2-8681

Union for Private Economic Enterprise
bul. Stamboliiski 2a
BG-1000 Sofia
    Tel: 359-2-659-371 or 659-366 or 874-522
    Fax: 359-2-659-411
President: Valentin Mollov

Union of Small- and Medium-sized Enterprises
ul. Ekzarkh Yossif 14
BG-1000 Sofia
    Tel: 359-2-8421 or 878-417
    Fax: 359-2-872-604
    Telex: (865) 23523 or 23607

Arbitration Court
bul. Al. Stamboliyski 11a
BG-1040 Sofia
    Tel: 359-2-972-631
    Telex: (865) 22374

Association of Bulgarian Enterprises for International Automobile Transport &
Roads
bul. Emil Markov 56, block 15
BG-1680 Sofia
    Tel: 359-2-591-113 or 592-117
    Telex: (865) 23616
Services: Issues and registers TIR carnets and AGT manifests.

"Balkan" Bulgarian Airlines
Sofia Airport
BG-1540 Sofia
    Tel: 359-2-712-01
    Telex: (865) 22342 or 22299
Services: Passenger and freight for domestic and international.

Bulgarinterautoservice
Kiril & Metodi St.
BG-1309 Sofia
    Tel: 359-2-220-518
    Telex: (865) 23582
Services: Repair, servicing, towing, and transport of automobiles.

Balkantourist
bul. Anton Ivanov 100
BG-1000 Sofia
    Tel: 359-2-624-151
    Telex: (865) 22797
Services: Main tourist agency.

Bulfracht
ul. Gurko 5
BG-1000 Sofia
    Tel: 359-2-875-581
    Telex: (865) 22161
Services: Maritime transport.

Bulgarkonsult
130 Tsar Boris
BG-1000 Sofia
    Tel: 359-2-884-820 or 872-355 or 802-729
    Telex: (865) 23201
Services: Study, design, consulting, technical assistance, and other engineering
services for urban planning.

Bulgarkontrola
ul. Parchevich 42
POB 613
BG-1000 Sofia
    Tel: 359-2-874-092
    Telex: (865) 23318
Services: Specialized independent quality and specification control of trade
goods.

Bulgarreklama Agency
ul. Parchevich 42
BG-1000 Sofia
    Tel: 359-2-85-151
    Telex: (865) 22318
Services: Advertising agency; arranges official exhibitions.

Bulstrad
ul. Dunav 5
BG-1000 Sofia
    Tel: 359-2-851-91
    Telex: (865) 22564
Services: State insurance agency.

Center for Congress Events, State Committee for Tourism
ul. Lenin 1
BG-1000 Sofia
    Tel: 359-2-841-31
    Telex: (865) 22583 or 22584
Services: Organizes international conferences, symposia.

Club Economic Alternative
Chervena zvzda 165 3a
BG-1390 Sofia
    Tel: 359-2-705-156 or 629-597
Services: Market research, consulting.

Cooptourist
ul. Rakovski 99
BG-1000 Sofia
    Tel: 359-2-8451
    Telex: (865) 22429 or 22349 or 22657
Services: Tourism.

Customs Administration (at the Ministry of Finance)
ul. Rakovski 102
BG-1000 Sofia
    Tel: 359-2-8491

Despred
ul. Slavyanska 2
BG-1000 Sofia
    Tel: 359-2-876-016
    Telex: (865) 22306
Services: International freight forwarders.

Eckopt-Escort
ul. Alabin 34
BG-1000 Sofia
    Tel: 359-2-803-558
    Fax: 359-2-881-311
    Telex: (865) 23960
Services: Consulting, conferences.

Foreign Trade & International Markets Center
ul. Kaloyan 8
BG-1000 Sofia
    Tel: 359-2-851-31
    Telex: (865) 22271
Services: Applied research and information services for the Ministry of Foreign
Economic Relations and others on foreign trade matters.

General Average Adjuster's Office (at the Chamber of Commerce & Industry)
bul. Al. Stamboliyski 11a
BG-1040 Sofia
    Tel: 359-2-872-631
    Telex: (865) 22374
Services: Determination of averages, issuance of adjustment statements at the
request of ship owners, insurance companies, cooperation with foreign adjusters,
and mediation for voluntary settlement of claims.

Inflot
ul. Burko 5
BG-1000 Sofia
    Tel: 359-2-882-771
    Telex: (865) 22376
Services: Agency for foreign ships in ports; ticket sales.

INFORMA (Information Center for Technology Transfer)
ul. A. Chapaev 55a
BG-1574 Sofia
    Tel: 359-2-700-281 or 718-003 or 718-153
    Fax: 359-2-704-145
    Telex: (865) 23178
Services: Consulting, market research, specialized exhibitions.

Institut za Prouchvane i Vuzdeystvie na Pazara
bul. Dondukiv 41
BG-1000 Sofia
    Tel: 359-2-878-449
Services: Institute for market research and marketing.

International Plovdiv Fair Economic Enterprise
bul. G. Kimitrov
BG-4018 Plovdiv
    Tel: 359-32-531-91 or 543-21
    Telex: (865) 44432
Services: Administers Plovdiv fair exhibitions.

Jusauthor Copyright Agency
Slaveikow Sq. 11
POB 872
BG-1000 Sofia
    Tel: 359-2-879-111
Services: Registers copyrights.

Law Office for Foreign Legal Matters
ul. Alabin 31
BG-1000 Sofia
    Tel: 359-2-877-782 or 870-316
    Fax: 359-2-890-581
    Telex: (865) 22104
Services: Legal protection of interests of foreign natural and legal persons in Bulgaria and those of Bulgarian nationals abroad in civil, administrative, criminal, and other matters; legal consultancy and other legal assistance.

Lyudmilia Zhivkova Palace of Culture
bul. Bulgaria 1
BG-1463 Sofia
    Tel: 359-2-515-01
    Telex: (865) 23643 or 23644
Services: Conference center; also organizes various publicity activities and has its own printing center.

Mezdounarodni Prevozi
Gorublene 438
BG-1000 Sofia
    Tel: 359-2-781-121
    Telex: (865) 22356 or 22380
Services: International transport.

Patent & Trademark Bureau, Chamber of Commerce & Industry
bul. Al. Stamboliyski 11a
BG-1040 Sofia
Tel: 359-2-872-631
Telex: (865) 22374
Services: Representation of foreign national and juridical persons in patenting of inventions and registration of trademarks in Bulgaria.

Rousse International Free Zone
ul. Blagoev 5
BG-7000 Rousse
POB 17
Tel: 359-82-722-47
Fax: 359-82-700-84
Telex: (865) 62285
Services: Offers optimal location for a wide range of activities such as: manufacture and assembly; sales and distribution; transshipping, storing and processing; providing services to companies within the Zone such as banking, insurance, and leasing; organizing the transport flows, including container services and bunkering ships; freight forwarding.

Sofcommerce
ul. Moskovska 41
BG-1000 Sofia
Tel: 359-2-393-339
Telex: (865) 22670
Services: Commercial and financial operations; engineering and leasing operations; import-export of machinery, equipment, and consumer goods; renting offices and sales against foreign exchange; advertising and tourist services. FTO of Sofia's city council.

Sofia Press Agency
ul. Slavyanska 29
BG-1040 Sofia
Tel: 359-2-885-831
Telex: (865) 22622
Services: Press agency and multimedia support services.

Vangelia-A
bul. A. Vitosha 62
BG-1463 Sofia
Fax: 359-2-800-102
Services: Trade and investment consulting.

Foreign Trade Organizations (FTOs)

Interpred Association
Bulgaro-Sovetska Druzhba 16
BG-1057 Sofia
    Tel: 359-2-714-646-46 or 714-635-13
    Telex: (865) 23284 or 23285 or 23286 or 23287
Services: Unlike FTOs in neighboring countries, Bulgaria's agencies (with the exception of Bulpharma) are organized primarily according to the geographical "client" rather than the industrial sector.

Members of the Association are all located at the address above:

Bulpharma
    Telex: (865) 023284
Specializes in chemicals and drugs.

Kom
    Telex: (865) 023284
Specializes in German firms.

Lozen
    Telex: (865) 022379 or 023284
Specializes in Italian, French, and Swiss firms.

Lyulin
    Tel: 359-2-881-665 or 873-191 or 873-192 or 873-193
    Telex: (865) 023284 or 022578
Specializes in Japanese and British firms.

Mourgash
    Tel: 359-2-874-765 or 873-191 or 873-192 or 873-193
    Telex: (865) 023284
Specializes in Scandinavian and Japanese firms.

Moussala
    Telex: (865) 023284 or 023285
Specializes in Greek and Benelux firms.

Pirin
    Telex: (865) 023284
Specializes in British and American firms.

Rila
    Telex: (865) 023284 or 022571
Specializes in Italian, French, and Swiss firms.

Rouen
    Telex: (865) 023284 or 022571
Specializes in Austrian, German, and Swiss firms.

Shipka
    Telex: (865) 022650
Specializes in American, Japanese, and French firms.

Trakia
    Telex: (865) 023283
Specializes in Balkan firms.

Vitosha
    Telex: (865) 023284
Specializes in American, Italian, Swiss, and British firms.

Trade Agencies Outside the Interpred Association

BUL-AWT
2 Sofiiska Koumuna
BG-1000 Sofia
    Tel: 359-2-8551
    Telex: (865) 22032
A joint venture of the Bulgarian Foreign Trade Bank and AWT-Internationale Handels und Finanzierungs AG (Austria).

IKO-Economic & Consulting Complex
ul. Kostur 16
POB 621
BG-1058 Sofia
    Tel: 359-2-581-711
    Telex: (865) 23666

IZZT "INFORMA"
ul. Tschapaev 55a
BG-1000 Sofia
    Tel: 359-2-706-581
    Telex: (865) 23178

Technoimpex
ul. Tsar Kaloyan 8
BG-1000 Sofia
    Tel: 359-2-881-571
    Telex: (865) 22950

Tourisinvest Ltd.
ul. Trijadiza 6
BG-1000 Sofia
    Tel: 359-2-885-723

Scientific Institute for International Foreign Cooperation & Foreign Economy
j.k. Chervena Zvezda
ul. 165 N 3a
BG-1113 Sofia
    Tel: 359-2-714-81
    Fax: 359-2-705-154
    Telex: (865) 22271

Governmental Financial Institutions

Bulgarian National Bank
ul. Sofiiska Komuna 2
BG-1000 Sofia
    Tel: 359-2-8551
    Telex: (865) 22031
President: Todor Vulchev (Central bank of Bulgaria)

State Savings Bank
ul. Moskovska 19
BG-1000 Sofia
    Tel: 359-2-881-041
(Bank for domestic private accounts)

Bulgarian Foreign Trade Bank
ul. Sofiiska Komuna 2
BG-1000 Sofia
    Tel: 359-2-8551
    Telex: (865) 2203)1
(Bank for foreign commercial transactions)

Commercial Banks

The Agricultural & Cooperative Bank
ul. G. Dimitrov 37
BG-4018 Plovdiv
    Tel: 359-32-238-946 or 231-876
    Telex: (865) 44324

Bank for Agricultural Credits
bul. Hristo Botev 57
BG-1000 Sofia

Biochim
ul. Ivan Vazov 1
BG-1000 Sofia
    Tel: 359-2-874-911 or 899-888
    Fax: 359-2-541-378
    Telex: (865) 23862

The Construction Bank
ul. Dunav 46
BG-1000 Sofia
    Tel: 359-2-838-41
    Fax: 359-2-835-223
    Telex: (865) 22182 or 22183 or 23887

The Economic Bank
ul. Slavyanska 9
BG-1000 Sofia
    Tel: 359-2-851-61 or 870-741
    Fax: 359-2-885-526
    Telex: (865) 23910

Elekronika
ul. Chapaev 55/6
BG-1574 Sofia
    Tel: 359-2-735-51
    Telex: (865) 23745

Mineralbank
ul. Lege 17
BG-1000 Sofia
    Tel: 359-2-801-737
    Telex: (865) 23390 or 23391 or 23392

The Transport, Agriculture & Building Equipment Bank
ul. 9-ti Septemvri 126
BG-1618 Sofia
    Tel: 359-2-553-101
    Fax: 359-2-581-176
    Telex: (865) 22061 or 22062 or 23916

The Transport Bank
ul. N. Vaptsavro 69
BG-9000 Varna
    Tel: 359-52-233-71 or 223-71 or 223-073 or 237-378
    Telex: (865) 77515 or 77293 or 77303

Bulgarian Banks in the West

Bayerische-Bulgarische Handelsbank
Maffeistr. 2
D-8000 Munchen
Federal Republic of Germany
    Tel: 49-89-293-871
    Telex: (FRG) 5214166
(German-Bulgarian joint venture)

Foreign Trade Bank (branch office)
33 Eastcheap.
London EC3
United Kingdom
    Tel: 44-71-626-1888
    Telex: (UK) 886928

Litex Bank SAL (Dormant in February 1991)
Rue Maurice Barres
Beirut, Lebanon
    Tel: 0-251-480
    Telex: (Lebanon) 208
(Branch of Foreign Trade Bank)

Bulgarian Foreign Insurance & Reinsurance Company

Bulstrad-Bulgarsko Vunshno Zastrhovatelno i Prezastrahovatelno
ul. Dunav 5
BG-1000 Sofia
    Tel: 359-2-851-91
    Telex: (865) 22564

Darzhaven Zastrakhovatelen Institut (State Insurance Institute)
ul. Rakovski 102
BG-1000 Sofia

Foreign Banks in Bulgaria

Banco di Napoli
c/o Interpred/Vitosha
bul. A. Stamboliiski 2
BG-1000 Sofia
    Tel: 359-2-874-52
    Telex: (865) 23284

Societe Generale
c/o Interpred/Vitosha
bul. Rakovski 153
BG-1000 Sofia
    Tel: 359-2-800-267
    Telex: (865) 22010

CZECHOSLOVAKIA

CZECHOSLOVAKIA

In a Nutshell

		Urban Population
Population (1992)	15,654,000	67%

Main Urban Areas		Percentage of Total
Prague (Capital)	1,211,207	7.74
Bratislava	435,710	2.78
Brno	389,789	2.49
Ostrava	330,602	2.11
Kosice	232,362	1.48
Pilzen	174,625	1.11

Land Area	49,370 square miles
	125,870 square kilometers
Comparable European State	Slightly smaller than Greece
Comparable U.S. State	Slightly larger than New York State
Language	Czech (western region)
	Slovak (eastern region)
Common Business Language	German is common but
	English is preferred
Currency	Koruna (Crown) (= 100 Heller)
Best European Air Connection	Frankfurt (Lufthansa, Delta)
Best Ground Connection	Vienna to Prague (309 kilometers)
	Vienna to Bratislava (30 kilometers)
	Frankfurt to Prague (500 kilometers)
Best Hotel	Intercontinental Prague
	($190 per night as of 1/92)

CHAPTER CONTENTS

INTRODUCTION AND REGIONAL ORIENTATION

Geographical and Historical Background

Czechoslovakia was created in the aftermath of World War I to provide a nation for the Czechs and Slovaks who were minorities in the former Austro-Hungarian empire. Today, Czechs outnumber the Slovaks by approximately two to one. In general, the Czechs favor a more centralized federal republic, and the Slovaks favor a looser confederation.

In spite of this difference of opinion, the prospects for a stable and competent government in post-Communist Czechoslovakia are excellent. Since the November 1989 "velvet revolution," which led to the downfall of the Communist leadership, Czechoslovakia has sought to open its political and economic systems, rid itself of Soviet influence, and assert its independence in the global arena. At the same time, the "new" Czechoslovakia is actively looking westward for ideas, advice, and economic assistance.

A number of significant changes have occurred in Czechoslovakia. Restrictions on the media, political activities, and artistic freedom have been lifted to a large degree, and many new newspapers and journals have appeared. Civic organizations have sprouted up everywhere in the country. Laws on educational reforms, language policy, and human rights have been passed. Most state security forces have been restructured and purged.

Free elections have been held, and a multiparty political system based on law and on checks and balances between the executive, legislative, and judicial branches has been established. The post-Communist government is decidedly proreform and has been working hard to create the conditions necessary for Czechoslovakia's re-entry into the international community. Structures left over from the totalitarian regime are being dismantled, and new democratic institutions are being created.

In the past, the foreign policy of Czechoslovakia was subordinated to the Soviet Union. Current diplomatic initiatives reflect the country's new independent foreign policy orientation. Membership is also being sought in important international institutions and bodies governing political, military, and economic relations, especially in Europe.

Czechoslovakia recently became a member of the International Monetary Fund in 1991 and was granted most-favored-nation status by the United States. In addition, Prague was selected as the permanent site of the Conference or Security and Cooperation in Europe in November 1990. Clearly, Czechoslovakia's goal is full integration with the economies of the West on all levels.

However, Czechoslovakia's process of self-transformation will be difficult. Internal tensions between the Czechs and Slovaks, particularly those stemming from

Slovakia's demands for greater autonomy, have become more open since the new leadership headed by President Vaclav Havel came to power.

In response to such pressure, a new power sharing agreement was reached in December 1990 and will effectively reduce the authority of the federal government in favor of the republics. Some view this measure as a first step toward a confederation arrangement. In any case, it appears that the central leadership in Prague is trying to avoid exacerbating the type of ethnic tensions that are tearing apart the federations in the former Soviet Union and Yugoslavia.

Extreme nationalists in Slovakia, although a minority, favor outright separation. However, according to polls in 1991, most Slovaks do not think that a separate and independent Slovakia is practical at the present time and favor greater autonomy within a republic of Czechs and Slovaks. Nevertheless, some Slovak politicians indicate that they would like to see Slovakia become an equal and independent member of the European community, along with the Czech lands. With the process of accession to the European Community solidified in October 1991 (with only a single "seat" for CSFR), the Slovak Separist movement is all but extinguished.

A variety of external challenges, such as the crisis in the Persian Gulf, the loss of cheap oil from the Soviet Union, and the disintegration of traditional trading relationships, have tested the abilities of the new leadership. Trade with countries belonging to the Council for Mutual Economic Assistance (CMEA) fell by more than 14% in 1990. Foreign debt increased slightly to US $7.6 billion. In 1991, the Soviet Union reduced its oil deliveries with Czechoslovakia from the previous year. The terms of Czechoslovakia's trade with the former Soviet Union still need to be worked out in view of the now independent republics.

Disruptions in the economy resulting from these external factors and ongoing reorganization of the internal system have become evident. Unemployment and inflation have risen, industrial production and real personal income have declined, and the euphoria of the revolution is giving way to the realization that tough times are ahead. Thus, not surprisingly, debates between those who advocate taking a more cautious approach toward reform and those who favor more radical changes continue.

The economy of the Slovak region of the country has been hit harder by the effects of economic transformation. Steel, aluminum, and chemical plants leftover from the Communist era are not profitable and have survived up until now through government subsidies. Weapons plants, once a source of hard currency, are being shut down or are being forced to convert to nonmilitary production. In brief, Slovak leaders fear that they will not be able to attract Western investment like the Volkswagen deal with Skoda in the Czech lands. Volkswagen of Germany won a bid to be the joint venture partner for Skoda to produce passenger cars.

Following the Communists' fall from power in 1989, the government in Prague rapidly drafted legislation governing banking, taxation, foreign exchange, and the establishment of new economic entities, such as state enterprises, cooperatives, joint ventures, and foreign-owned companies. The new legislation seeks to give far greater freedom to these economic entities. The goal seems to be the replacement of old rules that required permission to conduct foreign trade with a new system that only requires interested parties to register.

A new law passed in April 1990 by the Federal Assembly allows citizens the right to establish their own businesses and places no limits on the number of employees or amount of property that entrepreneurs can own. In addition, a constitutional amendment was passed that grants equal status to owners of private, cooperative, and state property.

Vaclav Claus, the current Minister of Finance, favors rapid privatization of the economy. The National Assembly, however, appears to be wary of the social disruptions that a rapid transition may cause. Debates on the subject of economic reforms have dragged on, causing some Czechs and Slovaks to question the resolve of their lawmakers.

Two laws on private enterprise were passed in October 1990. One concerned the return of nearly 70,000 shops, hotels, and restaurants that were nationalized in the 1950s and 1960s. The other concerned small scale privatization. Under the terms of the new law, some 100,000 enterprises will be auctioned off by the government in two scheduled rounds of buying, the first of which will be open only to resident citizens of Czechoslovakia.

The first round of auctions, which took place in late January 1991, was deemed a success by the authorities, although some bidders complained that Westerners had conspired with Czechoslovak citizens to illegally buy property in the first round. Others suspected that backing came from black marketers. In any case, the bidding for the first property, a green grocer, opened at koruna 11,000 and closed at koruna 580,000. Foreigners will not be permitted to bid until a second round of auctions is held for properties which did not meet the minimum calling price in the first round.

Debate on a law concerning large scale privatization has been postponed indefinitely because of dwindling interest from foreign investors. Under the terms of proposed legislation, portions of large enterprises will be privatized on the basis of vouchers "investment points" issued to all adult, resident citizens of Czechoslovakia. These vouchers may not be sold to foreigners or Czechoslovaks living outside the country. The conversion of state-owned entities into joint stock companies will be organized by the enterprises themselves and began in October 1991. Such conversions may favor the sale of stock to employees. The major influence on these types of reforms comes mainly from Western Europe, especially Germany.

Private businesses are springing up rapidly. In November 1989 there were approximately 15,000 private businesses in Czechoslovakia. By September 1990, there were about 300,000, most of which, however, were very small.

Prices in retail stores have almost doubled since price controls were lifted in January 1991, alarming consumers and causing officials to doubt the prospects of a smooth transition to a market economy. Some officials have blamed the sharp increase in prices to the delays in dismantling state monopolies on retail outlets. They pointed out that if the large government chains of stores had been broken up into small units, competition would have developed and prices would have been kept lower. However, as the auctions of state-owned stores and wholesalers proceed, the retail monopolies should be broken up rapidly.

Despite the fact that Parliament has been slow in adopting a law on the privatization of large companies, the government went ahead with price liberalization plans at the beginning of the year. The Ministry of Trade and Tourism of the Czech region has reported that prices for retail goods, excluding gasoline, have increased 80% to 100% since the last survey taken in September 1990.

The population for the most part seems to be responding stoically by making due with less for the time being, sensing that the increase in prices is a painful but necessary part of economic reform. Compounding the misery will be the government's plan to generally limit wage increases to only 8%. Wage increase above that level will be highly taxed.

The current situation has led to inevitable criticism of the government from other political parties and from within the government. Finance Minister Vaclav Klaus complained that the state-owned trading organizations were making profits, "many times higher than normal." The profits on baked goods, for example, had tripled or even quadrupled, while the costs had only increased an average of 40% during the period of October 1990 to October 1991.

Despite the introduction of anti-inflationary measures, inflation rose to 14% at the end of 1990 but has held stable at between 3% to 5% since May 1991. Industrial production fell approximately 3% to 4% during the first three quarters of 1990. Trade with the West increased nearly 5% during the same time period.

APPROACHING THE MARKET

Foreign Trade and Investment Decision-Making Infrastructure

The present foreign trade environment in the Czech and Slovak Federal Republic (CSFR) is being built on new relationships established multilaterally and bilaterally, as well as by new laws changing the legal framework for conducting foreign trade.

Multilateral Infrastructure

The important new multilateral relationships include: the accession to the General Agreement on Tariffs and Trade (GATT) and the granting of most-favored-nation status; the entry into the Economic Community (EC); and the entry into the European Free Trade Association (EFTA). Entry into these associations is accomplished by meeting prescribed conditions and graduating into full membership. It is expected that the CSFR will become part of the EC by the year 2000. A declaration of cooperation was signed between the European Free Trade Association (EFTA) and the CSFR on June 13, 1990. Provisions included cooperation in trade, science and technology, industry, economics, tourism, transportation, and environmental protection. Such cooperation will reduce obstacles to trade; promote trade through seminars, trade fairs, and exhibits; provide financing for projects; and launch joint ventures.[1]

Bilateral Infrastructure

Czechoslovakia, bilaterally with the United States, signed a trade agreement in July 1990 that went into force on November 17, 1990. The pact gives most-favored-nation status to the CSFR with respect to the United States and obligates Czechoslovakia to further protect intellectual property and ease administrative constraints. In addition, Czechoslovakia has requested to be designated a beneficiary under the Generalized System of Preferences (GSP), thereby allowing very low tariff rates to encourage fledgling trade in developing countries. This designation has been used customarily with countries in the process of development. It was granted GSP status during 1991.

Czechoslovakia entered the world market economies by agreeing to the GATT conditions and by waiving the Jackson-Vanik amendment, thereby gaining most-favored-nation status and becoming eligible for U.S. programs of the Export-Import Bank and the U.S. Trade and Development Program. (See section in this chapter on "Financing and Capital Markets.") COCOM restrictions on U.S. exports of certain high technology products were eased in May 1991, thereby encouraging joint ventures and trade in high tech industries. High tech joint ventures will be further encouraged by the fact that the CSFR passed legislation in December 1990, safeguarding imports of high technology and instituting an export licensing regime to track high technology imports.[2]

Dissolution of Old Foreign Trade Structure

These new relationships are evolving as Czechoslovakia's old trading relationships within the COMECON or CMEA are dissolving. The CMEA is the common market for the former nonmarket economies of Eastern Europe and the former Soviet Union.

In addition, Czechoslovakia's main trading partners for the last 40 years have been the former German Democratic Republic (GDR) and the Soviet Union. Since the unification of Germany, the former East German market has been lost. Most COMECON countries today want to trade in hard currency rather than the barter or countertrade methods used in the past. For Czechoslovakia, the former Soviet Union's requirement that oil payments be made in hard currency has increased the difficulty of economic reform and controlling inflation. Furthermore, the former Soviet Union does not have hard currency to pay for the industrial goods it has bought in the past from the CSFR. Some form of countertrade may be necessary as an interim measure while the former nonmarket economies are readjusting to world market conditions.

New Legal Framework

The new bilateral and multilateral relationships would not have been possible without the simultaneous liberalization of trade, pricing, and currency convertibility. The Foreign Trade Act, effective May 1, 1990, and the Foreign Exchange Act, effective January 1, 1991, combined to liberalize trade with the CSFR, conforming to the market-oriented international trading regime. The Foreign Trade Act opened the process of participating in foreign trade, while the Foreign Exchange Act, implementing the critical factor of internal convertibility, made implementation practical.

The Foreign Trade Act, or the Act on Economic Relations with Foreign Countries (Act No. 102/1988 Coll.), applies to both goods and services (for example, transportation, communications, education, medical care, insurance, and banking). It also regulates activities of mediators between the CSFR and foreigners, inspections of international trade, sea-shipping operations, consignments of goods traded internationally, and international activities of Czechoslovak media (television and press). The Foreign Trade Act does not regulate the export and import of foreign exchange or banking activities reserved for the purview of the Central Bank and approved banking and financial institutions.

Businesses desiring to engage in foreign trade must register in the Companies Register. Authorization is required for certain regulated industries, such as the defense industry. Until the early spring of 1991, foreign companies who wanted to engage in foreign trade in the CSFR had to be licensed; now only a registration is required in nonregulated sectors.

The Foreign Trade Act opened trade to Czechoslovak private citizens and businesses (other than the state-owned Foreign Trade Organizations or FTOs); streamlined administrative procedures, specifically replacing licensing by registration and authorization of trading enterprises; allowed foreigners to participate in trading activities; and instituted an import and export licensing system for certain products, replacing the old authorization system.

Deputy Minister of Foreign Trade Zdenek Cerveny stated the following:

> The only control instruments will be the customs duty, export and import licenses, and licensing procedures connected with the setting up of branches of foreign companies.... All licensing procedures concerning foreign trade will be abolished for all subjects authorized to work in Czechoslovakia on the basis of a permission of the magistrate or the court. This does not apply to trading organizations handling the production and marketing of selected goods, such as arms and ammunition designed for defense purposes (not sport), narcotics, production endangering the environment, alcohol, and tobacco.[3]

Mr. Cerveny stressed the importance of the role of the Czechoslovak Chamber of Commerce and Industry as part of the triad with the government and the trade unions. He also discussed the role of compulsory economic chambers at the national (republic) and federal levels; these chambers will represent the interests of entrepreneurs to the government.

Although FTOs no longer have a monopoly on foreign trade, many continue to be influential due to their expertise and established relationships. Contacting the appropriate FTO in the product area of interest can be accomplished by the U.S. Embassy Commercial Section, the U.S. Department of Commerce (EEIBEC), the Czechoslovak Embassy in Washington, D.C., or the Czechoslovak Chamber of Commerce and Industry.[4]

It should be noted that when the first Minister of Foreign Trade under the Havel presidency left office, he was not replaced. Some believe that the position will eventually be dissolved.

Recent Trade Trends

U.S. imports from Czechoslovakia increased slightly between 1989 and 1990 from US $86.9 million to US $87.0 million, while U.S. exports increased from US $53.7 million to US $89.1 million. In 1989 CSFR exports to the United States totaling US $320 million, consisted mostly of chemicals, glass products, machine tools, and agricultural products.[5] Products predominantly imported in 1990 from the CSFR include manufactured goods, machinery and transport equipment, food and live animals, and, to a lesser extent, other commodities, beverages, and tobacco, and chemicals. Primary 1990 exports from the United States included machinery and transport equipment, crude materials (except fuels), chemicals and related products, manufactured goods, and beverages and tobacco.

In 1989, Czechoslovakia's trade with European Community (EC) countries accounted for 18% of the CSFR's foreign trade turnover; exports to the EC were 18.1% of total exports and imports were 17.8% of total imports. Total trade with EFTA countries in 1989 was US $2.7 million, up from US $2.6 million in 1988. The CSFR's total exports to EFTA totaled US $1.2 million and EFTA imports were US $1.5 million; this was 8.4% of Czechoslovakia's total export trade and 10.5% of its total import trade.[6]

State and Private Consulting/Legal Services

There are no state consulting services in Czechoslovakia, although both domestic and foreign consulting firms do exist. Official agencies providing trade and investment information are the Federal Agency for Foreign Investment, the Czechoslovak Chamber of Commerce and Industry, and the technical advisory service of the World Bank being established in Prague. Most major U.S. consulting firms — Price Waterhouse, KPMG, Ernst and Young, Coopers & Lybrand, and Arthur Andersen & Co. — have offices in Prague. The Czech and Slovak Consultancy Association, located in Prague, may also be of assistance.

Since the legal and business environments are changing rapidly, the services of a local lawyer or a U.S. law firm with CSFR offices could be quite useful. There is a lawyers' counseling service in the CSFR called Advokatni Poradna. Lists of both consulting firms and law offices are kept by the Commercial Section of the U.S. Embassy in Prague and at the Eastern Europe Business Information Center (EEBIC) at the Department of Commerce.

Sales Promotion, Fairs, Conferences, and Advertising

One of the best ways to make business contacts in Eastern Europe is to attend one of the many trade fairs. Fairs are important for promoting products, assessing the competition, finding sales representative and distributors, making direct sales to retailers and wholesales of consumer goods, and renewing old contacts. Historically, since the first recorded fair at St. Denis (near Paris), France, in 710 A.D., fairs have been an essential component in marketing strategy throughout Europe.

Three of the most important fairs are: the International Engineering Fair, INCHEBA, the International Exhibit of the Chemical Industry, and the Universal Prague Exhibition, a centennial exhibition with two-week long revolving shows. For in-depth information on trade fairs, see *European Trade Fairs: A Key to the World for U.S. Exporters,* prepared by Maryanne Lyons, Office of Western Europe, International Trade Administration, U.S. Department of Commerce. Lists of fairs are also available through EEBIC at the Department of Commerce and through the

Commercial Section of the U.S. Embassy in Prague and the Consular Office in Bratislava.

Advertising or publicity for foreign firms is conducted primarily by two established organizations in the CSFR: 1) CTK — MADE IN PUBLICITY, which provides advertising, translation services, and organizes conferences; and 2) RAPID. Both are located in Prague. Private companies, including some major U.S. advertising and public relations firms, are also in the CSFR. One of the U.S. companies is Young & Rubicam who invested in AB Line Studios to provide advertising services.

Agents and Distributors

Formerly, the FTOs acted as agents and distributors for foreign trade. The new market-oriented distribution structure is not yet in place. Current law allows independent and wholly owned representation of foreign firms in the CSFR. The Commerce Department has an Agent/Distributor Service (ADS) assisting firms to find potential agents.

Consignment and Re-Export

Consignment is regulated by the Ministry of Foreign Trade. Licensing is required for only a limited number of exported goods from the CSFR, typically in regulated industries such as armaments and narcotics. A license is also needed to export and import petroleum products. There are some restrictions placed on CSFR exports by its trading partners in the areas of textiles, steel, and agricultural products. For example, the CSFR agreed in 1990 to put voluntary restraints on the export of steel to the United States for the next two years.[7]

Setting Up Offices, Retail Stores, and Service Facilities

A company setting up representative offices must find office space and set up space within 30 days of registration. Since office space is limited, most companies find office space first and then register.

Foreign companies, exclusive of banking and insurance companies, register with the Ministry of Foreign Trade, Section 13, Politickych veznu 20, 11249 Prague 1; Tel, (42/2) 236-0297. Banking and financial companies register with the state bank, and insurance companies register with either the Czech or Slovak Ministry of Finance, Prices, and Wages.[8]

INVESTMENT CLIMATE

Privatization

The three cornerstones of Czechoslovakia's Scenario for Economic Reform are the rapid transformation of property rights — the "wholesale privatization" of the economy, a sound macroeconomic policy including restrictive monetary and fiscal policies, and the liberalization of prices, foreign trade, and foreign exchange rates.

Two independent acts are the basis of privatization in the CSFR: the Small Privatization Act and the Large Privatization Act. In October 1990, the Czechoslovak Federal Assembly approved the Small Privatization Act allowing small businesses to be sold through an auction system.

The privatization of small- and medium-scale entrepreneurial businesses, such as restaurants, retails shops, and hotels began in early 1991; however, the larger scale privatization involves a more complicated and time-consuming process. The industrial sector, including construction, will privatize first, followed by the service sector (i.e., large banks, public transportation, power production, and utilities). Some companies may not be transferred to private hands in the initial stages of privatization. According to Tomas Jezek, Czech Minister of Privatization, these companies include railroads, post and telecommunications companies, electric power plants, and other strategic companies.[9]

Large Privatization

The Large Privatization Act, passed in February 1991, returned the nationalized industries — or State Owned Enterprises (SOEs) — to the private sector through a voucher system and the formation of joint stock companies. The large privatization is being accomplished by a three-step process: 1) the sale of shares of government-owned joint stock companies to the citizens of Czechoslovakia in return for "vouchers;" 2) the sale of shares of SOEs to Czechoslovak citizens or institutional investors for korunas; and 3) the sale of shares of SOEs to foreign investors.

The Voucher System

The voucher system was devised because personal savings in Czechoslovakia are too low to meet requirements for capital investment. The value of savings in Czechoslovakia is estimated at 335 billion CSK (US $12 billion, which includes 270 billion CSK in deposits and 65 billion CSK in circulation), about a tenth of the expected need.[10] Using the voucher or "investment coupon" involves the broadest section of the population in the privatization process by offering them shares at a nominal cost. The vouchers, a form of restricted currency, may only be used to purchase stock in the newly formed joint stock companies (formerly SOEs).

Each voucher represents a portion of the state's property and is a means to distribute the national wealth among Czechoslovak citizens, thereby augmenting the wealth of the population. The vouchers will not be distributed all at once, but rather in waves concomitant with each group of enterprises being privatized.[11]

Adult citizens (over age 18) have the right to purchase nontransferable coupons (or vouchers) redeemable for shares in companies being privatized by the voucher method. The government plans to authorize banks to set up mutual funds to assist citizens in investing their coupons or money and to manage the investment fund. Citizens could redeem coupons for shares in a mutual fund investing in privatized companies, or they could invest independently. The Czech government plans to open a stock exchange in Prague as soon as feasible to facilitate equity trading.[12]

The Scenario for Economic Reform of August 1990 stated that participation of foreign investors who are excluded from the voucher system is limited by the degree of coupon privatization.[13] However, the emphasis in 1991 was to attract foreign direct investment (FDI) at an earlier stage.

Companies to be privatized by the voucher method are those without a domestic or foreign partner, according to Tomas Jezek, the Minister of Privatization for the Czech Republic. Mr. Jezek stated that he prefers an investor who pays in cash — i.e., the direct method. The individual ministries had until the end of June 1991 to compile the list of companies to be sold and their assets and liabilities. The Czech Republic approved the principles of compiling the list of companies to be sold at the end of May 1991, and the Slovak Republic approved its list of companies in September for sale in October 1991 and February 1992.

The Czech and Slovak republics will have virtual autonomy in governing the privatization process within their jurisdictions.[14] The Agency for Foreign Investment and Assistance of the Czech Republic has been operational since October 24, 1990, and is headed by Ladislav Chrudina, Vice Minister, Ministry of Economic Policy and Development. The respective Slovak Republic Agency for Foreign Investment and Assistance became operational in the spring of 1991; Ladislav Lysak is the contact located in Bratislava. The role of the Federal Agency for Foreign Investment, headed by Dr. Zdnek Drabek, is to provide information and coordination as Czechoslovakia moves to a market-oriented economy.

Formation of Joint Stock Companies

Apart from the nonstandard coupon system of privatization, other standardized methods are being used. They include: 1) sales of property shares, or of the entire privatized enterprise, to domestic and foreign investors at market prices; 2) investment of joint-stock capital in joint ventures with foreign capital participation; and

3) leasing arrangements involving either parts of, or the entire enterprise, to private bidders. [15]

Each company selected for privatization is required to devise its own privatization scheme (or project) based on the needs and development potential of the enterprise. This plan, prepared by the company management and the responsible ministry, includes a company valuation, company structure, and a plan for share distribution. In addition, anyone may submit a privatization plan for a given company to the appropriate Ministry of Privatization. At the federal level, the Ministry of Finance is in charge of privatization; at the republic level, the Czech or Slovak Ministry for Management of State Property and Privatization is the appropriate body.

The privatization plan will be approved by the respective ministry at the federal or republic level. [16] Industries under federal jurisdiction (energy, telecommunications, or transportation), use the appropriate federal ministry; otherwise, the appropriate republic ministry approves the plan. Formerly, under the centralized economy, ministries were organized by sector according to "branches" with authority over particular industries. Under the present system, ministries are organized functionally. The relevant ministry for reviewing and approving privatization plans is referred to as the "founder," whether at the republic (referred to as "national" in Czechoslovakia) or federal level.

Each privatization project will be approved by a government commission — i.e., a joint body composed of representatives from company management, the appropriate federal or republic ministry, the Ministry of Privatization at the federal or republic levels, company employees, local authorities, and the National Property Fund(s). Once a plan is approved, the assets of the company are transferred to the National Property Fund(s) (one federal and two republic funds) so that shares of the newly formed joint-stock company can be distributed using either the voucher or auction method — and eventually a proposed stock exchange.

Detailed regulations regarding the implementation of the Large Privatization Act were published last year and addressed such issues as: 1) technical and organizational aspects of voucher privatization; 2) method of selection of companies for privatization; 3) guidelines for a privatization plan; and 4) guidelines for investment companies.

Current methods for privatization, revised from the Scenario for Economic Reform, give no preference to employees with regard to sales of shares and allow no Employee Stock Option Programs (ESOPs). The precise measures will depend on the company's privatization plan. [17]

In order to accomplish the commercialization or denationalization of the State Owned Enterprises (SOEs), the enterprises are being organizationally and financially restructured. Large, monopolistic SOEs are being dismantled to establish strong economic units which can attract capital. Commercially nonviable enterprises will either be sold off or their assets will be liquidated, while viable enterprises are being appraised and transformed into legal structures conducive to privatization – in most cases, joint-stock companies run by directorates appointed by the National Property Fund(s).

The National Property Fund(s)

Established by the Large Privatization Act to be executor of ownership rights on behalf of the government, the fund will temporarily own the "transformed" state-owned joint-stock companies, prior to privatization.

The National Property Fund(s) will also receive payments from the sale of SOEs. In the first wave of privatization, the government will select only 400 to 600 enterprises to be sold directly or through the sale of government shares. The government expects the privatization of at least 300 of the most attractive firms to be completed by the end of 1991.[18]

Over 3,000 SOEs, including industrial and trade companies as well as banks, are to be privatized under the Large Privatization Act; the majority will be privatized by the voucher method and restructured into joint-stock companies. Privatized companies can form joint ventures with foreign investors.[19]

A World Bank study, quoted by the U.S. Chamber of Commerce, expects that 50% to 60% of the SOEs will be viable, 20% to 30% will require an immediate influx of foreign capital, and 10% to 20% will be closed.[20] More conservative estimates are that only 20% to 30% of the SOEs will be able to survive in a competitive marketplace.

The Consolidation Bank

Created by the Ministry of Finance, the bank aims to restore financial viability to companies preparing to be privatized and to purge nonperforming assets from commercial bank portfolios by converting long-term loans into commercial loans. The Consolidation Bank, a nonprofit institution, began operations March 1, 1991, and it is eventually expected to merge with the National Property Fund(s).

Former SOEs accumulated perpetual, nonperforming bank loans to cover the costs of raw materials and intermediary goods. This was the result of extremely high taxation which eroded away their working capital base. In addition, although loan amounts were small when the program originated in the 1960s, a high debt accumulated since enterprises could finance their operations at very low cost and, *de facto,* there was no need to repay the loan. At the introduction of internal convertibility and other reform measures in January 1991, the banks attempted to recall these loans.[21] However, to do so would have resulted in the technical insolvency of many of these companies. An interim solution was the creation of the Consolidation Bank.

These perpetual loans have been converted into assets (i.e., commercial loans) of the Consolidation Bank (CB). They represent a "replenishment of the working capital of industrial enterprises," not new loans.[22] In effect, these CB assets will create quasi-equity in the privatizing companies.

The assets resulting from the perpetual loans are valued at about CSK 120 billion, or 30% of the operational credits of the portfolios previously held by the commercial banks. The CB also took over the monetary resources, or liabilities (i.e., household deposits, Central Bank loans, etc.) to cover those assets from the commercial banks. The CB will now charge interest on these assets at a rate covering the cost of the resources, 13% per annum, representing the dividends on the assets. The companies will repay the CB in 16 installments over eight years, beginning in January 1992.

During the privatization of the former SOEs, the Consolidation Bank will be the preferred creditor, with its assets paid from the proceeds of privatization. The CB will be paid after the commercial banks are paid. This is guaranteed by an agreement held with the Ministry of Privatization and the National Property Fund(s), with whom they have collateral security for the CB assets. In other words, if the CB assets are not paid off from the proceeds of privatization of a particular firm, the shortfall will be paid to the CB by the National Property Fund(s) from whatever profits are accumulated by the privatization process. The extent of cooperation to this effect will be specified in forthcoming regulations.

A substantial influx of equity capital is expected (foreign direct investment) as a result of the large privatization. Since an evaluation of assets is required as part of the privatization of each enterprise, companies in the CSFR will seek assistance from international accounting and auditing firms.[23]

Restitution Laws

In addition to the Small and Large Privatization Acts governing the commercialization of former SOEs, Czechoslovakia has passed two other important laws concerning land and business ownership. The Restitution Law returned businesses and other property confiscated by the former government to original owners or their heirs. Former owners, or their heirs, had until the end of September 1991 to file claims; only permanent residents were allowed to lay claim to their property.

This law applies to approximately US $11 billion of nonagricultural property expropriated by the communist government between 1948 and 1989; property taken between 1945 to 1948 is excluded. Agricultural property will be reprivatized under separate legislation. Only small- and medium-sized companies not eligible for restitution will be reprivatized; restitution and large privatization will occur concomitantly.[24]

Property (real estate, nonagricultural land, and industrial property) will be returned in its present condition to the original owners or heirs, if possible. If the property value has increased, the new owners must pay the difference; if the value has decreased, the claimant can opt for financial compensation rather than restitution. If the property has substantially changed — for example, it has been attached to other property making restitution impossible — claimants may also be financially compensated. Compensation is in the form of cash (up to the equivalent of US $1,000 or equivalent to about nine month's average wage in Czechoslovakia)[25] and securities in the newly privatized companies. An earlier law passed in the fall of 1990 applied to the return of property confiscated since 1955.[26]

Small Privatization

The republic and local government authorities are the primary actors in the small privatization process. The respective Czech and Slovak Ministries for Management of State Property and Privatization created regional commissions to implement the small privatization. These commissions include "representatives from local administrations, founders of the enterprise to be privatized, the 'Town and Village Union,' delegates from the republic's national council, and representatives of pertinent trade unions."[27]

The commissions decide which properties will be privatized and prepare an inventory of the enterprises' obligations and claims. The enterprises are then auctioned publicly throughout the country, with auction rules being set by the two republics. The Small Privatization Law required the minimum bid to be 50% of the state auditor's assessed value (i.e., the residual book value of the capital assets); or, if depreciation is not taken into account, 20% of the original procurement cost as found in the enterprise's records.[28]

According to the U.S. Chamber of Commerce, over 100,000 small- and medium-sized enterprises will be privatized by the auction method. The first round of bidding took place in January 1991. Only Czechoslovak citizens could bid in the first round; however, foreign investors can be invited by the winning bidder to be joint venture partners with either majority or minority equity holdings.[29] According to the U.S. Department of Commerce, foreigners can also use third parties to purchase firms, even though direct sales to foreigners for hard currency is prohibited during the small privatization.[30]

If a business does not sell in the first round, foreigners participate in a second round of bidding where a business may be sold at a lower price. A two-year waiting period is required before a privatized enterprise may be resold. At the end of May 1991, Deputy Minister Muron of the Czech Ministry of Privatization announced that 4,500 small- and medium-sized businesses had been sold, raising over 2 billion CSK (over US $70 million).[31] The selling price for these companies surpassed the original price in most cases.

Caveats for Investors

Potential foreign investors evaluating a privatizing Czech or Slovak company must overcome internal issues including corporate inertia and insolvency. According to Jan Klacek, head of the Economics Institute of the Czechoslovak Academy of Sciences, corporate inertia may be the most intractable problem to solve. A major external factor is the collapse of traditional markets, specifically the Soviet Union and the former German Democratic Republic. The most seriously affected industries include armaments, textiles, and leather.[32]

Asset valuation is another critical issue for any potential investor. The foreign investor should be prepared to work with the Czech or Slovak counterpart to ensure transparency and competition. Antitrust ramifications must be considered for any large transaction as specified under the new Law on Protection of Economic Competition, effective March 1991. The Competition Law is relevant primarily in two situations: 1) when a new joint-stock company holds 30% or more market share for a specific market; and 2) when a merger involves a company with more than 30% market share. In the first case, the National Asset Fund prepares an analysis of potential market abuse, to be reviewed by the Competition Office. The appropriate jurisdictional governmental body can overrule a disapproval. In the second case, the standard to be applied is whether the "'detriment' to competition resulting from the merger is 'less important' than the advantages to be thus gained." The law does not specify if appeal is possible in this case.[33]

Investment Protection and Dispute Settlement

Dispute Settlement for Ventures in Foreign Trade

The *U.S.-Czechoslovakia Bilateral Agreement on Trade Relations* of 1990 states that each party shall receive national treatment regarding access to courts and administrative bodies. Neither country shall claim immunity from taxation on commercial transactions except as provided in other bilateral agreements.

Commercial disputes will be settled by arbitration provided for in agreements or contracts between nationals or companies. The parties may apply for arbitration under any internationally recognized arbitration rules, including United Nations Commission on International Trade Laws (UNCITRAL) rules; an appointing authority under those rules should be designated in any country other than the United States or the CSFR. A place of arbitration should be mutually decided by the parties. Unless otherwise agreed, any country other than the United States or the CSFR, which is party to the 1958 U.N. Convention on the Recognition and Enforcement of Foreign Arbitral Awards, is acceptable. The trade agreement, however, does not limit the preferred means of arbitration mutually agreed by the parties. Both the CSFR and the United States shall ensure the enforcement of arbitral awards within its respective territory.[34] (See section on foreign trade, "Approaching the Market," for further information on the U.S.-Czechoslovakia Bilateral Agreement on Trade Relations.)

The Act on Economic Relations with Foreign Countries (April 19,1990; effective May 1, 1990), Article 47, named the Arbitration Court at the Czechoslovak Chamber of Commerce and Industry as the permanent body to settle disputes concerning property claims in international trade relations. Rules of procedure for the Arbitration Court are proposed by its board and announced by the Federal Ministry of Foreign Trade in the Collection of Laws.

Dispute Settlement with Regard to Foreign Investment

In the investment arena, disputes between joint ventures and other Czechoslovak enterprises will use the same arbitration procedures as Czechoslovak enterprises, unless another procedure is identified in the joint venture contract, according to Bohuslav Klein, who was Chief of the Legal Department, Czechoslovak Chamber of Commerce and Industry, in 1989. If the parties agree on the arbiters, arbitration can be done on an "ad hoc" basis; otherwise, the dispute is settled by the Czecho-slovak State Arbitration Board. Arbitration is conducted according to the joint venture contract for all other disputes, including those between joint venture partners; the contract may specify arbitration by an international body, such as the International Chamber of Commerce.[35]

It is important to note that the United States and Czechoslovakia signed an agreement on the Protection and Promotion of Investment in 1991, forcing changes in the arbitration process for joint ventures or for wholly owned subsidiaries. In addition, the CSFR Commercial Code was revised in 1991, affecting foreign trading activities, including dispute settlement.[36]

Section 22 of the Joint Venture Law, officially entitled, The Enterprise with Foreign Property (or Capital) Participation Act (effective May 1, 1990, amending Act No. 173 of 1988, Coll.), states that property of the joint venture may *only* be expropriated "in accordance with the rules of an act." The acts referred to are those such as the Construction Act and the Air Transport Act, which allow the CSFR government the right of *eminent domain*. An investor in a joint venture should find assurance in the fact that major construction projects have five- to ten-year lead times. Additionally, the Joint Venture Law provides compensation to the company at the current value at the time of the enforcement of the expropriation. This compensation is freely transferable abroad, and it is made in the currency in which payment was made for the shares by the foreign investor, or in the currency of the country in which the corporation is domiciled.[37] (For further information on dispute settlement, see section on "Licensing, Patents, and Trademarks.")

Joint Ventures and Wholly Owned Subsidiaries

The movement toward a market-oriented economy has necessitated a rapid and comprehensive overhauling of laws and regulations in Czechoslovakia. According to Deputy Minister of Foreign Trade Zdenek Cerveny, 600 laws and 3,000 regulations must be changed.

In addition, some laws were written specifically for the transition period and are being amended as needed to implement the economic reform. More than 40 laws were slated to be adopted or amended by December 31, 1990, in such areas as banking, stock exchanges, bonds and obligations, and import and value-added taxes.[38]

One example is a February 1991 revision of the Joint Venture Law liberalizing the establishment of joint ventures in cases in which the Czechoslovak partner is a private person or the company is a wholly owned subsidiary of a foreign enterprise. This liberalization allows a company to forego the license formerly required; the company only needs to register with the Company Register in the District Courts. A license from the Ministry of Finance, however, is required if the joint venture partner is a Czechoslovak State-Owned Enterprise.[39]

One reason given by Prime Minister Calfa for this recent liberalization of joint ventures is that although the number of joint ventures is increasing, the volume of equity capital is still low. As of March 1991, 70 of the joint ventures have an initial capital of more than 10 million CSK; 12 joint ventures have over 100 million CSK; and three joint ventures have more than one billion CSK.[40]

The Joint Venture Law, more technically called the Act Concerning Enterprises with Foreign Capital (Equity) Participation, was originally passed in November 1988, effective January 1, 1989 (Coll. No. 173/1988); it was amended effective May 1 1990 (Act 112/1990). The highlights of those changes included the following:[41]

1. Allows both Czechoslovak natural and juristic persons to participate in enterprises with foreign capital participation or joint ventures;

2. Allows 100% foreign ownership, i.e., wholly owned subsidiaries;

3. Allows foreign partners to buy into an existing Czechoslovak enterprise without having to form a new legal entity;

4. Simplifies licensing procedures; the single authority is the Federal Ministry of Finance in agreement with the national (republic level) Ministries of Finance, Prices, and Wages. For banking, the authority is the Czechoslovak State Bank. (Note: amended February 1991. Procedures were further liberalized, requiring only registration except in certain strategic industries such as armaments.)

5. Allows a choice of legal code other than that of the CSFR to govern joint ventures and its ensuing relations;

6. Reduces the obligatory reserve funds from three to one;

7. Introduced the obligatory offering of foreign currencies by the enterprise (at least 30%) to a competent bank and allowed enterprises to open foreign currency accounts at a foreign bank, subject to approval by the Czechoslovak State Bank. (Note: amended by foreign exchange act of November 28, 1990, effective January 1, 1991, requiring 100% sale of foreign currencies, except for equity capital, to a foreign exchange financial institution.)

Because laws, decrees, and regulations are changing the business environment very rapidly, provisions of the 1988 law and its 1990 revision have not only been altered by the new Foreign Exchange Act, but also by the following:

- Tax regulations
- A recent clarification by the State Bank on transfers of income from foreign investments. (See Announcement of the State Bank of Czechoslovakia No. 15, under section "Financing and Capital Markets: Payment Modalities" later in this chapter.)
- Amendments announced in February 1991 to further simplify starting a business.

It is, therefore, essential for any business to check on the most recent reforms with regard to licensing, registration, foreign exchange, and taxation. For example, a new tax code is expected to be developed by 1993 and a new commercial code was enacted during the summer of 1991.

The most recent amendment to the Joint Venture Law (Act 112/1990, effective May 1, 1990), added the following liberalizing provisions:

- Transfer of profits to a foreign country out of foreign currency generated by the company is possible;

- If a company is liquidated or participation is reduced, a foreign investor may transfer his or her shares to a foreign country in the original paid-in currency;

- Foreign employees may transfer their income to foreign countries without limit;

- Monies for social insurance, pension schemes, and other benefit programs may be freely transferred for foreign employees; but only foreign currencies generated by the company may be used for this purpose.

According to the Joint Venture Law, joint ventures may be established in all areas, except for those in the defense arena or impinging on the security of the country. Regulated sectors for investment include railroads, the post, telecommunications, and armaments.[42] Regulated sectors for foreign trade include armaments, drugs, and tobacco.

The Economic Code

The economic code regulates the legal form of a company as well as governs relations of entrepreneurial activities of legal and natural persons authorized to conduct such activities. Legal forms permitted in Czechoslovakia include stock companies, associations, limited liability companies, special partnerships (societe commandite), special stock partnerships, and ordinary business partnerships. The Economic Code (Act No. 103/1990) also governs State-Owned Enterprises, unless regulated by special laws — "the commercial company, the silent company, the consortium, and the joint venture; the register of enterprises; economic penalties; and the organs of economic establishments ...which manage economic activities."[43]

Private Entrepreneurship in Czechoslovakia

Czechoslovak citizens who are private entrepreneurs are governed by the Private Enterprise Law (Act No. 105/1990). The latest amendment to this act removed a number of requirements. It states the following:

- It is no longer necessary to obtain a permit from the local government.

- It is no longer a requirement to hire only family members.

- There are no longer restrictions on the acquisitions and ownership of property or production facilities.

Presently, companies operate under three different codes: the Civil Code, which governs relationships with private citizens; the Economic Code, which governs relationships with entrepreneurs and legal persons, such as Czechoslovak corporations or organizations; and the Czechoslovak Foreign Trade Code, which governs relationships with foreign parties.

The Act on Private Enterprise (Act No. 105/1990) (also called the Act of April 19, 1990 on Private Entrepreneurial Activities of Natural Persons) outlines the rights of private citizens to engage in entrepreneurial activities. These regulations, however, must also be considered in conjunction with many other statues and laws, as well as the new amendments to the constitution. Examples include the Commercial Code, which was revised in July 1991; various tax acts; the Labor Act; the Joint Stock Companies Act; the State-Owned Companies Act; and the Act on Economic Relations with Foreign Countries.

Private entrepreneurs may now engage in activities which were formerly permitted only to certain organizations, provided they can meet the regulations related to those activities. Areas excluded from this act, which will be regulated separately, include: health care, legal advice, auditing, copyrights, and agriculture.[44]

Private entrepreneurs are not subjected to obligations in the State plan for economic and social development. They may hire as many employees as needed and may acquire unlimited property for the purpose of conducting business. Relationships between employer and employees are governed by labor laws, presently under development.

To engage in business, the entrepreneur must be 18 years of age, have no criminal record, have the qualifications for the proposed business, and be capable of legal acts. The entrepreneur must register in the Company Register within the municipality. This registration has implications for tax treatment and requires the company to pay sales tax and to satisfy special accounting regulations.[45] In addition, foreign residents are required to obtain an authorization, which will be attached to the application, from a central government department of either the Czech or Slovak Republic.

Accounting principles for entrepreneurs are set forth in separate laws. The Ministry of Finance will be stipulating the amount of allowable depreciation. If the entrepreneur engages in business relationships with other countries, he or she must be registered to do so either under the Joint Venture Law or the Law Dealing with Economic Relations with Foreign Companies (Foreign Trade Law).[46]

Finally, certain behavior that is an abuse of economic power is prohibited by this law. Such behavior might include gaining a disproportionate advantage over other competitors by restricting supply of one's product or hiding or accumulating product. This law is modeled after the German type of unfair competition law that prohibits a wide range of behaviors in order to protect consumers or competition.[47]

Opportunities for Investment

Priority sectors for investment in 1991, as identified by the Federal Ministry of Economy, include the following:

1. Transportation — Highways, railways, air terminals in Prague and Bratislava to create a transportation system compatible to United Nations EDIFACT/DOCIMEL system;

2. Telecommunications — Digital telephone system, public data and cellular phone systems;

3. Environment — Pollution control, hazardous waste treatment facilities, reduction of nitrous oxide emissions, production of nonasbestos sealing and friction materials, and water treatment systems;

4. Chemicals — Value-added chemical and petrochemical products;

5. Light Industry — Sugar refineries, packaging technology, wood processing;

6. Energy — Upgrading and creating new nuclear and natural gas resources; application and development of flue-gas desulphurization technology for coal-fired power plants; and thermal insulation;

7. Metallurgy — Development and production of specialty steels; aluminum production;

8. Tourism — Preservation of historical centers;

9. Services — Market distribution, banking, and insurance.[48]

These sectors may qualify for tax incentives and credit guarantees. The Federal Foreign Investment Agency in the Ministry of the Economy can provide more information on the investment approval process, regulations, and other matters. The contact is Richard Sumann at Agentura Pro Zahranicni Investice (Federal Foreign Investment Agency), Federal Ministry of Economy, Nabrezi Kpt. Jarose 1000, Prague 7; Telephone (42-2) 389-2627; Fax (42-2) 375-659; Telex 121044.

Each republic also has a foreign investment agency as mentioned earlier. No information is available on the Slovak agency. The functions of the Agency for Foreign Investment and Assistance of the Czech Republic include the following:

1. To provide information on investment opportunities, economic conditions, and government regulations.

2. To provide advice to potential foreign investors, to recommend joint venture partners, and to provide analytical support to municipal administrations.

3. To facilitate negotiations and contacts between foreign parties and Czech enterprises.

4. To implement privatization and foreign investment objectives of the Federal and Czech governments, including coordination with similar agencies and, when necessary, evaluation of joint venture proposals.[49]

Czechoslovaks particularly seek joint ventures which will involve technology transfer to assist in making their enterprises internationally competitive. In addition to telecommunications, transportation, and environmental protection mentioned previously, such areas include robotics, precision engineering, biotechnology, medical diagnostics, and pharmaceuticals. Traditional industries of strength for Czechoslovakia, which are good candidates for joint ventures, are aviation, the automotive industry, machinery, and nuclear energy stations.[50]

The U.S. Foreign Commercial Service in Prague prepared a list of the "Best Prospects for Trade and Investment, 1991." These prospects include the following:

- microcomputer systems and software applications
- water pollution testing and control equipment
- mineral extraction equipment
- processing and packaging machinery for fruit, vegetables, milk, and cheese
- beef, pork, and poultry slaughtering equipment and facilities
- hotel and restaurant equipment
- airport cargo handling equipment
- highway and railway engineering services
- insurance services
- advertising and public relations services
- management training services
- financial services for valuation, assessment, and auditing
- medical equipment for cardiac and cancer treatment

Price Waterhouse has identified other growth areas for joint ventures. Some of these include the following:

- consumer goods, especially for leisure activities (e.g., bicycles, skateboards, and tennis shoes
- household appliances and durable goods (e.g., refrigerators, microwave ovens, furniture)

- modules, components, and materials for industrial technology (e.g., electronics, precision hydraulics, pneumatic equipment, engines, dyes, ceramic materials)
- ecological engineering to solve pollution problems (e.g., powder separators, sensors, water cleaners, monitoring equipment, desulphurating equipment)
- communications networks and equipment
- machinery (e.g., in the areas of construction, woodprocessing, road building, agriculture, small transport aircraft, and sports aircraft)
- medical and health care.[51]

Recent investments in Czechoslovakia range from hotels to telecommunications to automotive manufacturing. In the tourism industry, Raiffeisen Zentralbank of Austria is financing the construction of a 500-bed hotel in Prague which will be built by Penta, a subsidiary of Lufthansa. The Hotel Palace is a $26 million joint venture between Cedok, the Czechoslovak tourist agency; Hotelinvest, a well-known Czechoslovak hotel operator; and the Austrian construction firm Varimpex. Tesla Prague negotiated a multibillion dollar deal with U.S. West and Bell Atlantic, which commenced in early 1991, to create a telecommunications joint venture. Czechoslovakia's first joint venture with a foreign firm was created in 1987 with Senetak of Denmark in the field of chromatography; this technique is used in the pharmaceutical and food industries as well as for testing in the biological and environmental fields. As mentioned previously, Volkswagen of Germany won a bid to be the joint venture partner for Skoda to produce passenger cars.

Czechoslovakia is looking for large investments which will bring in new technology. As of the fall of 1990, the Ministry of Foreign Trade listed 82 contracts for joint ventures. Fifty-six joint ventures were operating at the end of 1989. They broke down into the following sectors:

1. Industrial production — 16

2. Travel and tourism — 14

3. Services — 8

4. Technology — 7

5. Agriculture — 5

6. Software — 4

7. Construction — 2

Strong candidates for foreign investment are those areas in which Czechoslovakia is traditionally strong: chemicals, textiles, shoes, glassware, porcelain, bicycles, cars, and aircraft. Key sectors which should not be excluded include tourism and other services, foodstuffs, and household goods.[52]

Cooperation Agreements, Leasing, and Franchising

Cooperation Agreements

Cooperation agreements, in this context, include any type of arrangement to conduct business with a foreign partner — minority joint venture, majority joint venture, trading partnership or contract, licensing, subcontracting, or franchising. The foreign partner must decide which form is best for his or her individual firm as well as the type of business in which he or she is engaged. The greater the involvement, the higher the risk. For example, there is a higher risk, due to higher up-front costs and a longer pay off time, associated with foreign direct investment (such as a joint venture or a wholly owned subsidiary).

Less risky relationships are licensing, exporting and importing, and franchising arrangements. In such arrangements, less capital is invested; profits are realized more rapidly; and it is easier to extricate one's firm from a deal. A typical first step into the international market is to export product; the degree of risk is associated with the type of credit which can be obtained and the degree of trust between the trading partners. A later step may be to set up an overseas sales office or to work through sales or representative offices of an associated firm in the new foreign market.

Leasing

Two areas need to be addressed in discussing leasing in the CSFR: 1) leasing property for a business; and 2) buying equipment from abroad under a leasing arrangement. Foreigners are permitted to lease, but not buy, land for businesses. It should be noted that when purchasing a company, three sets of property rights and associated sales can be negotiated: the property on which the business is located; the equipment and machinery used to carry out the business; and the actual "business" of the business.

Leasing is being developed as a financing tool in the CSFR; for that reason, few instances of lease-purchase of equipment and goods such as automobiles can be cited. However, it is considered to be very popular, due to tax advantages. Special permission is needed to set up a leasing company.

Franchising

No laws or regulations specific to franchising exist in Czechoslovakia, although various laws do impinge on how franchising can be done in the CSFR. For example, a potential franchiser should pay attention to the trademark protection laws, land ownership laws, the Competition Law, and laws pertaining to the termination of relationships. The franchiser must be in a position to provide exclusive service, under a protected trademark, with a specified operator or franchisee within a particular territory — and he or she must be able to terminate a franchise if necessary.[53]

Other issues which a franchiser must address include repatriation rights and currency convertibility; costs and procedures for obtaining trademark and service protection; and remedies for infringement of those protections. In addition, franchisers may be subject to bureaucratic delays associated with obtaining the appropriate permits and approvals (i.e., zoning, health, building, etc.) necessary to conduct such a business.[54]

Law firms such as Brownstein, Zeidman, and Schomer; Rudnick & Wolfe; and Adlers of London are specializing in franchising in Eastern Europe. These companies have joined forces with a Canadian consortium to establish EastEuropeLaw, an enterprise specializing in franchising, real estate, and commercial law in Eastern Europe.[55] EastEuropeLaw is exploring the applicability of franchising in the privatization of State-Owned Enterprises.

According to Michael Brennan, a partner in Rudnick & Wolfe, franchising in Eastern Europe requires one to adjust standard lease approaches to real estate property, since a government agency may act as a franchiser. In the United States, a company like McDonald's Corporation usually owns the property on which the restaurant sits and then leases it to their franchisees; other companies sign "head leases" and then sublease to franchisees. If a government agency in Eastern Europe acts as the franchiser, the franchise is often held in a self-liquidating trust that returns the property to the agency if the franchise fails.[56]

Franchising in Eastern Europe is usually undertaken as a joint venture, because very few private entrepreneurs have the capital to purchase a franchise. However, franchising to individuals and private businesses is expected to be not far off. Sectors in which companies are seeking franchising partners include fast foods, lodging, and business services.

Problems associated with franchising in Eastern Europe in addition to lack of capital, include uncertainty as to land title; quality and delivery of supplies; the length of time it takes to set up an operation (three to five years compared to half that in the United States); and lack of local entrepreneurial expertise, particularly in sales, advertising, and marketing. Franchising is seen as a boon to the free-market economies of Eastern Europe in that it can provide access to financing, marketing expertise, and know-how.[57]

The foreign investor also gains advantages from franchising: 1) it enables a company to side-step the state controlled distribution systems, which are antiquated and have no incentives to meet delivery deadlines; 2) it provides greater control over quality and price; and 3) lowers the investment risk, bringing sales and brand recognition at a lower cost than joint ventures.[58]

Third-Country Projects

A foreign enterprise is permitted to contract with a Czech or Slovak firm to do a project in a third country, such as Kuwait. A foreign company subcontracting to a Czech or Slovak firm will need to investigate areas such as import or export licensing; taxes or surcharges on products or services; method of making a contract legally binding and enforcing it; means of payment; and, generally, the rules for conducting business.

Taxation and Regulatory Conditions

The Ministry of Finance, Department of Taxes, is the jurisdictional body for the regulation of taxes. Enterprise taxes are governed by Act No. 157/1989 Coll. of Laws; they include the Income Tax and the Wage Tax. The basic provisions of the tax laws and regulations include the following:

Income/Profit Tax

The tax rate for the first 200,000 CSK of profit is 20% for companies with foreign capital participation; above that, 40% if foreign equity participation is equal to or more than 30%. If a company makes more than 200,000 CSK profit and has less than 30% foreign equity participation, the tax rate is 55%. The tax rate on banks was reduced from 75% to 55%.[59]

Tax Holidays

Tax holidays may be requested for two years after initial business operations begin.[60]

Wage Tax

The wage tax is usually 50% of the wages paid out; in selected areas, such as services, it is 20%.

Dividend Taxes

The general tax rate on dividends for foreign participants is 25%. Agreements exist with 22 foreign governments as well as with the former CMEA countries to prevent double taxation; the lower tax rate applies, which may be 0%, 5%, 10%, or 15%. For subjects of the CSFR, the "tax on dividends is added to their profit which is then taxed as a whole."[61] The tax is 25% for CSFR individuals and 50% on CSFR companies with no foreign participation. The tax on dividends and also on profits as currently written results in double taxation for CSFR entities; this law will be changed in the new tax code expected in 1993. This double taxation does not affect joint ventures with foreign participation or wholly-owned foreign subsidiaries.

The government is preparing a major reform of the taxation system for 1992 to 1993. They are planning to overhaul the profits tax, introduce a unified personal income tax, and replace the turnover tax with a value-added tax. Appropriate administrative changes will occur concomitantly. The reform is intended to reduce the burden on the private sector and to replace taxes used with the former system of controlled prices.

Retail taxation was previously based on the turnover tax, levied according to the difference between wholesale and retail prices. As of January 1, 1991, four turnover tax rates were set, ranging from 0% to 32% of the purchase price. Also introduced at this time was a consumer tax on such items as petroleum products, alcoholic beverages, tobacco products, and passenger cars. These tax rates are higher than the turnover tax rates.

The government is also in the process of abolishing both domestic and foreign trade subsidies. Domestically, the phasing out of retail subsidies, the "negative turnover tax," has been part of the process of price liberalization formally instituted January 1, 1991. Food subsidies began to be eliminated in June 1990; the removal of the remaining subsidies, primarily for energy products, is to be completed as soon as feasible.[62] According to Pavol Parizek, Head of International Finance, Ministry of Finance, regulated prices remained on approximately 10% to 15% of products as of May 1991. The products with controlled prices are limited in number, applying to cases in which there is a monopoly position (such as energy prices) — to basic foods (such as meat, bread, and potatoes) — and to certain intermediate industrial goods.[63]

Taxes on international trade were dependent on the system of controlled prices prior to price and trade liberalization instituted on January 1, 1991. The old system of foreign trade levies and subsidies, known as FENZO, was abolished at that time.[64]

FINANCING AND CAPITAL MARKETS

Banking and Other Financial Institutions

The Central Bank of Czechoslovakia — referred to in the CSFR as the State Bank of Czechoslovakia (Statni Banka Ceskoslovenska) — performed both central bank and commercial bank functions under the nonmarket system. The previous regime to President Vaclav Havel's instituted reforms to segregate these two functions, but they were not implemented. Portions of the former State Bank which had dealt with commercial banking were set up independently, although the State Bank continued to be a major shareholder. Presently, the banking system is in a period of flux as new banks are being set up to provide service according to Western standards and activities. The new system of banks includes representational offices of foreign banks as well as foreign joint venture banks.[65]

The State Bank is reorganizing the banking system in conjunction with the International Monetary Fund and the World Bank as well as with bilateral cooperation. The State Bank will also help create the new stock market and the foreign exchange market. Two important acts — a Securities Act and a Financial Companies Act — have yet to be created.

The State Bank holds shares in two commercial banks which conduct foreign exchange transactions: Czechoslovenska Obchodni Banka (Foreign Trade Bank) and Zivnostenska Banka, whose primary business has historically been foreign exchange transactions. Three other commercial banks were created from the old Central Bank: Komercni Banka in Prague; Investicni Banka, which supports government investments; and Vseobecna Uverova Banka (General Credit Bank) in Bratislava. In addition, two former savings banks now serve commercial clients as well as households — Ceska Statni Sporitelna and Slovenska Statni Sporitelna.

Mr. Josef Tosovsky, President of the State Bank, describes the system as still very monopolistic, but the number of commercial banks is growing. Foreign banks are creating branches, subsidiaries, as well as the newly created "joint-stock banks."

Examples of these joint venture banks include Agro-Banka, with participation of Creditstalt of Vienna, and Tatra Banka of Bratislava, with participation of Reifeisen Zentral Bank of Austria, Credit Suisse First Boston, and private Austrian investors.[66]

Payment Modalities (Convertibility, Foreign Exchange, and Bank Accounts)

Convertibility and Exchange Rate Policy

As part of the macroeconomic reforms instituted as Czechoslovakia moves to a market economy, the government introduced a single exchange rate on December 28, 1991, and on January 1, 1992 it adopted internal convertibility.

Convertibility is the ability to trade a specific currency, in this case the koruna or crown, on the world currency market. Internal convertibility means that companies are entitled to purchase hard currency (i.e., freely convertible currencies such as Deutsche marks, French francs, or U.S. dollars) with Czechoslovak crowns to conduct current account transactions. Current account transactions are the purchase and sale of goods and services.

The second phase of convertibility — full convertibility — will include capital account transactions and the trading of currency abroad. Presently, these transactions are controlled by the State Bank. No specific date has been set for full convertibility.

The single exchange rate set for the crown against the dollar in December 1990 was 28 crowns per U.S. dollar, devalued from a former commercial rate of 14.25 per dollar and revalued from a tourist rate of 30 crowns per dollar. Since January 1, 1991, the crown has floated against the dollar within a set band.[67] This rate is established on a daily basis by the Interbank Foreign Exchange Market, which consists of the State Bank and the commercial banks.

The central bank — State Bank of Czechoslovakia — can intervene in the market to stabilize exchange rate fluctuations. The World Bank and the International Monetary Fund have created a stand-by facility to provide foreign exchange reserves for the stabilization program.[68]

Foreign Exchange Policies and Bank Accounts

On November 28, 1990, the Czechoslovak Federal Assembly passed the Foreign Exchange Act, effective January 1, 1991, which provides the basis for internal convertibility. The new Foreign Exchange Law abolishes the old quota requirements on foreign exchange denominated accounts; allows unlimited current account transactions in foreign currencies; requires companies registered in Czechoslovakia to surrender all foreign exchange earnings to appropriate financial institutions for crowns; and requires companies to maintain business accounts only in crowns.[69] At the same time, financial institutions are required to sell foreign currency on demand at the daily market rate so that businesses can conduct current account transactions.

Some exceptions with regard to surrendering foreign exchange and the holding of foreign exchange accounts are allowed for private individuals and joint ventures. Private individuals may hold foreign exchange denominated accounts up to certain limits, to be used primarily for tourist purposes. Joint ventures are considered Czechoslovak legal entities and are treated as domestic companies; however, a joint venture may keep the foreign equity capital of the foreign partner in a separate foreign exchange denominated account with transferability guaranteed. Foreign citizens and foreign companies may also keep foreign exchange denominated accounts in CSFR banks, with guaranteed transferability, according to Pavol Parizek, Head, International Finance, Ministry of Finance.[70]

In order for a Czechoslovak company, including joint ventures and wholly owned subsidiaries registered in the CSFR, to obtain foreign currency for any purpose, it presents an order to exchange available crowns for a designated foreign currency to the State Bank or authorized financial foreign exchange institution (banks). The purchase may be for imported components or making distributions to foreign shareholders. However, there are several precautions to foreign investors. To transfer foreign exchange abroad from a koruna denominated account — to pay dividends, to purchase foreign imports, or to repatriate profits — the enterprise must present the appropriate financial statement to prove that the transaction is a current account transaction and that funds were generated out of profits from the business. Such financial statements include the balance sheet, a profit and loss statement, or the invoice for the imported goods.[71]

Additionally, there are two important limits. A 20% surcharge is assessed on the import of certain consumer goods, primarily for finished products; however, it is expected to be phased out in the near future. Of more import for joint ventures and wholly owned subsidiaries is a special set of exemptions from internal convertibility. A special permission of the State Bank is required to buy foreign exchange for the purpose of purchasing immovable assets or securities from abroad or to receive a foreign exchange credit from a foreign bank or financial institution. The latter could be detrimental for companies who plan to obtain foreign currency financing.[72] Transfers of profits and dividends on investments will be subject to the bilateral investment treaty.

In Announcement No. 15 from the State Bank of Czechoslovakia, a clarification of the Foreign Exchange Law was made on the transfers of income from foreign investments in the CSFR. The following were determined:

1. Investment income is considered part of the current account and can be transferred abroad.

2. Investment income includes profits from businesses, interest, capital gains, income from equities and securities, and fees from intellectual property.

3. Income in koruna gained primarily from the sale of goods and services provided by a foreign exchange expatriate (nonresident individual or company) is not considered investment income.

4. Transfers of income are executed under the Foreign Exchange Act (#528/1990); upon the request of a registered company or entrepreneur, a licensed Czechoslovak financial institution is obliged to transfer to a foreign investor the foreign exchange equivalent of the amount of his or her koruna investment income.

5. Proof of origin of the funds must be provided with the request for the transfer of investment income (i.e., balance sheet, profit and loss statement, list of holders of equity and securities, etc.).

6. The transfer of investment income may be abroad or to an foreign currency denominated nonresident account with a financial institution in the CSFR.

7. A foreign investor can instruct a juridical person (company in the CSFR) to deposit his or her income in "his [or her] Czechoslovak currency denominate nonresident account with a financial institution."

8. A foreign exchange license from the State Bank is required to conduct transactions as in number 7 above. The license requires proof of origin.

9. These procedures are in effect until they are superseded by an international agreement on the protection and promotion of investment to which the CSFR is a signatory.[73]

Countertrade and Buybacks

The generic name for a *quid pro quo* transaction is "countertrade;" a buyback is actually a form of countertrade. More specifically, countertrade is a "generic name for reciprocal trade, which contractually links purchases of goods and services by an importer with exports of goods from the importing country. Countertrade arrangements include counterpurchase, buyback (or compensation), and barter — or various combinations of these forms. Sometimes this term is used interchangeably with the term 'offset.' Buyback or compensation is the sale of plant, equipment, and/or technology in return for products resulting from the facility once it is functional; it usually requires 5-20 years for completion."[74]

Countertrade may be used as a financing tool, a marketing tool, or a tool for economic development. Prior to the breakup of the Eastern bloc and the move to develop market economies, countertrade was the type of trade and investment conducted with COMECON countries (the common market of the former USSR and the Eastern bloc). Due to the lack of convertibility of currency, creative financing arrangements were necessary to transfer currencies. The problem of "blocked currencies," still exists to the extent that foreign exchange reserves are limited. For example, the former Soviet Union used many industrial and manufactured goods from the CSFR which need to be serviced; however, there is a lack of foreign exchange for such payments. This systemic barrier was pointed out by Mr. Pedrik, Vice Minister of Foreign Affairs, at an Atlantic Council briefing on Czechoslovakia in February 1991.

In general, countries entering a free market system prefer to be paid in hard currency, so that they may use that foreign exchange in world markets. Although countertrade and buyback may be used for the short and medium term, one can expect that this form of trade and investment will be discouraged; it is also considered to be trade inhibiting and against the principles of such multilateral agreements as the General Agreement on Tariffs and Trade (GATT).

Equity Finance and Privatization (U.S. Assistance Programs)

The Overseas Private Investment Corporation (OPIC) now offers insurance and financing to U.S. investors in Czechoslovakia; the Export-Import Bank of the United States provides insurance and loan and credit guarantee programs to U.S. exporters. These activities became possible after the United States and the CSFR signed bilateral agreements permitting such activities.

OPIC, an independent agency of the U.S. government can now insure U.S. investors against political risk and political violence, expropriation, and currency inconvertibility for CSFR investments. OPIC provides direct loans of $.5 to $6 million to small- and medium-sized companies, or loan guarantees, usually between $2-$25 million (although they can be up to $50 million) to U.S. lenders (banks) for projects. OPIC works with other lenders, such as the Multilateral Investment Guarantee Agency, the International Finance Corporation, and the European Bank for Reconstruction and Development in the development of loan packages. OPIC provides some limited consulting services to link U.S. and CSFR companies, specifically through their database, the "Opportunity Bank"; additionally, it leads investment missions to Czechoslovakia. OPIC is also participating in the organization of a private mutual fund, the Central and Eastern European Growth Fund, to be managed by Salomon Brothers. This fund will leverage investments in certain countries of Central and Eastern Europe, including Czechoslovakia, Poland, Hungary, the former "East Germany," and Yugoslavia.

The Export-Import Bank, or "Ex-Im Bank," also an independent agency of the U.S. government, provides three basic financing programs to increase the sale of U.S. exports overseas: direct loans, loan guarantees, and insurance. Direct loans are made to the foreign buyers of U.S. exports. Guarantees are made to U.S. banks for the financing they extend to a foreign bank or a foreign importer of U.S. goods. Credit insurance policies can be extended (usually for short-term transactions of less than one year) to a U.S. bank or a U.S. exporter who is extending financing (typically through a letter of credit, an open account, or a promissory note) to the foreign purchaser.

Project financing can also be obtained through the U.S. Agency for International Development (USAID) and the U.S. Trade and Development Program (USTDP). USAID presently is offering a multimillion indefinite quantity contract for the privatization of Eastern Europe, including the CSFR. USAID is also funding through the Department of Commerce a "Consortia of American Businesses in Eastern Europe." Under this pilot program, a maximum grant of $500,000 will be provided to nonprofit organizations (the consortia) to set up offices with appropriate staff so that U.S. companies can establish a commercial presence in Eastern Europe. (*See* Office of Export Trading Company Affairs, U.S. Department of Commerce for further information.) U.S. assistance to Eastern Europe is coordinated through the Office of the Special Advisor to the Deputy Secretary for Coordinating Assistance to Eastern Europe, headed by Ambassador Barry.

The U.S. Trade and Development program provides funds for feasibility studies to U.S. businesses for programs which will promote the sale of U.S. exports overseas. TDP will have signed more than $1.5 million in grants by the end of 1991 for such studies in the areas of hazardous waste, upgrading coal-fired power plants, and the modernization of Czechoslovakia's steel industry.

The U.S. Congress recently approved the establishment of the Czech and Slovak-American Enterprise Fund under the SEED II program. The $60 million fund was established in the spring 1991 and is chaired by John R. Petty, former chairman and CEO of Marine Midland Bank. The fund is to encourage the development of the private sector by lending to, or investing in, small- and medium-sized enterprises in the CSFR directly, or indirectly through the American joint venture partner. The funds can also be used for technical and managerial assistance as well as training.[75]

Tapping International Aid Institutions (Multilateral Programs)

Funding is available from the following institutions: the World Bank and the International Monetary Fund, the European Bank for Reconstruction and Development (EBRD), and the International Finance Corporation, an agency within the World Bank.

Czechoslovakia rejoined the World Bank Group and the International Monetary Fund (IMF) on September 20, 1990. The World Bank Group includes the International Bank for Reconstruction and Development (IBRD), the International Development Association (IDA), the Multinational Investment Guarantee Association (MIGA), the International Finance Corporation (IFC), and the International Center for the Settlement of Investment Disputes (ICSID). The CSFR also expects to join the European Community (EC) before the end of the decade; this is a lengthy process, with associate membership being a first step.

Czechoslovakia was a founding member of the World Bank in 1945; its membership was withdrawn in 1954 due to political reasons. The impact of its rejoining is twofold, according to Josef Tosovsky, President, State Bank of Czechoslovakia. It provides technical assistance in moving toward a market-oriented economy as well as financial support (the stand-by facility or stabilization fund), and it bestows its imprimatur on the provision of commercial banking assistance to the CSFR.[76]

World Bank and IMF teams have been working closely with the government of Czechoslovakia to created the economic and financial infrastructure for a market economy, including the establishment of the new banking system and the forthcoming stock market. The IMF program has focused on economic liberalization (e.g., foreign trade, prices, foreign exchange) and appropriate monetary and fiscal policies.[77] Most immediately, it has provided a stabilization fund to provide foreign currency reserves to facilitate internal convertibility.

The International Finance Corporation (IFC) provides direct project financing for private investment in developing countries. The IFC promotes the private sector by offering long-term project loans; providing equity investment, technology, and access to foreign markets through joint ventures; developing capital markets; providing financial and technical services to businesses; and providing advice to governments on investment incentives and privatization programs.[78] Specifically, the IFC is assisting the CSFR to design a mutual fund system to aid the privatization process; it will also support joint ventures in the private sector.[79]

Czechoslovakia attended meetings to establish the European Bank for Reconstruction and Development (EBRD). EBRD was set up to assist the transition of Central and East European countries to market economies and pluralistic democracies. The CSFR's participation in the EBRD is 120 million European Currency Units (ECUs); loans were expected to be available from the EBRD by the second half of 1991, according to Josef Tosovsky of the State Bank.[80]

LICENSING, PATENTS, AND TRADEMARKS

Licensing Policy, Procedures, and Payments

Licensing is a matter of contract law in the CSFR as it is in the United States. Licensing may involve a range of transactions including the licensing of the use of a trademark, licensing of a production process or a technology, or the licensing of a franchise (discussed in this chapter under "Investment Climate"). There are no restrictions on licensing. Licensing fees and royalties are treated like rents, i.e., they are considered part of the current account and can, therefore, be transferred out of the CSFR.

Trademark, Patent, and Copyright Protection

Czechoslovakia participates in the Berne, Paris, and Universal Copyright Conventions. The 1991 International Trade Commission (ITC) Report on Czechoslovakia stated that the record on the protection of intellectual property is "generally good;" however, copyright coverage for cinematographic work covers only 25 years, in violation of the 50 years required under the Berne Convention.

Trademarks may be granted to enterprises with foreign partners or wholly-owned subsidiaries of foreign companies. The new Law on Inventions, Industrial Design, and Rationalization Proposals (No. 527 of Nov. 27, 1990), recognizes exclusive rights of owners of patents and industrial designs. Owners may be either individuals or enterprises who funded the work leading to the invention or design. Excluded from applicability are: 1) discoveries, scientific theories, or mathematical models; 2) external aspects of products; 3) schemes, rules, and methods for performing mental acts; 4) computer programs; and 5) presentations of information.

Patents are granted by the Federal Office for Inventions and are in effect for 20 years. A "license contract" is granted to work the invention; it may be revoked if the patent is not being used or if an important public interest is endangered. The address provided by the U.S. Embassy in Prague for the office concerned with patents and copyrights is: Institute for Patents and Innovations, Vaclavske namesti 19, 113 46 Prague 1; (Tel) (42/2) 235 2152.

Industrial design is the "external aspect of a product, which is new and which is susceptible of industrial application."[81] Industrial designs must be registered with the Register of Industrial Designs. As with patents, the right to an industrial design may lapse from lack of use or expiration of registration.

Prior use clauses exist for both patents and industrial designs; these clauses protect persons or enterprises who had been working independently on the patent or industrial design prior to the rise of the priority right.

A patent may also apply to a production process; the effect of this patent covers identical products to that produced by the patented production process, unless there is proof to the contrary.[82] In addition, the creator of any technical, manufacturing, or operational improvement—or solutions to health, safety, and environmental problems—shall have the right to disseminate such improvements (i.e., "rationalization proposals").[83]

Disputes arising with regard to inventions, industrial designs, and rationalization proposals are to be decided by the courts or economic arbitration boards, unless where this law asserts they will be decided by the Federal Office for Inventions. In the areas of health, biotechnology, and the environment (specifically, in relation to prevention, diagnosis, and treatment of the human body and of animals as well as in protection of plants from pests and diseases), certificates are offered to appropriate individuals and enterprises subject to Decrees from the Ministries of Health (for humans) and the Ministries of Agriculture (for animals and plants) in the Czech and Slovak Republics.

The principal of reciprocity is observed, providing the same rights and duties to foreign persons or enterprises as those held by Czechoslovak subjects. Provisions of international agreements binding the CSFR are not affected by this law.[84]

Czechoslovakia's new patent laws bring it into compliance with international treaties, including the U.S.-Czechoslovak Bilateral Agreement on Trade Relations which outlines U.S. conditions for most-favored-nation status. As stated under the bilateral agreement, both parties agreed to provide "adequate and effective protection and enforcement for patents, trademarks, copyrights, trade secrets and layout designs for integrated circuits." Each party also agreed to the following:

- Enact or enhance measures to protect, by copyright, computer programs and databases as literary works.
- Extend protection of audiovisual works to 50 years from date the work is made public.
- Provide protection for sound recordings for 50 years from date of publication and prevent unauthorized distribution, reproduction, and importation.
- Provide protection of integrated circuit layout designs. .Provide product and process protection for technology, exclusive of materials used in atomic weapons.
- Provide comprehensive protection for trade secrets.

It was agreed that the legislation necessary to implement these obligations would be submitted to the respective legislative bodies by December 31, 1991; a "best effort" would be made to implement the legislation by this date as well.[85]

VISITING AND LOCATING

The Short-Term Business Visitor

Visas and Currency

A visa is not required for entering the CSFR for stays up to 30 days. There is no obligatory exchange of currency as one enters, nor is there a limit on the amount that can be brought in. However, one must advise customs officials of the amount brought in so that it may be taken out again. The Czechoslovak currency — the koruna or crown — may not be imported or exported; it may only be used within the country. Currency may be converted at banks and certain travel agencies, stores, and hotels in the CSFR.

Hotel Accommodations

Hotel reservations should be made in advance due to a shortage of rooms and great demand; in summer, a two-month lead time is suggested. Average prices may exceed prices of equivalent accommodations in Western Europe. Reservations may be made either through a travel agency such as CEDOK (for beds in hotels), PRAGOTOUR (private accommodations), or through a hotel. Forum, Palace, Intercontinental, Jalta, Alcron, Panorama, Esplanade, and Praha are some hotels suggested by the U.S. Embassy in Prague. The hotels in downtown Prague are conveniently located close to most ministries (within 20 minutes by public transportation). Most hotels now have fax services. Czechoslovakia uses the metric system; its standard voltage is 220 volts, 50 hertz.

Health Precautions/Medical Care

The traveler need not take unusual health precautions in Czechoslovakia; tap water is usually safe. However, the environmental problems that plague Eastern Europe should not be overlooked, particularly if one is traveling to an industrial area. Needed medications should be brought into the country; if medical treatment is needed while in country, the patient must pay. Diagnostic equipment is not on a par with U.S. standards, but doctors are well-trained.

Car Rental

Car rental in the CSFR is expensive, and few Western-made cars are available. Some travelers have suggested that visitors may choose to enter through Germany or Austria, renting a car at a more reasonable rate there. Cars may be rented at the

Prague's Ruzyne airport, which is about ten kilometers from the city center. However, one must also pay attention to the availability and price of gas, since Czechoslovakia's primary supplier — Russia — is renegotiating supplier contracts and requiring hard currency payments. Taxis are available at the airport; it costs approximately $10 to $15 U.S. dollars to travel from the airport to a downtown luxury hotel.

Internal Transportation

Ground and air transportation within Czechoslovakia are extensive, including bus, rail (metro and tram), and air. In Prague, three lines of metro provide service every two minutes during rush hour; 25 tram lines provide 5-minute rush hour service and 10-minute nonrush hour service. Seventy bus lines, which reach the outskirts of Prague, provide five minute service in rush hour. Prices are inexpensive (about $.15 per ride); tickets may be bought in advance or for a single journey. Season tickets are also available for one month, three months, and one year (about $40.00).

Telephone

Telephone numbers in Czechoslovakia vary in length from three to nine digits. A "USADirect" service allows travelers within the CSFR to make collect or credit card calls on the AT&T network; the service is reached by dialing (00 420 00101). There is a six hour time difference between the East Coast of the United States and the CSFR.

Tourist Information

To obtain information on tours, museums, restaurants; to find photocopying, typing, or facsimile services; or to enjoy American snacks, contact the American Hospitality Center, Male namesti 14, 110 00 Prague 1; Tel — (42/2) 269 738. CEDOK, the state travel and hotel corporation, can arrange accommodations, travel, and tours. They have an office at 10 E. 40th St., New York, New York 10157, (212) 689-9720; in Prague at Na prikope 18, 11 35 Prague 1, (42/2) 223 770.

Business Hours/Interpreters

Office hours in the CSFR are typically from 8:00 a.m. to 4:00 p.m.; punctuality is highly valued. Interpreters may be found through the Prague Information Service (PIS), Za Poricskou branou 7, 180 00 Prague 8, (42/2) 264 094 or 266 800; the names of other services can be provided by the U.S. Embassy in Prague.

U.S. Embassy/Consulate

The U.S. Embassy in Prague is located at Trziste 15, 125 48 Prague 1; the mailing address from the United States is c/o AmConGen (PRG), APO, New York 09213. The phone is (42/2) 536 641/9; fax, (42/2) 532 457; telex, 121 196. Shirley Temple Black is the Ambassador; the Commercial Attache is Robert Shipley. The U.S. Consulate in Bratislava is located at Hviezdoslavovo nam. 4; phone, (42/7) 330861; fax, (42/7) 330263. The mailing address from the United States is AmEmbassy Box 5630, APO, New York 09213-5630. The Consul in Bratislava is Paul Hacker.

CSFR Embassy

For further information about Czechoslovakia, contact the Embassy of the Czech and Slovak Federal Republic, 3900 Linnean Avenue, Washington, D.C. 20008; phone, (202) 363-6315.

For Further Information

The information in this section was provided predominantly from the booklet *CZECHOSLOVAKIA: Directory for Trading and Investing*, prepared by the Office of East European and Soviet Affairs and the Commercial Section of the U.S. Embassy in Prague (updated February 1991). Additional information can be obtained from the U.S. Department of Commerce, Eastern Europe Business Information Center (EEBIC), Room 6043, 14th and Constitution Ave., N.W., Washington, D.C. 20230; phone, (202) 377-2645; fax, (202) 377-4473. EEBIC is an information clearinghouse for Eastern Europe; it can refer questions to Commerce's Czechoslovak Desk Officer.

The Expatriate

In addition to the information needed by the short-term visitor, the expatriate needs to know how to set up bank accounts; how to find housing and where to live; the nature of the school system for expatriates; and holidays observed.

Bank Accounts

An expatriate may open both foreign exchange denominated and crown denominated accounts. Foreign exchange brought into Czechoslovakia can be taken out of the country when the expatriate so desires.

Foreign exchange can be freely converted into Czechoslovak crowns, the daily exchange rate set by the State Bank and based on market conditions. The single exchange rate is a floating rate set against the dollar within a certain band. The exchange rate of December 1991 was 30 crowns per dollar and is fairly stable. An expatriate may also open a domestic currency account. (*See* section "Foreign Investment" for information relating to transfers of funds and setting up bank accounts for private enterprises in the CSFR.)

Czechoslovak Chamber of Commerce and Industry

The Czechoslovak Chamber of Commerce and Industry cooperates with the U.S. Chamber of Commerce and participates in the joint body, the Czechoslovak-U.S. Economic Council. It has locations in Prague and Bratislava. Publications on trading and investing in the CSFR are available in English as are copies of recent laws.

The contact for the Czechoslovak-U.S. Economic Council in the United States is Tad Kopinski, Director for Central and Eastern Europe, U.S. Chamber of Commerce, 1615 H St., N.W., Washington, D.C. 20062; (PH) (202) 463-5482; (Fax) (202) 463-3114.

Education System

The Ministry of Education, Youth, and Sports of the Czech Republic or Youth and Sports of the Slovak Republic are the responsible parties for education. For schools available to U.S. expatriates, contact the U.S. Embassy in Prague or the U.S. Consulate in Bratislava.

Freight Forwarding

International air freight service is provided to the CSFR by DHL Worldwide Express, Federal Express, and United Parcel Service among others. CECHOFRAT handles international freight forwarding and chartering CSFR and foreign vessels; it also buys and sells ocean-going vessels. COS is also an ocean shipping business; Prague to New York service is provided by Elco Freight International/Walter Sea Service. (Addresses are provided in *Directory for Trading and Investing* produced by the U.S. Embassy in Prague.)

Housing/Office Space

Housing is difficult to locate due to tight market conditions. Foreigners may not own land, but long-term leases are available for both housing and office space. However, businesses incorporated as Czechoslovak companies ("juristic persons") — i.e., joint ventures with Czechoslovak partners or wholly-owned subsidiaries — may hold land as an asset. Local authorities still control most of the real estate. For further information on housing and office space, contact the following organizations in the

CSFR: The Mayor's Office in Prague, The Towns and Municipalities Association in Prague, and the Slovak Commission for Housing Reform.

Public Holidays

The following are public holidays:

- January 1, New Year's Day
- Easter Monday
- May 1, May Day
- May 9, Liberation Day
- July 5, Day of the Apostles
- July 6, John Hus Day
- October 28, Independence Day
- December 24-26, Christmas

ENDNOTES

1 Oldrich Schmied, "Czechoslovakia and EFTA," *Czechoslovakia Foreign Trade 31* (January 1991): 22-23.

2 U.S., Department of Commerce, International Trade Administration, "Czechoslovakia: 1991 Trade Report," Fact Sheet prepared by the U.S. Embassy in Prague, January 1991, 3.

3 Pavla Podskalska in an interview with Deputy Minister of Foreign Trade Zdenek Cerveny, "Liberalization of Foreign Trade," *Czechoslovak Foreign Trade* (Prague, CSFR: Journal of the Czechoslovak Chamber of Commerce and Industry) 31 (January 1991): 2.

4 U.S. Embassy in Prague, Office of East European and Soviet Affairs and the Commercial Section, *CZECHOSLOVAKIA: Directory for Trading and Investing*, February 1991, 7.

5 American Czechoslovak Society, "CSFR Approves Trade Accord," *ACSNEWS*, Vol. 1, No. 7 (September 13, 1990): 3.

6 See note 1. above.

7 See note 5. above.

8 U.S. Embassy in Prague, Office of East European and Soviet Affairs and the Commercial Section, *Czechoslovakia: Directory for Trading and Investing* February 1991, 13.

9 Milan Ruzicka, "Czech Government Finalizing Plans for Large Industrial Privatization," *Journal of Commerce*, (May 17, 1991): 3a.

10 Personal Interview with Pavol Parizek, Head, International Finance, Czechoslovak Federal Ministry of Finance, and Humphrey Fellow, American University, Washington,

D.C., April 8, 1991; personal interview with Jiri Jonas, Assistant to the Executive Director, International Monetary Fund, Washington, D.C., May 31, 1991.

11 Interview with Pavol Parizek, Head, International Finance, Ministry of Finance, Washington, D.C., April 8, 1991.

12 Milan Ruzicka, "Czech Government Finalizing Plans for Large Industrial Privatization," *Journal of Commerce*, (May 15, 1991): 3a.

13 See *Scenario of the Economic Reform* (August 1990), "Major Privatization"; also, *SWB*, "CZECHOSLOVAKIA: Federal Government Approves Bill on Large-Scale Privatization," Nov. 5, 1990.

14 See note 9. above.

15 See *Scenario of the Economic Reform*, "Major Privatization," 17-19.

16 Pavol Parizek, "Privatization and Restitution Laws Approved in the Czechoslovak Parliament," unpublished article, Washington, D.C., April 4, 1991, p.2; and personal interview with Pavol Parizek, Washington, D.C., April 8, 1991.

17 See note 11. above.

18 Pavol Parizek, "Privatization and Restitution Laws Approved in the Czechoslovak Parliament," *ACSNEWS* (April 1991): 2.

19 U.S. Chamber of Commerce, Central and Eastern European Trade and Technical Assistance Center, "DATAFILE: CZECHOSLOVAKIA," (Winter 1990-1991): 5.

20 Ibid, 6.

21 Personal interview with Jiri Jonas, Assistant to the Executive Director, International Monetary Fund, Washington, D.C., May 29, 1991.

22 Pavol Parizek, "Privatizaton and Restitution Laws Approved in the Czechoslovak Parliament," unpublished article, Washington, D.C., April 4, 1991, p. 3.

23 Ibid, 2.

24 U.S. Department of Commerce, International Trade Administration, "Czechoslovakia Privatization Information," Factsheet (February 1991): 1-3.

25 See note 21.

26 American Czechoslovak Society, "CSFR Returns Seized Property," *ACSNEWS*, Vol. 2, No. 1 (March 1991): 8., and Pavol Parizek, "Privatization and Restitution Laws Approved in the Czechoslovak Parliament," unpublished article, (March 1991): 1.

27 U.S. Department of Commerce, International Trade Administration, "Czechoslovakia Privatization Information," Factsheet (February 1991): 1.

28 Ibid.

29 See note 11.

30 U.S. Department of Commerce, International Trade Administration, " Czechoslovakia Privatization Information," Factsheet (February 1991): 2.

31 Speech by Prime Minister M. Calfa to the Federal Parliament of Czechoslovakia, "Report on the State of the Economy and Further Orientation of the Economic Policy," March 27, 1991, edited and translated by Pavol Parizek (April 4, 1991): 2; updated figures provided in personal interview with Jiri Jonas, Assistant to the Executive Director, International Monetary Fund, Washington, D.C., May 29, 1991.

32 See note 9.

33 Daniel Arbess, "Czechoslovakia Opens for Business," *Financial Times* (London, March 7, 1991): 23.

34 U.S. President, *Agreement on Trade Relations Between the Government of the United States of America and the Government of the Czech and Slovak Federal Republic*, Article 14: "Dispute Settlement."

35 U.S. Department of Commerce, Unclassified Telegram from American Embassy in Prague, Ref: A. Prague 2739, "Answers to Questions on Czechoslovak Joint Venture Law," by Bohuslav Klein, Head, Legal Dept. CSFR Chamber of Commerce and Industry, April 1989.

36 See note 11.

37 See note 35 above.

38 "Czechoslovakia: A Nation on the Move," *The Wall Street Journal*, 26 October 1990, Advertorial, "Informing U.S. Investors."

39 Speech by Prime Minister M. Calfa to the Federal Parliament of Czechoslovakia, "Report on the State of the Economy and Further Orientation of the Economic Policy," March 27, 1991, edited and translated by Pavol Parizek (April 4, 1991): 2.

40 Ibid.

41 "National Economy of the Czech and Slovak Federal Republic," *Economic Digest* (June 1990): 7-11.

42 Jiri Brabec, Deputy Minister, Foreign Trade, CSFR, Presentation before the U.S. Chamber of Commerce, April 17, 1991.

43 CSFR, *The Economic Code*, Act 103, 1990 Amendment, Section 1, para. 1-3.

44 KPMG, "Czechoslovakia: Paving the Way to a Free Economy — A Guide to Legislation Governing Company Establishment and Investment in Czechoslovakia," (May 10, 1990), p. 1.

45 KPMG, "Czechoslovakia: Paving the Way to a Free Economy," p.2.

46 KPMG, "Czechoslovakia: Paving the Way to a Free Economy," p.2.

47 A.H. Hermann, Unpublished document commenting on selected texts of new statutes in the CSFR, p.117.

48 U.S. Department of Commerce, International Trade Administration, "Czechoslovakia Investment Opportunities and Contacts," Fact Sheet (December 1990).

49 Czech and Slovak Federal Republic, Czech Ministry for Economic Policy and Development, Agency for Foreign Investments and Assistance, "Purposes and Activities of the Agency," Fact Sheet (December, 1990).

50 "Czechoslovakia — A Nation on the Move," *The Wall Street Journal*, Special Advertising Section, 26 October 1990.

51 Price Waterhouse, "Business Opportunities for U.S. Companies in the Czech and Slovak Federal Republic," Report of the East European Services Group (January 1991): 5.

52 "Czechoslovakia — A Nation on the Move," *The Wall Street Journal*, Special Advertising Section, 26 October 1990.

53 Interview with Philip Zeidman, Esq., Brownstein, Zeidman, and Schomer, Washington, D.C., May 1991.

54 Philip F. Zeidman, Esq. and Michael Avner, Esq., "Franchising in Eastern Europe and the Soviet Union," draft article to be published in *Business Law Journal* (De Paul University, Summer 1991): 35.

55 Eleanor Kerlow, "Property Lines: Taking Real-Estate Law to Eastern Bloc," *Legal Times*, (April 2, 1990): 15.

56 Ibid, 14-15.

57 "Marketplace: Franchisers See a Future in East Bloc," *The Wall Street Journal*, 5 June 1990.

58 *The Economist*, "Franchising in Eastern Europe: McGouslash to Go," (April 6, 1991).

59 Personal interview with Jiri Jonas, Assistant to the Executive Director, International Monetary Fund, Washington, D.C., May 30, 1991.

60 KMPG, "Czechoslovakia: Paving the Way to a Free Economy — A Guide to Legislation Governing Company Establishment and Investment in Czechoslovakia," (May 10, 1990): 4-5.

61 *Economic Digest*, "National Economy of the Czech and Slovak Federal Republic," Issue No. 6/90 (June 1990): 12.

62 Interview with Jiri Jonas, Assistant to the Executive Director, International Monetary Fund, Washington, D.C., May 30, 1991.

63 Personal interview with Pavol Parizek, Head, International Finance, Ministry of Finance, Washington, D.C., May 5, 1991.

64 See note 62.

65 U.S. Department of Commerce, International Trade Administration, "Czechoslovakia: 1991 Trade Report," Fact Sheet prepared by U.S. Embassy in Prague (January 1991): 1.

66 Personal interview with Josef Tosovsky, President, Statni Banka Ceskoslovenska, Washington, D.C., September 26, 1990.

67 U.S. Department of Commerce, International Trade Administration, "Czechoslovakia: New Foreign Exchange Regime Effective 1/1/91," Fact Sheet (undated): 1.

68 Pavol Parizek, "Convertibility in the CSFR," *ACSNEWS*, Vol. I, No. 11 (January 1991): 2.

69 Ibid.

70 Ibid.

71 CSFR, Statni Banka Ceskoslovenska, "Transfers of Income from Foreign Investments in the CSFR," Announcement of the SBCS No. 15, Prague, April 1991.

72 Daniel Arbess, "Czechoslovakia Opens for Business," *Financial Times* (London, March 7, 1991): 23; CSFR, *Foreign Exchange Act of November 28, 1990,* Section 4: "Assumption of Financial Liabilities to Foreign Exchange Expatriates and Their Payment," Para. 1, p. 9.

73 CSFR, Statni Banka Ceskoslovenska, "Transfers of Income from Foreign Investments in the CSFR," Announcement of the SBCS No. 15, Prague, April 1991.

74 Ann Elizabeth Robinson, "A Comparative Study of the Economic Effects of External and Internal Linkages Achieved through Compensatory-Type Investments: The Mexican Automotive Industry," (unpublished Doctor's dissertation, The George Washington University, 1988, p. 302). See *Dissertation Abstracts International*, Vol. 49, No. 10, 1989.

75 U.S. Department of Commerce, International Trade Administration, "Czech and Slovak-American Enterprise Fund," Fact Sheet, March 20, 1991.

76 Personal interview by Ann Elizabeth Robinson, Ph.D., with Josef Tosovsky, President, Statni Banka Ceskoslovenska, Washington, D.C., Sept. 26, 1991.

77 U.S., The White House, Office of the Press Secretary, "U.S. Assistance to Czechoslovakia," Fact Sheet (undated): 3.

78 International Finance Corporation, *IFC IN CENTRAL EUROPE*, Brochure, (Washington, D.C., March 1991): 1.

79 U.S., The White House, Office of the Press Secretary, "U.S. Assistance to Czechoslovakia," Fact Sheet (undated): 4.

80 Personal interview by Ann Elizabeth Robinson, Ph.D., with Josef Tosovsky, President Statni Banka Ceskoslovenska, Washington, D.C., September 26, 1991.

81 CSFR, *Law on Inventions, Industrial Designs, and Rationalization Proposals*, "Notion of an Industrial Design," para. 36/1/, No. 527 of Nov. 27, 1990.

82 CSFR, *Law on Inventions, Industrial Designs, and Rationalization Proposals*, Part I, Sect. 13, para, 2, No. 527 of November 27, 1990, p. 5.

83 CSFR, *Law on Inventions, Industrial Designs, and Rationalization Proposals*, Part Four, "Rationalization Proposals," Sect. 72, para.1, No. 527 of November 27, 1990, p. 22.

84 CSFR, *Law on Inventions, Industrial Designs, and Rationalization Proposals*, Part Five: "Relationship to Foreign Countries," Section 76, Paras. 1 and 2., No. 527 of Nov. 27, 1990, p. 23.

85 U.S., President, *Agreement on Trade Relations Between the Government of the United States of America and the Government of the Czech and Slovak Federal Republic*, Article 10.

CZECHOSLOVAKIA

KEY CONTACTS FOR BUSINESS

U.S. Embassy—Czech & Slovak Federal Republic (May 1991)

Prague

Trziste 15-12548 Praha
American Embassy Prague
c/o Amcongen (PRG)
APO, NY 09213
   Tel: 42-2-53-6641/9
   Telex: j 121196 AMEMBC

Ambassador: Shirley Temple Black
Deputy Chief of Mission: Theodore E. Russell
Political: Clifford G. Bond
Economic: Harvey D. Lampert
Commercial: Janet G. Speck
Congressional: Richelle Keller
Administrative: Steven J. White
Military: Robert V. Daly
Agriculture: Robert J. Svec
Military: Thomas Hull
Military: Col. Edwin J. Motyka

Czech & Slovak Federal Republic Key Ministries (March 1991)

Federal Ministries

Foreign Affairs
Ing. Jaroslav Kubista
U.S. Desk
Loretanske nam. 5
125 10 Prague 1, CSFR
   Tel: 2193-111
   Telex: 122085

Fuels and Energy
Ing. Jiri Martinek
Chief, Foreign Relations
Vinohradska 8
120 70 Prague 1, CSFR
  Tel: 2353969
  Telex: 122083
  Sec: 262698

Communications
Zdenek Strnad
Chief, Foreign Relations
Olsanska 5
125 02 Prague 1, CSFR
  Tel: 714-1111
  Telex: 111410

Transport
Ing. Vladimir Junek
Foreign Relations Department
Na prikope 33
110 05 Prague 1, CSFR
  Tel: 2122-1111
  Telex: 111410

Foreign Trade
Jiri Skvara
U.S. Desk
Politickych veznu 20
112 49 Prague 1, CSFR
  Tel: 21262112
  Telex: 121808

Agriculture and Food
Ing. arpad Szabo, CSc.
Chief, Foreign Relations
Tesnov 17
110 01 Prague 1, CSFR
  Tel: 2862111
  Telex: 121041

Metallurgy, Engineering, and Electrotechnology
Ing. Miroslav Florian
Chief, Foreign Relations
Gorkeho 32
113 87 Prague 1, CSFR
    Tel: 2318745
    Telex: 122900

Finance
Ing. Frantisek Pavelka
Deputy Minister
Letenska 15
118 10 Prague 1, CSFR
    Tel: 514-1111
    Telex: 121868

Czech Ministries

Health
Dr. Jiri Macke
Chief, Foreign Relations
W. Piecka 98
101 00 Prague 10, CSFR
    Tel: 2118-457
    Telex: 121602

Industry
Ind. Ladislav Kubicek
Chief, Foreign Relations
Na porici 24
111 80 Prague 1, CSFR
    Tel: 232-1111
    Telex: 121104

Slovak Ministries

Health
Ing. Milos Ihnat
Foreign Relations
Cs. armady 6
813 05 Bratislava, CSFR
    Tel: 50946
    Telex: 92361

Industry
Ing. Dusan Gbelsky
Chief, Foreign Relations
Mileticova 1
824 64 Bratislava, CSFR
Tel: 374427
Telex: 92543

Additional Sources of Information

Czechoslovak Chamber of Commerce and Industry

In Bohemia:
Argentinska 38
170 05 Praha 7, CSFR
Tel: 87-24-111
Telex: 121-862

In Slovakia:
Gorkeho 9
816 03 Bratislava, CSFR
Tel: 33-38-46
Telex: 0935-86 Bratislava
Promotes foreign trade and disseminates information about the Czechoslovak economy. Has database/directory covering over 7,000 firms throughout Czechoslovakia. The person in charge of relations with the United States is Dipl. Ing. Karel Stasny.

CTK (Ceskoslovenska Tiskova Kancelar)
Opletalova 5
111 44 Praha 1, CSFR
Tel: 2147
Telex: 1-314-3
Provides promotional services for foreign firms in Czechoslovakia including advertising, translating services, organizing symposia, etc.

Transakta
Lentenska 11
118-19 Praha 1, CSFR
Tel: 514-444, 2142
Telex: 122-261
Provides consulting services on joint ventures, licensing arrangements, countertrade arrangements, and other forms of special types of international economic cooperation.

RAPID (Czechoslovak Advertising Agency)
28. rijna 13
112-79 Praha 1
Czechoslovakia
    Tel: 2139
    Telex: 121-142 REAG C
Engaged in agency publicity activities of all kinds relating to foreign trade.

CEDOK (Travel and Hotel Corporation)
Na prikope 18
11-35 Praha 1
Czechoslovakia
    Tel: 22-42-51-9
    Telex: 121-109
Provides services for travelers to Czechoslovakia.

Consulting Services for Foreign Investors in Czechoslovakia (March 1991)

Consulting Center of the Czechoslovak Chamber of Commerce and Industry

Mr. Jarosaw Svoboda
Pocernicka 64
100 00 Praha 10
    Tel: 42-770558
    Telex: 121862

Transakta FTO
Joint Venture Center
Mr. Gustav Svoboda
V Jame 1
110 00 Praha 1
    Tel: 42-2368427
    Fax: 42-220251
    Telex: 066/122938 TRAS c

Commercial Technical Group
Mr. Jaroslav Janzura
V Jame 1
110 00 Praha 1
    Tel: 42-2366157
    Fax: 42-5144220
    Telex: 066/122038 TRAS C

Pragoconsult
Mr. Miloslav Ciz
Tehovska 31
106 00 Praha 10
    Tel: 42-7810112

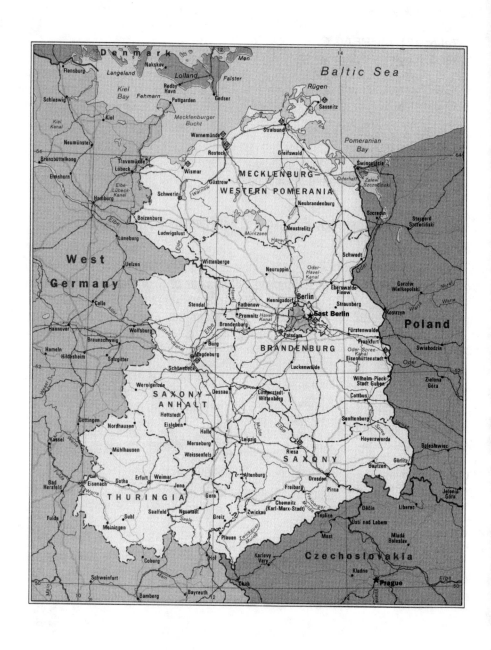

GERMANY (EAST)

GERMANY (EAST)

In a Nutshell

		Urban Population
Population (1992)	16,200,000	77%

Main Urban Areas		Percentage of Total
East Berlin (Capital)	1,284,535	7.93
Leipzig	545,307	3.37
Dresden	518,057	3.20
Chemnitz (Karl-Marx-Stadt)	311,765	1.92
Magdeburg	290,579	1.79
Rostock	253,990	1.57
Halle	236,044	1.45

Land Area	41,768 square miles
	105,980 square kilometers
Comparable European State	Moderately larger than Portugal
Comparable U.S. State	Slightly larger than Tennessee
Language	German
Common Business Language	English is prevalent
Currency	Deutsche mark (as of 7/90)
Best European Air Connection	Frankfurt to Berlin (Lufthansa)
Best Ground Connection	Hannover to Berlin
Best Hotel	Grand Hotel
	($275 per night as of 1/92)

CHAPTER CONTENTS

INTRODUCTION AND REGIONAL ORIENTATION

Geographical and Historical Background

The fall of the Berlin Wall in 1989 and the subsequent political reunification of Germany, unthinkable only a few short years ago, has proved thus far the most dramatic result of the changes taking place throughout Eastern Europe. With a single stroke, Germany has consolidated its position as the economic leader of Europe. However, the full impact — political, social, and economic — of the merging of East and West Germany remains to be seen. The quickness with which unification was achieved testifies to the determination of the people of Germany and the mandate for change existent in what was East Germany.

After October 3, 1990, the German Democratic Republic ceased to exist as a political entity and West German Chancellor Helmut Kohl became the leader of a united Germany. Before full political unification became official, representatives from both West and East Germany sought to reassure authorities in Poland that the Oder Neisse border would not be changed, despite revived claims from certain quarters for the return of territory that belonged to Germany before World War II. At the present time, the issue appears to be settled.

Despite early protestations from the member states of the Warsaw Pact (which itself officially disbanded in Spring 1991), United Germany has maintained its membership in the North Atlantic Treaty Organization. However, the presence of hundreds of thousands of NATO (mainly from the United States) and Soviet forces stationed on the territories of the former West and East Germanies, respectively, has presented particular problems. While the size of the NATO contingent will be reduced significantly, the withdrawal of the 360,000 Soviet troops and their dependents from Germany met with complaints over logistics from Moscow. In response, the former West German government offered the equivalent of $8 billion to help cover costs connected with the withdrawal, including millions to construct low-cost housing in the former Soviet Union to house the returning troops. This amount came in addition to some $3 billion already offered in guaranteed loans. Some observers feel that such munificence, on top of West Germany's absorption of the whole of East Germany, will overly burden the economy of newly unified Germany. Nevertheless, of all the European countries, Germany has been the most active in promoting expanded trade opportunities, credits, and aid in the East.

The Financial Times reported in August 1990 that of approximately 2,800 joint ventures initiated in what used to be East Germany, 95% were with West German companies.

Many have described the wheeling and dealing going on in former East Germany between the time of the opening of the borders with the West in the fall of 1989 and unification in October 1990, as something similar to sharks engaged in a "feeding frenzy." East Germany's attraction was based on the fact that it has maintained the highest per capita income in Eastern Europe and has been the largest CMEA exporter of manufactured goods, primarily to the Soviet Union and other CMEA countries in the East, and to West Germany, which provided it with special credit arrangements. Trade with the West increased significantly following Western recognition of the GDR in the early 1970s. Most Western countries have had normal tariff and credit preferences with the GDR, with Canada being the last major Western country outside the United States to grant most-favored-nation status when a long-term grain agreement was signed in 1983.

The economy of the German Democratic Republic under the former Communist regime had been carefully planned and was based on the Stalinist command model of the Soviet Union. Financial institutions, transportation, industrial and foreign trade enterprises were state owned, and the vast majority of agricultural land was collectivized. The capital stock of what was East Germany, while updated during the 1980s, was generally considered to be the best in Eastern Europe, though not up to the standards of the West. The overall level of skilled labor was viewed similarly. Together, these two factors gave the country a comparative advantage in Eastern Europe.

Shortly before unification, East Germany's economy began a rapid transformation towards a market-oriented system heavily based on private ownership. The advent of unification has accelerated this process further, primarily through the Trevhandanstalt in Berlin, although many obstacles will have to be overcome, including retooling factories, unemployment, re-education of the workforce, establishment of new legal structures, rapid inflation, labor shortages, debt burden of GDR, improvement of communications, and transportation infrastructure.

Despite the former East Germany's leading status among the economies of the East, many feel that earlier appraisals of the area's ability to be upgraded to Western standards were not realistic. Recent assessments, based on closer inspection of the economic landscape, have determined that the transition of the eastern part of Germany will be more costly and require more work than was previously anticipated. Ronald D. Asmus, a specialist on German affairs for the Rand Corporation, estimates that bringing the eastern part of Germany up to the standards of the western part over the next decade could cost nearly one trillion Deutsche marks. Equipment and technology is outdated and will have to be scrapped. Unemployment might reach 20% in the area of the former GDR. Economic growth in this region was expected to drop 15% in 1990, and by 5% in 1991.

In addition, pollution controls in industry were far below most Western standards, resulting in severe damage to the environment. East Germany's practice of importing (for a fee) the hazardous waste of its Western neighbors resulted in more damage and a crucial environmental problem that cannot be ignored any further.

The economy of the area of the former GDR is expected to pick up and "take off." Projections prepared by Deutsche Bank have the area achieving growth rates of 7.5% to 10% throughout the decade of the 1990s. Beyond its own borders, the German economic locomotive has the potential to pull the economies of other post-communist countries along the road to reconstruction and growth, thus facilitating efforts to achieve greater economic and political unity throughout all of Europe. However, energy shortages may result in the short term because the only nuclear power station in the former GDR, used to supply 11% of its electricity, is being shut down for safety reasons.

Demonstrations and violence over housing have broken out in Berlin and other East German cities. Strong concerns in the population of what was East Germany also exist regarding inflation, interest rates, and the rising cost of living.

Demographics

Trends in Consumer Demand

Unification will reinforce West Germany's position as Europe's strongest economy as the unified Germany becomes the world's third largest economy, after the United States and Japan. However optimistic this sounds, it will be years before the standards of living in the eastern part of Germany match those of the western part in most respects.

After an initial 7.5% jump in inflation in July 1990, prices rose only slightly in August 1990 and have remained stable since. The West German inflation rate rose only 3% in September 1990.

West Germany's 1989 GNP reached $1,078 trillion while East Germany's GNP reached $215 billion. Most of East Germany's trade was with the centralized economies of Eastern Europe. The united Germany will have a dominant trade position in the former East bloc, due in part to West Germany's $82-billion trade surplus in 1989.

Both East and West are particularly strong in engineering, cars, electronics, and chemicals. Forestry and fishing provide 11% of the jobs in the East and 5% in the West.

Germany is a member of NATO. Upon Moscow's request, no NATO troops will be stationed on former East German territory. East Germany's armed forces, which reached their highest figure in 1989 with 175,000 men, will cease to exist. Some of its former members will be absorbed into the Bundeswehr, limiting the German army to 370,000.

The economic recovery from 40 years of communist control in the GDR will be a slow and painful process. Local industry is generally in poor condition and few companies can be competitive in a free market. Privatization of the state-run industries is currently in process, and buyers are being sought for the surviving companies. Over the next few years high unemployment is anticipated, with 20% to 30% of the work force expected to be idle. The average monthly salary of those with work is approximately $750.

Political considerations have stolen attention away from changes taking place in the East German economy and the prospects for doing business in the GDR. Contracts written in East Germany by East German organizations before that time will be honored; however, in many cases, only the basics have been covered until political and economic uncertainties are resolved.

Disposable income is low but should increase rapidly as new investments improve the productivity of the work force. The Deutsche Bank predicts 7% average real growth for Eastern Germany over the next ten years. This "average" growth, however, will consist of flat growth rates in the initial years, with a double digit boom forecast in the second half of the period. Companies which are not risk averse should participate in the compounded return of this growth by entering the market now.

West German officials and business executives have been working feverishly to hammer out deals and agreements that, in effect, are uniting both East and West Germany faster than the actions of politicians and statesmen. The construction of new factories and the formation of joint ventures to manufacture and market products are being planned. For example, many West German automotive manufacturers, such as Volkswagen A.G., Daimler-Benz, and Adam Opel, have announced deals with counterparts in the GDR for the production of thousands of cars and trucks. Plans for improved transportation and communication links are also being proposed.

Trade experts agree that the potential for growth in East Germany — or what was East Germany — is tremendous and, moreover, that this area might serve as a way station to further investment in Eastern Europe.

Following the replacement of East German currency with the West German D-mark in July 1990, enterprises in the GDR are free to purchase whatever they choose. West Germany, presumably, will dominate supply channels. The bulk of purchasing and the main focus of imports has been on consumer rather than investment goods; indications are that this trend has now reversed.

With assets of approximately $10 billion in the West, the GDR can manage its net debt of between $9 and $10 billion, although a hard currency deficit of $1 billion was reported for 1989. East Germany's trade balance with West Germany showed an estimated DM 355 million deficit in 1989; however, the country maintained a positive balance of well over DM 250 million within the DM 850 million "swing" framework credit.

Foreign trade is being completely restructured. Traditional foreign trade organizations have lost their monopolies, and former trading partners are operating under new names or newly created legal forms. Many FTOs are being reorganized as trading houses, hoping to adapt to the changeover to a market economy. Given their narrow experience in this area, it is unlikely that they will survive unification unless they can cultivate strong ties with Western partners. Strict divisions by industrial sector will fade as the FTOs, reorganized as stock companies, bid for all the business they can get and begin to work more along the lines of trading houses. Many will deal on their own account, taking title to goods which pass through their hands. Western firms in the future may expect to deal with end-users dealing on their own, with newly modified FTOs, or with wholly new traders or trading agencies.

Firms are no longer required to have an agent in the former East Germany. Companies receiving approval to do business in the East may acquire office space wherever they find it.

Industrial production in 1990 was well below the levels recorded for the previous year given labor shortages and problems securing supplies, particularly materials and components, arising from the abrupt abandonment of central planning and the crumbling system of trade. Enterprises can now order supplies themselves directly, but most do not know how.

According to some East German estimates, as much as 75% of industry is not viable. Outdated equipment and technology, often with poor pollution controls, will probably be scrapped. It is assumed that much of the GDR's industry will be replaced by unused West German capacity.

It is expected that there will be energy shortages; however, these can be met by electricity imports. Agreements for the importation of electricity from West Germany and Austria already exist and will be expanded.

The continuous outpouring of thousands of skilled laborers has delivered a devastating blow to the East German economy. On March 20, 1990, the government in Bonn decided to cut aid to East Germans who move to the West. Public opinion in West Germany is hardening against the East German settlers. Two states, Bremen and Saarland, have declared themselves closed to more East Germans. It is uncertain whether such actions will stop East Germans from traveling West.

On July 1, 1990 the currencies and social benefits of the two countries were merged as a first step toward unification. A plan formulated by the Bundesbank, the central bank of West Germany, in late March 1991 called for the exchange of all East German funds except private savings up to 2,000 GDR marks to be exchanged at a two-to-one rate; savings accounts of 2,000 GDR marks or less were to be converted at a one-to-one rate. By July 1990, however, the one-to-one ratio was applied to all currency instruments.

Strong concerns over rising interest rates and spiraling inflation resulting from the monetary union have worried some in the West but have yet to materialize. The official East German exchange rate was three GDR marks for one Deutsche mark prior to unification.

The introduction of the Deutsche mark as the new currency of the GDR and the withering away of CMEA creates an interesting situation. East Germany's enterprises have no use for anything except hard currency in its dealings within the former CMEA. Existing commitments, especially those to the USSR, will have to be met or renegotiated; thus, certain inefficient and unprofitable enterprises will have to be kept alive (at least in the near term). Subsidies will be necessary to meet obligations at previously negotiated low prices.

Political/Institutional Infrastructure

Election Timetable

The newly formed country will assume the West German Basic Law and political structure. The lower house of Parliament, the Bundestag, will have 663 members. The enlarged upper house, Bundersrat, will represent the 16 federal states, or Lander. The first all-German elections took place on December 2, 1990.

Elections

The first free elections in the history of East Germany were held on March 18, 1990. The conservative Alliance for Germany (comprising three parties — the Christian Democratic Union, the German Social Union, and Democratic Awakening), led by Lothar de Maiziere of the Christian Democrats, won 49% of the vote. The Christian Democratic Union and its allies are likely to seek a "grand coalition" with the Social Democratic party in order to achieve the two-thirds majority necessary to change the constitution and clear the way for unification. The Alliance for Germany, actively supported by West German Chancellor Helmut Kohl, strongly advocates rapid reunification with West Germany. Mr. de Maiziere has been named the country's first non-Communist prime minister. Sabine Bergmann-Pohl, a member of the Christian Democrats, was elected Speaker of the Volkskammer, or Parliament. Regional elections were held on May 6, 1990.

When Helmut Kohl proposed a ten-point plan for the unification of Germany in November 1989, he sought to reassure all concerned that the process would be carried out in a gradual and orderly manner and that a united Germany would not dominate and disrupt the political and economic balance of Europe.

Finance and Investment Policies

The unification of East and West Germany may be viewed as a first step toward the greater unification of Eastern and Western Europe. The result of which will be a larger and more dynamic economic power providing greater opportunities for growth and eventually a Europe that is better able to compete against the United States and Japan. By spending the equivalent of hundreds of billions of dollars to rebuild East Germany and its neighbors, West Germany — the so-called "locomotive of Europe" — will drive growth in the East and, ultimately, the whole of Europe.

During the first quarter of 1990, the East German government estimated that more than 700 new deals were struck with entities in the GDR. Of that number, "more than 96%" were with partners based in West Germany. The remainder, according to one knowledgeable East German official, were primarily with Fortune 500 firms such as Philip Morris, Procter & Gamble, Coca Cola, and mammoth Japanese trading firms — which the source characterized as moving cautiously and deliberately.

Policies to Attract New Business

Loan and Grant Programs for Investment

German and foreign investors are equally eligible for credit supports. U.S. companies with German subsidiaries are good candidates for these subsidized programs, with the application made through the German subsidiary. For U.S. companies, qualification is based on the combined turnover of both the U.S. parent and the German subsidiary. In the case of a European Recovery Program (ERP) loan, for example, the combined turnover of the U.S. parent and German subsidiary could not exceed DM 50 million. U.S. companies desiring to participate in an investment loan from the Kreditanstalt für Wiederaufbau, (KfW), program have the option of establishing a German subsidiary for this purpose. The stipulation is, of course, that the proceeds of the loan be used in Eastern Germany for one of the purposes stated in the following loan and grant agreements/programs.

1. European Recovery Program (ERP) - Loans for New Businesses and Investment

   - Tourism
   - New businesses
   - Environmental protection
   - Modernization

2. Investment Loans from the Deutsche Ausgleichsbank

- Establishment of an independent business
- Moving the location of a business
- Growth investment
- Innovation

3. Equity Capital Assistance Program from the Deutsche Ausgleichsbank

   - Establishment of a private enterprise
   - Acquisition of a company or individual plant
   - Investment to stabilize a private firm

4. Investment Loans from the Kreditanstalt für Wiederaufbau

   - Establishment, security, or expansion of enterprises
   - Improvement of the environment

5. Investment Grants

Preferred Foreign Investment Projects

The U.S. Embassy reports the following opportunities for American companies during the rebuilding of the area of the former GDR.

Construction. Modernization of retail establishments, hospitals, transportation, telecommunications, tourism, and environmental protection.

Housing. Renovate and expand the existing stock of housing. About one-fourth of current housing does not have indoor toilets.

Hospitals. One-half of the existing medical facilities need renovation.

Retail Outlets. Retail space in Eastern Germany is expected to double over the next six years.

Transportation. Half the rail system needs to be rebuilt; most roads need work.

Energy and Environment. Energy and environmental facilities must be raised to Western standards.

Tourism. The tourism infrastructure must immediately be upgraded. Restaurants and two and three star hotels are particularly needed.

Telecommunications. Billions of dollars will be required to modernize the phone system.

Investment Incentives and Privileges

Germany is providing generous incentives for foreign investors in Eastern Germany. The investment allowance will stand at 12% for at least two years.

With the adoption of the United Federal Republic of Germany's tax and commercial laws, Germany will have three advantages that will not be available in the rest of Eastern Europe for years: hard currency, useable commercial law, and a reasonable tax system.

APPROACHING THE MARKET

Foreign Trade and Investment Decision-Making Infrastructure

Possessing a vast, untapped market for industrial and consumer products, as well as access to West German cash and ingenuity, East Germany is a new frontier for investment opportunity. Despite the enticements, including established commercial ties throughout the Eastern bloc, there are business risks and important issues facing U.S. companies wishing to enter the East German market. The fundamental issue of ownership and its regulations has not yet been resolved. The value of real estate and capital equipment has never been realistically defined and is likely to fluctuate in the future. Rents have been stagnant since the end of 1990, when it began to rapidly increase. Another risk involves acquisition regulations, comprised of complex and unclear technicalities. Finally, locating the "correct" authorities to approve ventures is no small task.

Setting Up Business Operations

Until recently, the East German economy was organized around kombinats, or business units. First, there were the so-called Z-Kombinats, which were centrally coordinated by the state. Second, there were B-Kombinats — kombinats that were organized by the districts. Finally, there were a few small, privately owned firms. All of the kombinats have been dissolved and their ownership transferred to the body in charge of East German privatization — the Treuhandanstalt.

Any firm looking to buy shares in an East German company needs to contact the Treuhandanstalt, which owns all East German firms and is responsible for all negotiations concerning joint ventures and/or acquisitions (as of October 1990). Due to a restructuring of the organization's personnel, many joint ventures and acquisitions have been delayed. All firms are in the process of privatization, so to reach 100% Western ownership is only a matter of negotiation with the specific CEO and the Treuhandanstalt, since there is now no restrictive legislation.

Before any merger or acquisition can take place, an East German company must be transformed into a limited liability company (GmbH) or a publicly held corporation (AG) (Aktiengesellschaft). Due to substandard systems of accounting, this process will take significant time for most companies. When balance sheets are adjusted to conform to Western standards, most East German firms appear to be bankrupt. Many do have a chance of survival, but they will need much support from the Treuhandanstalt. Investment warranties and subsidies pose a further risk, since this issue has also yet to be clarified.

Rules of Doing Business

On July 1, 1990, the GDR adopted the commercial and economic structure of the Federal Republic of Germany. The German Deutsche Mark (DM) was adopted, giving the GDR hard currency, with full convertibility for the first time. With reunification on October 3, 1990, the entire legal system of the Federal Republic took effect in the five new eastern states: Brandenburg, Saxony-Anhalt, Thuringia, Mecklenburg-Vorpommern, and Saxony. With the exception of some transition regulations, there is no difference in the rules of business in the five new states and any other German state.

Germany has a free market system, with a commercial code similar to the United States and other western democracies. The five new states will also be included in the 1992 unification of the European Community (EC).

American firms should know the following regarding business operations:

1. As indicated, German commercial law now applies in all its states, with every form of European business incorporation allowed. Forms of legal organization include: a limited liability company (GmbH), a publicly held corporation (AG), a limited partnership (KG), or a sole proprietorship. It is also permitted to operate as a branch office of an American company, without formal local incorporation.

2. There are no restrictions on joint ventures. U.S. companies can buy all or part of the assets of a local corporation. All rules against holding a majority position in a company, as was the case in the former GDR, have been rescinded.

3. Profits from investments in Germany can be fully repatriated to the United States. There are no currency controls.

4. U.S. export control regulations for Germany have been unified, and the former G-GDR license has been abolished. The licensing procedures for Germany will apply equally in the eastern and western portions of the country.

5. The German tax system will be fully implemented in the east, and American companies doing business should plan on being taxed under German law. Information on German tax law is available from all major accounting firms. Currently the highest marginal tax bracket for corporations in Germany is 53%.

6. Clear title to real property is still a problem. There are numerous unresolved claims of property ownership resulting from the communist land confiscations and from pre-war Nazi expropriations. Clear title to land must be carefully researched, and claims from previous owners should be anticipated in some cases. As of October 1990, all claims for property should have been registered, resulting in the ability to determine if a clear title exists. The method of resolving claims is currently being formulated. Government guarantees have been created to protect investors from property claims.

Agents and Distributors

Under the former communist government, essentially all distribution of products was done through the "People's Combines," within state-dictated economic plans. Marketing, in the classic sense, was unknown, and virtually no modern systems are in place to sell and distribute products. Many of the larger state-owned businesses had contacts throughout the GDR, but their function was often only to deliver an assigned quota of products to a predetermined set of buyers.

New entrepreneurial companies are springing up at a rapid pace, many of which may be promising partners. They face the problem of being seriously undercapitalized and short on experience. While they may prove to be excellent long-term partners, these new companies will require strong financial support, extensive training programs, and a great deal of patience. American firms should not expect to sign on agents who can immediately generate large sales numbers.

With the impending financial crisis, opportunities to make direct sales will be limited, and independent agents and distributors will face difficult times. Aggressive agents should be able to sell to the entire German market, so American companies should not limit the territory of their agent too severely. Many potential distributors have experience in other Eastern European countries.

The local attitude toward new agencies and distributorships is not particularly positive. The government is anxious to attract capital to rebuild the country's production facilities. Individuals interested solely in imported foreign goods are viewed with some disdain. Given the current situation, importing of products will be a necessity, but companies concentrating only on imports can expect little assistance from local institutions.

It is highly unlikely, however, that an indigenous agent or distributor of the classic mold will be found in Eastern Germany. The following can be expected:

1. Almost any business partner will require financial support to distribute your product. Expect your local distributor to request you to invest in supplying initial product inventories, market penetration funding, and even participating in financing basic sales facilities.

2. Although your partner will probably have a solid basic technical background, he or she will require additional training with high level technologies or specialized products.

3. Extensive support will be required for a local agent to meet your expectations in logistics, selling, advertising, and distribution. Client acquisition is practically an unknown art. This lack of skills will often be compensated by an intense desire to succeed, a knowledge of the local market structure, and an ability to innovate.

4. Finding the right partnership is something which can be done now, but profitable sales may only come as the total market develops. In general, you should plan on two to three years for market development before the break-even point is reached.

Because of this situation, many American companies may choose to wait for conditions to normalize prior to attempting to enter this market or ally themselves with firms in West Germany. This strategy carries lower financial risk than immediate entry, but it may result in your company being blocked from the market by competitors who have taken the few qualified agents. Companies willing to provide the support and training to new agents will have a definite edge as the market develops.

Due to historical developments, the channels of distribution in this part of Germany are not the same as other markets. Sometimes selling directly to wholesalers, setting up your own distribution point, or employing an import trading company may be better than using an agent. Because the agent and distributor network is underdeveloped, locating and qualifying a potential agent or distributor may require an extensive search. Determining the qualifications of a potential partner will be as important as locating the individual.

INVESTMENT CLIMATE

Currently, numerous interesting opportunities are available for American investors. Risk is high, but so is the potential return on investment if you can find the right opportunity. Although the current economic situation is tenuous, companies entering on the ground floor will be in a good position to participate in the rapid growth expected in the eastern part of Germany over the next ten years. Investors should exercise caution to make certain the purchase price is fully discounted to reflect the portion of company debt to be assumed, the quality of the assets, and the responsibility for environmental problems.

Due to the dramatic changes of the last few years, the investment climate has become complex. To create a functioning private economy, it is necessary to privatize thousands of state-owned businesses (Volkseigende Betriebe). The task of forming private companies has been assigned to a "Trust Agency" (Treuhandanstalt), which will sell or liquidate all of the state-owned businesses. This job is anticipated to take several years, with a substantial percentage of the companies not expected to be salvageable.

Basically, the Trust Agency will sell the companies to the "best" bidder. This is not necessarily the highest bid, but the one which serves the best interests of Germany. Initially, the companies to be sold must produce a beginning balance sheet, an audited statement of assets and liabilities. The beginning balance serves as the basis of the company evaluation and is used to determine whether the firm is sold or liquidated. The Trust Agency decides on the disposal of each company on the basis of the bids received, how the bidder intends to deal with the employees, the prospects of the company as a going concern in relationship to its liquidator value, and other less tangible considerations.

The methods being used by the Trust Agency are not fully transparent and have been criticized by some American companies who have expressed concern that the procedures may not be fair. Some decisions of the Trust Agency are currently being tested in the courts. Several newly hired senior staff members are making rapid improvements in the Trust Agency's effectiveness.

Bids can be made for state-owned companies in many forms. In addition to total asset buyouts, minority positions, and consortia, joint ventures are also possible. The Trust Agency is open to most options; technology transfers, licensing agreements, contract production, distribution exchanges, or any hybrid partnerships are welcome for discussion. Financial investment with no management participation is also possible. Because of the currently depressed market, prudent capital placements may result in substantial growth potential.

Privatization, Investment Protection, and Dispute Settlement

The best opportunities in the next few years will be in the sectors where outside investment is greatest. Construction, environment, energy, transportation, telecommunications, and labor intensive crafts will all be strong industries. Initially, consumer goods sales will be sluggish, but will improve after infrastructure investments are made and the unemployment rate drops. Niche products will have the greatest success in all sectors.

The East German economy needs to rebuild its infrastructure and import large quantities of industrial goods and consumer products. Investment opportunities in infrastructure are estimated at $500 billion, while opportunities in the building industry total $400 to $500 billion. Similar figures are expected in the health care system. Almost all product and service areas offer unique opportunities.

Strategies for Penetrating the Market

Once East Germany has been selected as a business target, there are several ways to gain a market presence: trade fairs, offices or subsidiaries, licensing, co-marketing, and of course, joint ventures with East German partners. This latter option is often an attractive one, but should be planned and researched with care. The question is: "Should I transform an old player into a new player, or should I enter the market with fresh ideas and fresh blood?" It is impossible to give a generic answer to this question.

As for where to invest, the bulk of East Germany's industry is located in the south, with some concentration in Leipzig and Dresden, two highly industrialized cities. There are probably better opportunities for investment in the south than in the north, due to different levels of industrial production. The districts of Halle, Dresden, Leipzig, and Chemnitz account for 50% of East Germany's industrial production. Still, there are no hard and fast rules for the physical location of an investment. For U.S. companies, East Germany must be looked at as a long-term investment. The market will have its peculiarities and its complexities for some time. Far-sighted companies should make East Germany part of their long-term strategies for penetrating a new Eastern Europe and Europe broadly.

Joint Ventures and Wholly Owned Subsidiaries

American companies have been actively exploring possible joint ventures in Eastern Germany. The U.S. Embassy notes that while some Eastern German business sectors may be easier to enter than others, no one sector is saturated.

FINANCING AND CAPITAL MARKETS

Securities Market

It is now possible to buy shares in expertly managed portfolios of German stocks on the New York Stock Exchange. Any U.S. broker will handle the transactions for his or her regular commission, and all transactions are in U.S. dollars. Also, in today's constantly fluctuating market climate, you can buy $100 worth of top quality German stocks for $80. Four funds are actively traded now, a fifth is in registration, and more will be brought to market in the future.

A closed-end fund pools the money of investors for strategic placement. The fund issues a finite number of shares when it starts business, which are then traded on the stock exchanges as if they were shares of stock in individual companies.

The astute investor can magnify his or her gains with a closed-end fund. With a wise choice, the fund's portfolio will rise in value, raising the net asset value (NAV) and price per share. The bonus is that as the fund increases in public favor, its price-to-NAV discount tends to decline and may even move to a premium over NAV.

The oldest closed-end German fund on the NYSE is the Germany Fund, which came to market in 1986, managed by Deutsche Bank Capital Corp. At the end of December 1990, the Germany Fund sold at $11.13 per share, a 1% premium over NAV. The quality of the fund's portfolio is excellent, but bargain hunters may want to investigate its newer brethren: New Germany Fund (NYSE symbol GF), Future Germany Fund (symbol FGF), and Emerging Germany Fund (symbol FRG).

New Germany and Future Germany Funds went on the market in January and March 1990, respectively. Both are managed by Deutsche Bank Capital. But at the end of December 1990, New Germany was selling at $11.38 per share, an 11% discount from NAV, and Future Germany at $11.50 per share, an 18% discount. Emerging Germany Fund came to market in March 1990, managed by ABD Securities of New York, the U.S. investment bank of Dresdner Bank and Bayerische Hypotheken-und Wechsel-Bank. At the end of December 1990, Emerging Germany sold for $7.63 per share, a 20% discount from NAV.

None of the three newcomer funds has a track record at this point, but all are managed by seasoned German investment advisors. All have been beaten down in the worldwide market selloff that has accompanied the Persian Gulf crisis. So this may be the time to pick up a top-quality German stock portfolio on the bargain counter.

VISITING AND LOCATING

General Travel Checklist

Visas

No visas are required when traveling throughout Germany.

Currency

The national currency is the Deutsche mark or DM.

Getting Around

Frankfurt am Main is still the primary airline hub, although many carriers are now expanding into the second tier cities, particularly Berlin. The German rail system is superbly maintained and highly reliable. The world-famous German autobahn is also well maintained and easily accessible. Caution should be exercised in planning business meetings requiring long-distance auto connections, since five to ten kilometer traffic back-ups are common during peak hours. In March 1991, a new high-speed rail service was initiated between major population centers in the north and south.

However, the transportation infrastructure throughout the former GDR is in a state of severe disrepair. It is presently undergoing massive reconstruction, causing further delays and detours, especially surrounding the major population centers in the East.

Accommodations and Housing

Western-level accommodations are still relatively scarce, although most major hotel chains have announced plans to expand throughout the former GDR with full force.

GERMANY (EAST)

KEY CONTACTS FOR BUSINESS

Foreign Investor Center

Bundesministerium für Wirtschaft
Aussenstelle Berlin
Unter den Linden 44-60
O-1080 Berlin
   Tel: 49-30-399-85-100
   Fax: 49-30-399-85-235
   Telex: 115-2361

Economic Investment Corporations for the New Federal States

Wirtschaftsforderung Brandenburg GmbH
Mangerstrasse 39
O-1560 Potsdam
   Tel: 37-33-23581 or 23582
   Fax: 37-33-23582
   Telex:156184

Wirtschaftsforderung GmbH des Landes
Mecklenburg-Vorpommern
Wismarsche Strasse 152
O-2750 Schwerin
   Tel: 37-84-83604
   Telex: 812297

Wirtschaftsforderung GmbH des Landes Sachsen
Grunaer Strasse 2
O-8010 Dresden
   Tel: 37/51-487-4751 or 487-4696
   Fax: 37-51-495-2130
   Telex: 0692433

Wirtschaftsforderungsgesellschaft für das Land Sachsen-Anhalt

GmbH
Wilhelm-Hopfner Ring 4
O-3037 Magdeburg
   Tel: 37-91-613-056 or 613-600

Wirtschaftsforderungsgesellschaft Ostthuringen GmbH
Schlossstrasse 11
O-6500 Gera
   Tel: 37-70-64489 or 64481

Wirtschaftsforderung Berlin GmbH
Budapester Strasse 1
W-1000 Berlin 30
   Tel: 49-30-264-880
   Fax: 49-30-264-88239
   Telex: 184467

Other Institutions

Federation of German Industries
Gustav-Heinemann-Ufer 84-88
W-5000 Koln 51
   Tel: 49-221-370-800
   Fax: 49-221-370-8730

East-West Trade Committee of German Industry
Gustav-Heinemann-Ufer 84-88
W-5000 Koln 51
   Tel: 49-221-370-8417
   Fax: 49-221-370-8730

German American Chamber of Commerce
666 Fifth Avenue
New York, NY 10103
   Tel: 212/974-8830
   Fax: 212/974-8867

Representative of German Industry & Trade
(Association of German Chambers of Industry & Commerce/
Federation of German Industries)
1 Farragut Square South
Washington, DC 20006
     Tel: 202/347-0247
     Fax: 202/628-3685
     Telex: 248652

HUNGARY

HUNGARY

In a Nutshell

		Urban Population
Population (1992)	10,610,000	56%

Main Urban Areas		Percentage of Total
Budapest (Capital)	2,115,000	19.93
Debrecen	220,000	2.07
Miskolc	208,000	1.96
Szeged	189,000	1.78
Pecs	183,000	1.72

Land Area	35,919 square miles
	92,340 square kilometers
Comparable European State	Virtually the size of Portugal
Comparable U.S. State	Slightly smaller than Indiana
Language	Magyar (related to Finnish)
Common Business Language	English
Currency	Forint (= 100 filler)
Best European Air Connection	Frankfurt (Lufthansa, Delta)
Best Ground Connection	Vienna (265 kilometers)
Best Hotel	Forum Budapest
	($190 per night as of 1/92)

CHAPTER CONTENTS

INTRODUCTION AND REGIONAL ORIENTATION

Geographical and Historical Background

Hungary is located in the heart of Central-Eastern Europe, sharing national boundaries with Czechoslovakia, Austria, Yugoslavia, Romania, and the Soviet Union. In 1541, the Castle of Buda was captured by Turkish armies, and Hungary was divided between the Hapsburg empire, the Ottoman empire, and the Transylvanian empire. In the 19th century, Hungarian nationalism developed, based on Hungarian language and culture. The 1848-1849 revolution led to a temporary dethroning of the Hapsburg emperor as king of Hungary, but the Russian army assistance soon put down the rebellion. In 1867, a compromise dual monarchy in Vienna and Budapest was developed.

Hungary became an independent state with the collapse of the Austro-Hungarian empire following World War I. Like most other East European states, Hungary went through a series of different governments, including a brief period of communist rule under Bela Kun. The interwar governments became increasingly authoritarian.

Unhappy with the postwar settlements, Hungary became what can be classified as a revisionist state. Seeking to claim territory ceded to another state, it became an ally of Hitler during World War II. Soviet troops occupied the state after the war and played a role in the communist takeover of 1947.

A rebellion in 1956 was crushed by Soviet troops, but the people in Hungary during the 1960s grew continually more liberal, especially on the economic front. Early reforms included experiments with mixed markets and limited private ownership of agricultural plots. The transition to democracy began in 1988 when former communist party members began to compromise with opposition parties on reform measures.

Demographics

Socioeconomic Indicators and Conditions

The new government of Prime Minister Jozef Antall presented a "national renewal program" in May 1990 that called for the creation of a "social market economy," an end to inflation, short-term reorganization of the government and economic programs, and a three-year program of social, political, and economic restructuring. The main priorities of the program are refocusing Hungary's economy to the West and encouraging private entrepreneurship, while reducing economic problems.

Although the administration has been able to make significant personnel changes, complete new foreign policy initiatives with the West, withdraw from the Warsaw Pact and effect the removal of Soviet troops from Hungary, economic conditions and standards of living have been decreasing. Unemployment has increased due to reduction in trade with the former Soviet trading bloc CMEA. In addition, specific reform programs, especially on privatization, land reform, and the transition to a market remain vague.

Hungary's prospects for reform, however, may be somewhat better than those of other East European states. Some private economic activity was allowed under the communist system. Many workers moonlighted, working more than one job for extra money. Private land plots were also allowed. This extended exposure to market forces should aid reform and the development of a private sector. Managers and potential business partners are reported to be highly professional.

Still, a poorly developed infrastructure will not make it any easier for Hungary to overhaul its economy (Table 5-1). Hungary also had gross foreign debt of $20 billion at the end of 1990, and debt rescheduling is inevitable. Gross domestic product was projected to drop in 1991, and the economy is in a recession. The inflation rate was at approximately 35% for 1990 and leveled off to under 10% in 1991. Poor weather conditions will probably cause a drop in performance in agriculture.

Housing is scarce; a waiting list of approximately 80,000 names for subsidized housing in Budapest was reported in 1989. Market rents have seen dramatic increases as the housing crunch continues and government subsidies are reduced.

Table 5-1: Domestic Economy

	1987	1988	1989	1990*
Population (millions)	10.62	10.62	10.57	10.51
Population growth (percentage)	(0.1)	0	(0.5)	(0.5)
GDP (current dollars)	24.0	23.9	23.66	23.19
GDP per capita ($1)	2,260	2,250	2,238	2,206
GDP percentage change	4.1	(0.1)	(1.0)	(2.0)
Private enterprise (percentage of GDP)	N/A	N/A	14.6	18
Production and employment labor force (thousands)	4,885	4,885	4,800	4,750
Industrial production (percentage change in growth	3.8	(0.4)	(3.0)	(5.0)
Agricultural production (percentage change in growth)	(1.5)	(0.5)	(2.0)	(2.0)

* Estimated

Source: U.S. Department of Commerce. International Trade Administration. 1991. *Foreign Economic Trends and Their Implications for the United States—Hungary.* Washington, D.C.: Government Printing Office.

Political/Institutional Infrastructure

Hungary held free multiparty elections on both national and local levels in 1991, signals of the country's move toward democracy. The present government is based on a three-party coalition of Hungarian Democratic Forum, Independent Smallholders party and the Christian Democratic People's party.

Political Organization

Hungary has a multiparty republic, based on the constitution of October 1989. There is a Unicameral Parliament of 386 members, 176 elected from single-member constituencies, 152 from county lists, and 58 from a national list (Table 5-2). Supreme power is vested in Parliament. The prime minister is Jozef Antall and the president is Arpad Gonz.

Political Parties

The ruling coalition is made up of Hungarian Democratic Forum, Independent Smallholder's party, and the Christian Democratic People's party. Opposition parties include the Alliance of Free Democrats, Hungarian Socialist party, and the Alliance of Young Democrats. There are scores of smaller independent parties.

Table 5-2: Parties by Number of Seats in Parliament

Hungarian Democratic Forum (MDF)	164
Alliance of Free Democrats (SZDSZ)	94
Independent Smallholder's Party (FKgP)	44
Hungarian Socialist Party (MSZP)	33
Alliance of Young Democrats (FIDESA)	22
Christian Democratic People's Party (KDNP)	8

Federal/Regional/Municipal Organization

Hungary is divided into the capital, Budapest, and 19 other counties. Cities and communities have their own councils for local governance.

Election Timetable

Free parliamentary elections were held in March and April 1990.

Trade Flows

Top 10 Import/Export Trade Partners

Hungary's major trading partners include the Soviet Union, Germany, Austria, the Czech and Slovak Federal Republic, Italy, and Yugoslavia. Trade with former CMEA countries has increasingly been redirected to Western markets since 1990 (Table 5-3).

Table 5-3: Balance of Payments (Figures in $US 1 billion)

Convertible Currency Account	1987	1988	1989	1990*
Exports	5.014	5.50	6.45	7.40
Imports	5.011	5.01	5.91	6.60
Trade Balance	0.003	0.49	.054	0.80
Current Account Balance	(0.85)	(0.81)	(1.4)	(0.6)
Nonconvertible Currency Account				
Exports	4.91	4.48	4.1	3.0
Imports	4.87	4.39	3.5	3.0
Trade Balance	0.41	0.94	0.5	0.0
Current Account Balance	0.20	0.23	0.87	0.20

* Estimated

Source: U.S. Department of Commerce. International Trade Administration. 1991. *Foreign Economic Trends and Their Implications for the United States—Hungary*. Washington, D.C.: Government Printing Office.

Imports from CMEA amounted to 42.6% of Hungary's total imports in 1989 (Table 5-4).

Table 5-4: Hungary's Imports from CMEA and Non-CMEA Countries (1989) (Percentage of Total)

CMEA Countries	%	Non-CMEA Countries	%
Soviet Union	57.0	West Germany	31.9
East Germany	15.2	Austria	12.0
Czechoslovakia	12.5	Italy	6.4
Poland	7.4	Yugoslavia	5.2
Other	7.9	United States	2.8
		Other	41.7

Source: "Financial Currents," International Monetary Fund, (1990).

Table 5-5: U.S. Hungarian Trade (In $US 1 billion)

	1987	1988	1989	1990*
U.S. Exports to Hungary	0.095	0.078	0.121	0.17
U.S. Imports from Hungary	0.255	0.321	0.329	0.340
U.S. Share of Hungarian Convertible Currency Market				
Hungarian Exports	5.0	5.1	5.6	5.3
Hungarian Imports	1.80	1.3	1.6	1.8

* 1990 figures are estimated.

Source: U.S. Department of Commerce. International Trade Administration. 1991. *Foreign Economic Trends and Their Implications for the United States—Hungary*. Washington, D.C.: Government Printing Office.

Top 10 Import/Export Commodities

Top imports from the West include rice, textile yarn, polymers, synthetic fibers, nonelectrical machinery and tools, internal combustion engines, polyacetals and epoxide resins, organic-inorganic and heterocyclic compounds, telecommunications equipment and musical instruments, records and tapes. Principal U.S. exports to Hungary include: agricultural equipment, motor vehicles parts, tobacco, computers, telecommunications equipment, agricultural commodities, and aircrafts (Table 5-5).

Hungarian world trade has increased by approximately 40% since 1980. The trading partners have shifted from a 50-50 balance between the East bloc and the West to lean towards the West.

A number of areas have been identified by the U.S. government and private-sector as potential export opportunities, including: electronics production, computers, telecommunications, food processing and packaging technology, agricultural equipment, pharmaceuticals, pollution control equipment, chemicals, and transportation equipment.

Finance and Investment Policies

Hungary's government has taken a more conservative route to economic reform than the "flash cut" implemented in Poland. However, it has aimed to reduce the budget deficit, both on revenue and expenditure portions. In monetary policy, the government will try to control the amount of money in circulation, which should promote exports and reform measures, in addition to reducing inflation. The longer term goal is currency convertibility of the forint.

Policies to Attract New Business

Amendments to the Joint Venture code in March 1991 have eased requirements for approval, but some tax breaks for foreign investors have been eliminated. The Concessions Acts, which went into effect in 1991, allow private firms to operate in the public sector. A new law on land ownership is still under debate. The Privatization law will address transformation, protection of state property, and foreign investment.

Preferred Foreign Investment Projects

Targeted sectors for foreign investment activity include the following:

- electronics and electronic devices, such as the manufacture of computers
- telecommunications projects, computer-aided design technologies, and other technical devices
- manufacture of machine tools and vehicle components, as well as machines for agriculture, food processing, and forestry

Other key industries for foreign investment activity include package technology, pharmaceuticals and herbicides, veterinary science, energy saving technologies, and tourism. Special emphasis is also given to industries that will manufacture products to increase export of or decrease the convertible import in the agriculture and food industry.

Investment Incentives and Privileges

The government has passed favorable business laws for investment and the formation of joint ventures. Repatriation of currency is allowed.

Incentives to form joint ventures include guaranteed profit repatriation, 100% foreign ownership of subsidiaries, tax incentives, and guarantees against appropriation. Other incentives for investment include proximity to West European markets and the potential for rapid growth in the Hungarian and other East European markets.

The United States has also sponsored a number of investment-oriented incentive programs to assist Hungary's transition to democracy and a market economy. The Support for East European Democracy Act (SEED) provided funding to Hungary for various projects and confirms Hungary's eligibility to participate in U.S. government assistance programs. The Hungarian-American Enterprise Fund also authorized $60 million for loans, grants, and other equity investments.

The Eastern European Growth Fund is an equity-investment fund to provide capital to private enterprises in East Europe.

Tax Incentives

New foreign investment legislation has made it easier to register in Hungary, but has made it more difficult to qualify for tax incentives. Under the previous system, those companies with starting capital of more than Ft 25 million and with a foreign investor holding a 30% or more share, received a 100% tax holiday for five years and a 60% tax allowance for the sixth year. Any company in which a non-Hungarian invested more than Ft5 million or owned 20% of the capital was eligible for a 20% reduction of the tax, which is 40% on profits.

The 20% reduction has been eliminated under the new law. A company could qualify for a 60% reduction in the profits tax rate for the first five years and a 40% reduction in the second five years if the following conditions are met:

- It is established with capital of more than Ft 50 million.
- Foreign investors take at least 30% share of issued capital.
- More than 50% of the annual income is derived from manufacturing or operating a hotel built or renovated.

To be eligible for a full five-year tax holiday with a 60% reduction in the second five years, a company must meet the above conditions, as well as be involved in one of the priority sectors (electronics, vehicle components, machine tools, agriculture and food processing equipment, metal working equipment, packaging, pharmaceuticals and herbicides, animal fodder protein, animal husbandry, food and food from live animals, corn and wheat production, tourism and telecommunications, and certain transportation vehicles).

A company is eligible for a tax reduction of the profits tax if it receives investment of the dividends of a foreign investor.

Exemptions from value-added tax (VAT) and customs duties for goods and fixed assets contributed in kind by foreign investors are in force. However, if the assets are sold within three years, the VAT and duty become payable.

Free Trade Zones/Special Economic Zones

Companies with foreign participation may establish a customs-free zone under the customs authorities. These zones are subject to Hungarian taxation except for the VAT.

APPROACHING THE MARKET

Foreign Trade and Investment Decision-Making Infrastructure

The breakthrough for foreign investment in Hungary came in 1989 with the passage of the Act on Foreign Investment, the Companies Act, and the Transformation Act. These acts established investment incentives for foreigners, including the following:

- national treatment of firms
- allowance of 100% foreign ownership
- equity acquisition in existing companies
- a streamlined registration process
- ownership of real property
- hard-currency bank accounts
- duty-free imports of certain contributions to joint ventures
- guaranteed repatriation of profits
- state guarantee of compensation in the currency of original investment
- tax incentives
- low labor costs

There are, however, problems with foreign investment. Some of these include poor economic performance, the government's right to screen investment in which foreign participation exceeds 50%, a small internal market, and an inability to retain hard currency earned through exports. The infrastructure is poorly developed. Another difficulty of privatization has been the issue of compensation for property seized by the state under previous administrations. In April 1991, a bill was passed that provides for compensation to some whose land was confiscated under Communist rule. Property that was nationalized after 1949 will be returned. Farmers will receive up to 50 hectares of land. Those who owned urban land will receive vouchers, worth only a fraction of the current value of the land. The bill has opened the way for many speculators to file ownership claims. Also, ethnic conflicts were deepened, because land seized from ethnic Germans, Jews, and Gypsies predates the 1949 cutoff. The bill was a compromised way of returning some land, without bankrupting the state. In May 1991, a constitutional court ruled that the law was unfair in the compensation and that the 1989 cutoff date violates the rights of citizens whose land was confiscated prior to the Communist takeover.

State and Private Services

Market Research

Because the Hungarian market is small, market research is essential. Market research has been run by foreign trading companies in the past, but this situation has changed as foreign businesses try to tap into the Hungarian market. Companies may employ a local agent or broker—both are abundantly available, although most specialize in Budapest. They may establish representation or sales office registration, but no approval is necessary to form subsidiaries to promote products.

Setting Up Business Operations

Forms of Business Organization

Firms must be registered in the Trade Register, which can be done through the Metropolitan (Budapest) court. Businesses in which the foreign investor's share exceeds 49% must receive a state authority's permission to register. Registration regulations were streamlined in 1991.

Limited liability company. Those involved must report the date of the association contract, the date of starting activities, length of time of the company, sphere of activities, amount of primary stock, and names and domiciles of the Supervisory Board members to the auditor.

Sole traders and partnerships. Those involved must report the date of the association contract, the date of starting activities, length of time of the company, sphere of company's activities, and name and residence of legal entities or private person members.

Sales Promotion, Fairs, Conferences, and Advertising

The total advertising and promotion budget of Hungarian companies was approximately Ft 8 million in 1989, and approximately Ft 3 million of it was spent on radio and television commercials.

Advertising agencies in Budapest include: Young and Rubicam Hungary; Ogilvy & Mather Rt.; GGK Spott.; TOP Reklan; McCann-Erickson Interpress; Mahir; Grey-Multireklam; Saatchi & Saatchi Advertising Kft.; and DDB Needham.

Transportation and Freight (Air/Sea)

Hungary has a railway network of 7,765 kilometers, 1,147 of which are electrified. The road network is 140,000 kilometers of which 29,715 kilometers are national highways. National highways are typically well-maintained and are divided into four lanes. Hungary's airline, MALEV, has a fleet of 22 planes which flew 43 routes in 1989.

INVESTMENT CLIMATE

Privatization, Investment Protection, and Dispute Settlement

The first phase of a five-year privatization program covering 20 enterprises was announced in September 1990. The Budapest Stock Exchange opened in June 1990. Foreign investors are allowed to buy stock.

Joint Ventures and Wholly Owned Subsidiaries

Hungary experienced a surge in the number of joint ventures registered in 1990. Of the total 2,800 joint ventures registered, 200 are from the United States. The majority are from Germany.

Taxation and Regulatory Conditions

Sources of Income Liable to Taxation

Hungary has a profit tax on companies, personal income tax, a value-added tax (VAT), and local taxes which will be determined by local needs.

Company Tax

Although there is no tax on the capital or net worth of a company, companies are subject to profits tax of 40%. Certain tax exemptions apply. The goal is to reduce the relative amount of taxes on companies. More changes are likely to occur in 1992 when the Law on Accounting is passed.

Personal Income Tax

Hungary modified its personal income tax structure in 1991. The government's policy is currently focused on reducing inequalities in the taxation system, while decreasing the overall tax burden (Table 5-6).

Table 5-6: Taxable Income in 1991 (Forints)

	Percentage Rate
0-55,000	0
55,001-90,000	12
90,001-120,000	18
120,001-150,000	30
150,001-300,000	32
300,001-500,000	40
500,001-	50

Source: Hungarian Chamber of Commerce. *Hungary Bulletin 1991*.

Estate Duty

Estates are not taxed as entities.

FINANCING AND CAPITAL MARKETS

Banking and Other Financial Institutions

Bank reform has been another key measure instituted since the 1989 revolution. Since 1987 the banking system has been two-tiered. The Hungarian National Bank acts as an issue bank and the five major commercial banks provide services to companies. Foreign banks have also been established in Hungary. There were ten registered in 1990. However, foreign banking services are still dominated by Hungarian Credit Bank and Hungarian Foreign Trade Bank. The Hungarian National Bank is the sole bank allowed to borrow abroad. The Central European International Bank is exempt from foreign exchange rules and acts as an offshore bank, even though it is in Budapest.

Payment Modalities

The Currency

The Hungarian currency is the forint. The government is using a gradual process to move towards full convertibility (Table 5-7). In March 1, 1991, the Hungarian Commercial and Credit Bank guaranteed a purchase rate of Ft 77.05= US $1. In December 1991 the floating rate stood at Ft 75 = US $1.

Table 5-7: Hungarian Financial Profile

	1987	1988	1989	1990
Gross Convertible Debt	19.58	19.60	19.63	2.04
Net Convertible Reserves	2.16	1.98	1.46	1.20
Average Exchange Rate (x HFt = $US1)	46.98	50.42	60.0	70.0

*   1990 figures are estimated.
Source: U.S. Department of Commerce. International Trade Administration. 1991. *Foreign Economic Trends and Their Implications for the United States—Hungary*. Washington, D.C.: Government Printing Office.

Tapping International Aid Institutions

Hungary has the support of the World Bank for many programs. The United States has developed the SEED legislation which offers many forms of assistance. Hungary has been accepted as an observer to the European Community (EC) and hopes to become a full member.

Financial Market Operations

Money Market

There is limited trading in government bonds and company bonds on the Budapest Stock Exchange. The operation of the foreign currencies market is restricted.

Securities Market

The Budapest Stock Exchange reopened in June 1990. Most of the trading, which takes place every day for one hour, is over the counter. Only about 5% of the bonds and stocks are available through the exchange. In the first few months of trading, the average amount was $US 3-4 million per day. Trading bonds had been issued as early as 1983, a precursor to the exchange. Shares can be registered abroad and foreign securities may be listed in Hungary.

LICENSING, PATENTS, AND TRADEMARKS

Patents and other intellectual property rights in general extend for 20 years from the date of registration. Trademarks are valid for 10 years and copyrights are valid for the lifetime of the creator and for 50 years after death.

VISITING AND LOCATING

General Travel Checklist

Visas

Visas are a formality and are available at border stations and airport arrivals.

Currency

The Hungarian currency is the forint. In December 1991, $1 = 75 Ft. Major hotels, car rental agencies, or other firms that service foreigners may require that purchases be completed in hard currency. International travel tickets must be purchased in hard currency. Illegal currency transactions, especially trading on the street, should be avoided.

Getting Around

When driving, take note that Hungarians tend to pass on the right. Streets are poorly illuminated, and drivers are cautioned to watch for pedestrians, unlighted bicycles, carts, or other vehicles on the road. Hungarian police have the right to effect traffic fines on the spot.

Accommodations and Housing

Travel agencies and Hungarian travel offices can reserve accommodations prior to travel. While in Hungary, assistance may be obtained through travel offices, the service offices of hotels, and county tour offices. Major chains in Hungary include:

Hyatt Hotels, Hilton Hotels, Penta Hotels, Accor-Novotel Hotels, Minotels Hotels, Husa Hotels, InterContinental Hotels, Radisson Hotels, and Ramada Hotels.

Electricity Supply

Electrical appliances operate on 220 volts. Some hotels have transformers to lend to guests, and some may have 110 volt plugs or provide hairdryers.

Telecom, Postal, and Courier Services

The post office, recently split into three state-owned corporations, controls the postal service, telecommunications, and radio and television transmissions. These corporations are scheduled to be converted into joint-stock companies.

The post office is open on weekdays from 8:00 a.m. to 6:00 p.m. and on Saturdays from 8:00 a.m. to 2:00 p.m. The post office is closed on Sundays, except for 1062 lenin krt. 105 (Western Railway Station) and 1087 Baross ter 11/c (Eastern Railway Station).

Telephone service is inadequate by Western standards. Lines are difficult to get and may be static-filled; calls may be misdirected. Waiting lists for phones are common (generally more than a three-year wait). The public may wait years for a phone to be installed, while businesses receive quicker service. Paying in dollars also speeds up the connection time. A $300 million grant from the World Bank for telecom development is planned to improve the system.

Costs are currently two forints for a three-minute local call. International calls from Hungary are expensive; a Budapest to New York call costs as much as $2.40 per minute. Reversing the charges (New York to Budapest) is approximately $1.00 per minute. To make a call within Hungary, take the following steps: (1) dial tone; (2) 06 - inland dial tone; (3) area; (4) local number.

Business Hours

Offices are open from 8:00 a.m. to 4:00 p.m. Monday through Thursday and from 8:00 a.m. to 2:00 p.m. on Friday. Banks are open from 9:00 a.m. to 2:00 p.m. Monday through Friday.

Tipping

Customary restaurant tips are 10% of the total bill. Gypsy bands, if they play directly for you, should also be tipped.

Health Care

The U.S. Embassy in Budapest has an Embassy Health Unit which is open daily from 8:00 a.m. to 5:00 p.m. There is a limited supply of routine medicines. The staff nurse will assist Americans or help locate an English-speaking doctor if necessary. The Health Unit extension is 263. Outside of working hours, the nurse may be reached by contacting the Marine Security Guard.

First aid is free to all, but there is a charge for medical examinations and treatment. The ambulance number is 04.

The Media

There are approximately 13 major newspapers and monthlies distributed in Hungary. The major English-language daily in Hungary is the *Daily News*, published by MTI (Hungarian News Agency). An English-language monthly, *The Hungarian Observer*, is widely distributed outside of Hungary.

Availability of Foreign Products

Western goods are readily available in Budapest and are increasing in the secondary cities. Eight McDonald's restaurants have sprung up and are doing extremely well. Most are open until midnight. The Levi's Jeans store is notable in Budapest, in that it is the only store to frequently have long lines of prospective shoppers awaiting entry.

Shopping

Intourist shops are hard currency stores that cater to tourists, with specialty items such as Herend china. China, crystal, handicrafts, leather goods, antiques, and records and tapes can also be bought in the shopping district in Budapest. Prices are significantly lower than in the United States. Most stores do not close for lunch. There are street markets around Budapest.

Dining out

There are several fine restaurants within walking distance of Budapest's major hotels. Most restaurants are open between noon to 11:00 p.m. "The Gourmet's Guide" is a listing of restaurants in Budapest and can be obtained at the major hotels. Hungarian specialties include goose liver, jokai soup (bean soup with smoked ham) and gulyas soup, a paprika flavored soup with beef and potatoes. Chicken or veal paprikas, wild game, and grilled fogas (fish) are recommended main courses. Cucumber or tomato salads are common, as are rich desserts. Hungarian wines are of high quality. Budapest also offers a number of coffeehouses.

Entertainment

Classical music and opera are commonly available, as is legitimate stage theatre. Alternative theatre and pop music shows are growing quite common, but must be sought out by street-side posters and notices posted in music shops. Several "Parisian" type cabarets are ongoing, mostly in nightclubs adjacent to the major hotels.

Sightseeing and Tourist Information

Information is available at 1061 Budapest, Nepkoztarsasag utja 12, Tel: 118-667. Hours are Monday: 9:00 a.m. to 12:00 p.m. and 2:00 p.m. to 6:00 p.m.; Tuesday and Wednesday: 9:00 a.m. to 12:00 p.m.; Thursday: 2:00 p.m. to 6:00 p.m. and Friday: 9:00 a.m. to 12:00 p.m.

The Short-Term Business Visitor

Airlines Serving

Malev is the Hungarian national airline. Other airlines with direct flights to Hungary include: Aeroflot, Air France, Alitalia, Austrian Airlines, British Airways, CSA, E1 A1, Finnair, Interflug, KLM, LOT, Lufthansa, Sabena, SAS, and Swissair.

Limousine

Limousines are available through V.I.P. Limousine and Rent-A-Car, Budapest, Tel: 166-7466. The airport office is Tel: 157-8392. Automobile rental companies include: Hungar Motor Rent, Europcar, Avis, Budget, and Hertz.

Rent-an-Office Facilities

Renting an office in Budapest can be confusing, if not difficult. As reported in the Radio Free Europe/Radio Liberty's Soviet/East European Report, the shortage of office space in Budapest has driven prices up to nearly that of London or Paris. Some foreign business people are reported to be buying enterprises in order to access the real estate.

The Expatriate

In addition to the information needed by the short-term visitor, the expatriate needs to know how to set up bank accounts; how to find housing and where to live; the nature of the school system for expatriates; and holidays observed.

Hourly/Annual Mean Wages

The average Hungarian hourly wage is US $2.00. The average factory wage is around $150 US per month, according to a recent survey by the National Association of Manufacturers in Washington.

Immigration and Work Permits

Foreigners working in managerial capacity do not need work permits. Others must obtain a permit of up to one year. Long-term staff may obtain permanent residents' permits (for up to five years).

Labor Force

The Hungarian labor force is hard-working. Many are accustomed to working more than one job to earn extra money, as some private initiatives were in force during communist rule. Workers are highly educated, skilled, and motivated. Approximately 34% have college, university, or high school level education; 20% have basic education and industrial training; 30% have had at least eight grades of schooling; and 10% have had less education than eight grades of schooling.

Conditions of work. A standard work week is 40 to 42 hours. Equal opportunities for men and women are guaranteed constitutionally. Standard vacation time is 15 days.

Employment and medical insurance. The employer is obliged to pay a sum equal to a terminated employee's monthly pay for a period of prolongation, although a system of severance pay is not in effect.

Training. Most companies provide free or subsidized training.

HUNGARY

KEY CONTACTS FOR BUSINESS

U.S. Commercial Representation in Hungary

Embassy of the United States of America
Szavbadsag Ter 12
H-1055 Budapest V
(mailing address from U.S. is: APO New York 09213
Patrick Hughes, Commercial Counsellor
    Tel: 36-1-112-6450
    Fax: 36-1-132-8934
    Telex: 36-1-112-6450

Hungarian Commercial Representation in the U.S.A.

Embassy of the Hungarian Republic
Office of the Commercial Counsellor
150 East 58th Street, 33rd Floor
New York, NY 10022
    Tel: 212/752-3060
    Fax: 212/486-2958
Dr. Jozsef Heiszig, Director

Embassy of the Hungarian People's Republic
Branch Office of the Commercial Counsellor
139 East Randolph Drive
Prudential Plaza #1930
Chicago, IL 60601
    Tel: 312/856-1080

National Bank of Hungary
10 Rockefeller Plaza #1100
New York, NY 10020
    Tel: 212/969-9270
Imre Hollai, Chief Representative

Hungarian Government Trade and Investment Promotion Services—(In Hungary)

TRADE-INFORM (Hungarian State Office for Trade Promotion)
P.O. Box 133
Dorottya utca 4
H-1389 Budapest
   Tel: 36-1-118-5422
   Fax: 36-1-118-3732
   Telex: 22-5191

INVESTCENTER (Hungarian State Office for Investment Promotion)
Dorottya utca 4
H-1051 Budapest V
   Tel: 36-1-153-6064
   Fax: 36-1-153-3732
Judith Gergely, Director
Ferenc Salamon, Manager

Hungarian Chamber of Commerce
Foreign Investment Promotion Service
Kossuth L. Ter 6-8
H-1055 Budapest V
   Tel: 36-1-153-3333
   Fax: 36-1-153-1285
Peter Bunai, Director, Foreign Investment Services
Tibor Zselinszky, U.S. Desk Operator

Hungarian Government Economic Ministries

Ministry of Trade
Honved U. 13-15
H-1055 Budapest
   Tel: 36-1-153-0000
   Fax: 36-1-153-2794
   Telex: 36-1-131-4186
Gabor Horvath, U.S. Desk Officer
Janos Balassa, General Director, Joint Venture Department

Ministry of Telecommunications, Transport, and Construction
Dob. u. 75-81
H-1400 Budapest, P.O. Box 87
 Tel: 36-1-122-0220
  36-1-122-9478
 Fax: 36-1-122-8695
 Telex: 22-5729
Bela Doros, Deputy Minister

Ministry of Industry
85 Martirok utja
H-1024 Budapest
 Tel: 36-1-156-5566
 Fax: 36-1-175-3646 or 36-1-155-3482
Zolton Lehel, Director, International Department

Ministry of Finance
Jozsef Nador ter 2-4
H-1051 Budapest
 Tel: 36-1-118-2066
Istvan Tompe, Deputy Minister

Ministry of Agriculture & Food
Kossuth Lajos ter 11
H-1055 Budapest
 Tel: 36-1-153-3000

Hungarian Banks

National Bank of Hungary
Szabadsag Ter 8-9
1054 Budapest
 Tel: 36-1-153-2600
 Fax: 36-1-111-7437

Hungarian Credit Bank
Szabadsag ter 5-6
1054 Budapest
 Tel: 36-1-153-2600
 Fax: 36-1-131-5981

Foreign Trade Bank
Szent Istvan ter 11
Budapest V
    Tel: 36-1-141-4390 or 36-1-132-9360

General Banking and Trust Company
Szamuely utca 38
H-1055 Budapest
    Tel: 36-1-117-1255

Other Hungarian Government Offices and Organizations Dealing with Business Matters

Association of Entrepreneurs (VOSZ)
c/o Multicoop
Bogar U. 35-37
H-1145 Budapest
    Tel: 36-1-115-4179
Ferenc Mueller, President

Association of Industrial Cooperatives (OKISZ)
Thokoly U. 58-60
H-1145 Budapest
    Tel: 36-1-141-5124
Elek Bonyhady, President

Inland Revenue Office (Hungarian tax authority)
Szechenyi utca 2
H-1054 Budapest
    Tel: 36-1-112-1896 or 36-1-117-3071

Budapest Court of Justice ("Court of Registration")
Rozsa Ferenc utca 79
H-1064 Budapest
    Tel: 36-1-112-1629

National Authority of Wages/Labor
Roosevelt ter 7-8
H-1051 Budapest
    Tel: 36-1-132-2100

Hungarian Telecom Company
Krisztima krt. 6-8
H-1054 Budapest
    Tel: 36-1-156-8321
    Fax: 36-1-175-9890
    Telex: 22-1193
Dr. Krisztina Heller, Senior Advisor to the Vice President

Private Firms Offering Business-Related Services in Hungary

Legal, Accounting, and Business Consulting Services

Baker and McKenzie Law Firm
Pafrany U. 25
1026 Budapest
    Tel: 36-1-176-1138
    Fax: 36-1-175-9161
Dr. Lajos Schmidt, Manager

Price Waterhouse
Kosciuszko tade U. 14
1 EM 4
H-1011 Budapest
    Tel: 36-1-175-2603
Les Bonnay, General Manager

Interjurist - East/West Invest Ltd.
Szabadsag ter 5-6
1054 Budapest V
    Tel: 36-1-132-1133
    Fax: 311-1-131-5981

ECONOSERVICE Co., Ltd.
vaci U. 19-21
H-1052 Budapest V
    Tel: 36-1-118-7084
Ferenc Zental, Director

Union of Hungarian Accountants
Jozsef Nador ter 2-4
H-1051 Budapest
    Tel: 36-1-142-5777

Lawyers' Cooperative #4/4
Majakovszkij U. 93
H-1077 Budapest
    Tel: 36-1-142-5777
Dr. Peter Karpati, Counsellor

Neumann International Mgmt. Consultants
Budakeszi ut 55/D, P7 Building
1021 Budapest
    Tel: 36-1-176-7081
    Fax: 36-1-176-1843
Tamas Toth, Managing Director

Business Consulting Co.
Aranykez U. 3
H-1052 Budapest
    Tel: 36-1-3601-118-7200
Gyorgy Kovacs, Director

Ernst & Young/BONITAS Ltd.
Amerikaiut 96
1145 Budapest
    Tel: 36-1-183-3512
Dr. Gusztav Beinerth, Director

Coopers & Lybrand Ltd.
Pagony U. 18
1124 Budapest
    Tel: 36-1-117-1113
Mihaly Varga, Manager

SZENZOR Accounting Co.
Fo utca 68
H-1073 Budapest
    Tel: 36-1-115-5888

AUDIT Ltd.
Izabella utca 2
H-1073 Budapest
    Tel: 36-1-142-9938

Budapest Chamber of Law
Szalay utca 7
H-1055 Budapest
    Tel: 36-1-132-5330

Heminway Unimpex Consulting Co.
Felszabadulas ter 1
H-1053 Budapest
    Tel: 36-1-118-0383
    Fax: 36-1-138-2242

Young & Rubicam Hungary Ltd.
Prielle Kornelia u. 45
H-1117 Budapest
Ildio Takacs, Manager

Advertising

Aktiv-Color Advertising and Servicing Cooperative
Petzval Jozsef u. 12/c
H-1115 Budapest

Real Estate

IMMOBILIA Real Estate Agency Ltd.
Szamuely utca 3
H-1093 Budapest
    Tel: 36-1-117-6807
    Fax: 36-1-118-4199

Interreklam Marketing Co.
Ujpalotai ut 22
P.O.B. 197
H-1325 Budapest
    Tel: 36-1-149-0726 or 36-1-129-6245
    Telex: 22-5007

Market Research

ECHO
Budaorsi ut 45
H-1112 Budapest
    Tel: 36-1-185-0878
Contact: Sandor Richter

KOPINT-DATORG Institute for Market Research and Economics
Dorottya utca 6
H-1389 Budapest
    Tel: 36-1-118-6640
Contact: Andras Koves

Co-Nexus Corporation
Roham u. 1
P.O. Box 437
H-1371 Budapest
    Tel: 36-1-175-0375
    Fax: 36-1-156-9493

Banks in Hungary with Foreign Participation

Citibank Budapest, Ltd.
Vaci U. 19-21
H-1052 Budapest
    Tel: 36-1-118-8377
    Fax: 36-1-186-9301

UnicBank, Ltd.
Vaci ut. 19-21
H-1052 Budapest
    Tel: 36-1-118-2088
Dr. Ivan Gara, Director

U.S. Embassy—Republic of Hungary (May 1991)

Budapest
V. Szabadsag Ter 12
American Embassy
APO NY 09213
    Tel: 36-1-112-6450
    Telex: 18048 224-222
Commercial Development Center
    Fax: 36-1-132-8934
    Telex: 227136 USCDC H
    FBO Fax: 36-1-175-5924

Ambassador: Charles H. Thomas
Deputy Chief of Mission: Donald B. Kursch
Political: Thomas A. Lynch
Economic: Jeff Feltman
Commercial: Patrick Hughes
Congressional: Elizabeth Barnett
Administrative: Wayne K. Logsdon
Military: Kenneth Kayatin
SCI: Thomas A. Schlenker

Agriculture: Robert Svec
PRESS/CULT: Robert McCarthy
Military: Col. Ruth Anderson USA
AARMA: Sean Maxwell
IRS: Frederick Pablo (resident in Rome)

Republic of Hungary — Budapest
American Chamber of Commerce (AMCHAM)
Officers and Board of Governor Members
November 30, 1989

President
Michael J. Shade
Banking Technology Consultant
c/o Commercial & Credit Bank, Ltd.
Arany J.U. 24
Budapest 1051
    Tel: 36-1-117-2464
    Fax: 36-1-117-2485

Second Vice President
Les Bonnay, MBA, CMC
General Manager
Price Waterhouse
Kosciuszko Tade u. 14 I/4
Budapest 1751
    Tel: 175-2603

Board Member
Steven M. Bina
Director of European Operations
Schwinn Bicycle
P.O. Box 113
Budapest 1751
    Tel: 158-9356

Board Member
Zsuzsa Rajki-Local Manager
Dow Chemical
Vaci u. 19-21
Budapest 1052
    Tel: 36-1-118-8766

First Vice President
Daniel S. Fogel, Ph.D.
Academic Director & Dean
International Management Center
Pentz K.U. 1-3
Budapest 1221
    Tel: 36-1-173-0755, 138-5128
    Fax: 36-1-138-5340

Secretary-Treasurer
Bob Bellia
Director
Ernst & Whinney-Bonitas
Amerikai ut 96
Budapest 1145
    Tel: 36-1-183-7761
    Fax: 36-1-183-0502

Board Member
Theodore S. Boone
Attorney
Baker & McKenzie
Pafrany ut. 25
Budapest 1026
    Tel: 36-1-176-7138

U.S. Joint Ventures in Hungary

BCR and Lilly Co., Ltd.
Vaci U. 16
1052 Budapest V
Krista Abhar, Managing Director

Qualiplastic Co., Ltd.
2072 Zsambek
P.O. Box 32
Budapest
Bela Balas, Local Manager

Ogilvy and Mather - Mahir
u 1101 Ut. 51, III EM
1091 Budapest
Dr. Miklos Cseprigi, Office Manager

Babolna - McDonald's Restaurant
Bathory u. 3
1054 Budapest V
Endre Fazekas, Local Manager

Computerworld Informatics Ltd.
Hungarian American Joint Co.
Rakoczi Ut. 16
1072 Budapest
Deszo Futasz, Local Manager

Radelor Co.
Zsigmond Ter. 8
1023 Budapest II.
Bela Juhasz, Local Manager

Applied Technics Ltd.
Pozsonyi U. 36
1137 Budapest
Istvan Kondorossy, Director

Puski - Isis Ltd.
Corvin Ter 8 1/3
1011 Budapest
Laszlo Puski, Office Manager

International Management Center
Pentz Karoly U. 1/3
1221 Budapest
Zsuzsa Ranki, Local Manager

Hunguard Ltd. (Guardian Industries)
c/o Glass Industry Works
Beloiannisz u. 2/4
1055 Budapest
Lajos Sapi, Representative

McCann Erickson - Interpress
Budakeszi Ut 55/D
1021 Budapest II
Dr. Jane Serenyi, Local Manager

Kotoelem KFT
Vanyaleg U. 86
1225 Budapest
Jajos Stephen, Managing Director

Pangus Rubber Products Co.
c/o Taurus Gumiipari V.
Ujhegyi Ut 25
1108 Budapest X
Katalin Szantay, Local Manager

Hemingway Computing Int., Ltd.
c/o Szamalk
1115 Szakasits Arpad U. 68
Budapest XI
Dr. Ferenc Vamos

Fotex American - Hungarian JV Co.
Ferenchegyi Ut. 20
1025 Budapest II
Gabor Varszegi, Local Manager

Citibank Budapest Corp.
Vaci utca 19-21
1052 Budapest V
Mr. Robin M. Winchester, General Manager

Schwinn - Csepel Bicycles
P.O. Box 113
1751 Budapest
Laszlo Nogradi, Regional Manager

Levi Strauss Budapest Co.
Tanacs Krt 9 VIII/802
1075 Budapest
Andras Pinter, Local Manager

Corning Medical Corp. (medical instruments)
Corning, NY

ALM Holding Corp. (thermoplastic materials)
Wayne, NJ

IDG Communications (books/periodicals on computers)
Framingham, MA

Compumax Inc. (computer automation)
Menlo Park, CA

Dow Chemical - established JV in 1991 with Nitrokemia and Chemolimpex to
manufacture extruded polystyrene foam thermal insulation

First American - Hungarian Brokerage

Intercom (CAROLCO)

Concord Camera

Hisler - Radke Corp. (GMI)

General Electric / Tungsram

General Motors / Raba

Other U.S. companies recently active in Hungary:Unicum, Bear Stearns Inc.
(First Hungary Fund), Valmont Industries, Dupont, Estee Lauder, Pepsico,
Coca-Cola, UPS, DHL, Black and Decker, NCM, Remington, Union City
Body, Price Waterhouse, Seagate, Group 92 Int'l, Mister Minit, and VITA
(Volunteers in Technical Assistance).

U.S. Company Representative Offices in Hungary

International Trade Center
Bajcsy-Zsilinsky ut 12
1051 Budapest
(also Vaci ut 19/21, Budapest 1052)

Hartigay & Partners
Kelengyi ut 41/A
Budapest XI
Dr. Attila Agoston, Representative

Merck Sharp Dohme, Ltd.
Koscviusko tade u. 8
1021 Budapest
Dr. Veronika Biro, Manager

IBM
Menesi ut 22
1119 Budapest IX
Zsuzsa Branyik, Manager

Bechtel Hungarian Alliance
Ostrom utca 23/25
1051 Budapest
Mr. Lynn Curtis, Manager

Upjohn Tudomanyos Informacios
Batthyany u. 46. I/6
1051 Budapest
Brian Ellis, Manager

First U.S.-Hungarian Securities
Parisi U. 1
1051 Budapest
Jozsef Lupis, Manager

Rigler Electronics
POB 176
1364 Budapest

Bank Xerox
Nephadsereg u. 30
1055 Budapest
Racz Miklos

3M
Dozsa Gyorgy ut 102
1068 Budapest Vi
Dr. Ferenc Arvay, Manager

Price Waterhouse
Kocsiusszko tade u 14/1
1001 Budapest
Les Bonnay, Manager

Tektronix Technical Office
Horvath U. 2-12. lv/39
1024 Budapest
Gerhard Brychta, Manager

Hewlett Packard
Radvany utca 7
1118 Budapest
Laszlo Domokos, Manager

Hemingway Unimpex Corporation
Felszabadulas ter 1
1053 Budapest V
Mr. Pal Gacs

Honeywell
Teve U. 8-10
1139 Budapest
Ivan Matyas, Manager

Dow Chemical
Vaci utca 19-21
1052 Budapest V

Baker & McKenzie
Pafrany ut 25
1026 Budapest II
Dr. Lajos Schmidt, Manager

Ernst & Whinney
Tancsics Mihaly u. 1/3
1047 Budapest
Adam Tertak, Manager

Arthur Anderson, Inc.
Vaci u. 17
1052 Budapest
Hegedus Andras, Manager

Coopers & Lybrand
Pagony u. 18
1124 Budapest
Mihaly Varga, Manager

Estee Lauder International
Vaci u, 12
1052 Budapest
Judit Gonda, Manager

O.N.T. Inc.
Szerena u. 5/1
1025 Budapest
Eniko Pados

Interconcepts, Inc.
Beke ter 12
1139 Budapest
Charles Rudd, Director

Highland Import (Rockport)
Aranykez u. 6 VI/118
1052 Budapest
Istvan Zador, Manager

Pfizer Scientific Center
Alpari Gy u. 2
1051 Budapest
Hajnalka Vondra, Manager

BCR & Lilly Co.
Vaci u. 16
1052 Budapest
Crista Abhar, Director

DHL Worldwide Express
Vaci u. 7
1052 Budapest
Meszaroa Janos, Director

Business Contacts in Hungary: Telecommunications

Ministry of Telecommunications
Bem rakpart 47
H-1027
    Tel: 361-156-8000
    Fax: 361-122-8695
    Telex: 22-5571
Contact: Mr. Paul Banhalmi, Director of Int'l Affairs Dept.

Hungarian Telecom Company
Krisztina krt 6-8
H-1540 Budapest
    Tel: 361-156-8321
    Fax: 361-175-9890
Contact: Ferenc Valter, Director

Technoimpex Foreign Trading Company
P.O. Box 183
H-1390 Budapest
    Tel: 361-118-4055
    Fax: 361-118-6418
    Telex: 22-4171

Budavox Telecommunications Foreign Trading Co.
P.O. Box 267
H-1392 Budapest
    Tel: 361-186-8988
    Telex: 22-5077

Transelektro Foreign Trading Co.
P.O. Box 377
H-1394 Budapest
    Tel: 361-132-0100
    Fax: 361-112-7234 or 361-153-0308
    Telex: 22-4571

Elextroimpex Foreign Trading Co.
P.O. Box 296
H-1392 Budapest
    Tel: 361-132-8300
    Telex: 22-5771 elimp-h

Elektromodul Trading House for Electronics
P.O. Box 158
H-1390 Budapest
    Tel: 361-149-8340
    Fax: 361-140-2523
    Telex: 22-5154

BHG Telecommunications Works
Fehervari ut 70
P.O. Box 2
H-1509 Budapest XI
    Tel: 361-145-3300
    Telex: 22-5933

Hungarian Telecommunications Association
Gabor Aron u. 65-67
P.O. Box 33
H-1525 Budapest II
    Tel: 361-166-9873
Ivan Nemeskeri, Jozsef Oulicky, Directors

HITEKA Telecommunications Engineering Factory
Hunyadi J. U. 2
P.O. Box 10
H-1509 Budapest
    Tel: 361-166-9873
Lajos Rehling, Commercial Director

BRG Electronic Works
Polgar u. 8-10
P.O. Box 43
H-1300 Budapest
    Tel: 36-1-168-2080
    Telex: 22-5928

Computer Companies in Hungary

Graphisoft Co.
400 Oyster Point Blvd. # 520
San Francisco, CA 94080

Compudrug U.S.A., Inc.
13706 Research Blvd. # 216
Austin, TX 78750
    Fax: 512/331/4222

Muszertechnika
P.O. Box 225
1475 Budapest
    Fax: 36-1-157-0418
    Telex: 22-5460
Mr. Gabor Szeles, President

Microsystem
Varosmajor u. 74
1122 Budapest
    Fax: 36-1-155-9296
    Telex: 22-3768 MS
Mr. Peter Vadasz, President

Controll
Llai Ut 101
1091 Budapest
    Fax: 36-1-133-7392
    Telex: 22-3477
Mr. Geza Kelemen, President

SzKI
P.O. Box 19
H-1251 Budapest
    Tel: 36-1-15-08-99
    Fax: 36-1-35-01-80
    Telex: 22-5381
Mr. Pal Nemeth, Executive Director

Tudorg Information and Organization
Egry Jozsef U. 1-9
H-1111 Budapest

Szenzor Computer Center Ltd.
Lehel u. 11
1134 Budapest
    Tel: 36-1-401-539 or 202-850
    Telex: 225049

Compudrug, Ltd.
Furst S. U. 5
H-1136 Budapest
    Tel: 36-1-124-874
    Fax: 36-1-322-574

John V. Neuman Center for Computing Sciences
H-1368 Budapest
    Tel: 36-1-329-349
    Fax: 36-1-561-215

Optimum Software Co.
P.O. Box 206
H-1364 Budapest 4
    Tel: 36-1-496-706

Compexpo/Compfair
Beg U. 3-5
H-1022 Budapest
    Tel: 36-1-150-856
    Telex: 22-6708

KSH SZUV
Szuglo U. 9-15
H-1145 Budapest 14
    Tel: 36-1-642-000
    Telex: 22-6216

Multilogic Computing Ltd.
Csalogany U. 30-32
H-1015 Budapest

Business Contacts in Hungary:
Energy and Energy-Related Products

Chemokomplex Trading Co. for Chemical Industry Equipment
Nepkoztarsasag utja 60
P.O. Box 141
H-1389 Budapest
    Tel: 36-1-132-9980
    Telex: 22-5158
(Trades in variety of energy-related equipment.)

Interag Co. Ltd.
Rajk Laszlo u. 11
P.O. Box 184
H-1390 Budapest
    Tel: 36-1-132-6770
    Fax: 36-1-1532-0736
    Telex: 22-4776 intag h
(Interag is involved in a large number of oil/gas related projects, one of which is a joint venture with Shell Oil, under which Interag operates Shell retail gasoline and service stations in Hungary.)

Ganz Machinery Works
Kobanyai ut 21
P.O. Box 62
H-1087 Budapest
    Tel: 36-1-113-7020 or 133-5950 or 114-0840 or 134-0540
    Telex: 22-5575 or 22-5576
(Manufactures a variety of pumps and pumping components.)

Ganz Meter Factory
Voros hadsereg utja 64
P.O. Box 62
H-1701 Budapest
    Tel: 36-1-127-4800
    Fax: 36-1-127-4800
    Telex: 22-5486
(Manufactures measurement and monitoring systems for energy flows. Recently privatized, the company is now three-quarters owned by Schlumberger Industries of France.)

Hunicoop Foreign Trade Co.
Nepkoztarsasag utja 113
P.O. Box 111
H-1367 Budapest
    Tel: 36-1-142-4950
    Telex: 22-4435 hunic h
(Imports oil and gas pumps.)

Lampart Factory for Chemical Equipment
Gergely u. 27
P.O. Box 41
H-1475 Budapest
    Tel: 36-1-157-0111
    Telex: 22-5365, 22-5799
(Manufactures oil and gas pumps.)

Nikex Foreign Trading Company
Meszaros utca 48-54
P.O. Box 128
H-1809 Budapest
    Tel: 36-1-156-0122
    Fax: 36-1-175-5131
    Telex: 22-6406, 22-4971 nikex h
(Trades in oil, gas, and coal-related equipment.)

OBV National Co. for Mining Machinery
Baross u 91-95
P.O. Box 70
H-1325 Budapest
    Tel: 36-1-169-1416 or 169-1961
    Telex: 22-4764
(Manufactures mining equipment.)

OKGT National Oil and Gas Trust
Schonherz Z. u. 18
P.O. Box 280
H-117 Budapest
    Tel: 36-1-166-4413
    Fax: 36-1-166-2453 or 186-8405
    Telex: 22-5123, 22-4762
Istvan Zsengeller, General Manager
(Besides holding a monopoly over the entire oil/gas industry in Hungary, OKGT
exports and imports oil and gas-related equipment.)

Lignimpex Trading Company for Timber, Paper, and Fuel
Honved u. 20
P.O. Box 323
H-1393 Budapest
    Tel: 36-1-112-9850, 112-1800
    Fax: 36-1-132-2181
    Telex: 22-4251, -52, -53
(Trades in coal and fuels produced from coal and timber.)

Mineralimpex Trading Co. for Oils and Mining Products
Nepkoztaesasagutja 64
P.O. Box 130
H-1389 Budapest
    Tel: 36-1-131-6720 or 111-6470
    Fax: 36-1-153-1779
    Telex: 22-4651
(Trades in crude oil, natural gas, LPG, gasolines, and fuel oils.)

MVMT Hungarian Electricity Board
Vam Utca 5-7
P.O. Box 34
H-1251 Budapest
    Tel: 36-1-115-2600 or 135-8700
    Telex: 22-4382 mvmt h
(Production, transmission, distribution and sale of electric power; production and
maintenance of powerstations, substations, and networks.)

Geominco Geological and Mining Engineering Co.
Varsanyi I. u. 40-44
P.O. Box 92
H-1525 Budapest
    Tel: 36-1-115-5611 or 135-2187 or 135-4580
    Telex: 22-4442
(Does consulting, design and engineering for oil, gas, and coal exploration pro-
jects.)

ERBE Co. for Power Plant Investment
Szecheyi rkp 3
P.O. Box 17
H-1361 Budapest
    Tel: 36-1-111-6460 or 131-4100 or 112-3270
    Telex: 22-5442

Tranelektro Foreign Trading Co.
Munnich Ferenc utca 13
P.O. Box 377
H-1394 Budapest
    Tel: 36-1-132-0100
    Fax: 36-1-112-7234, 153-0308
(Trades in, among other things, equipment for power generating plants, including nuclear, and power transmission equipment.)

Megamorv Boiler Design and Research Co.
Ferenc Morvia, President
(Megamorv is a successful private company producing boilers, as well as refuse burners; can be contracted through the Commercial Section of the U.S. Embassy-Budapest.)

Business Contacts in Hungary:
Instrumentation and Process Controls

GANZ Measuring Instruments Works
Voros Hadsereg utja 64
H-1701 Budapest, P.O. Box 58
    Tel: 36-1-147-0740
    Telex: 22-4395 ganzi h

Hungarian Instrument Manufacturer's Association
Arany Janos u. 24
H-1374 Budapest, P.O. Box 563
    Tel: 36-1-131-7960
    Telex: 22-4330 miger h
Gyula Posch, President

MIGERT Instrument and Business Machine Distribution Co.
Nepkoztarsasag utja 2
H-1392 Budapest, P.O. Box 295
    Tel: 36-1-111-7090
    Telex: 22-4736 miger h

Metrimpex Trading Company for Instruments
Munnich Ferenc utca 21
H-1391 Budapest, P.O. Box 202
    Tel: 36-1-112-5600
    Telex: 22-5451

EMG Works for Electronic Measuring Gear
Cziraky u. 26-32
H-1631 Budapest, P.O. Box 5
    Tel: 36-1-183-7950
    Telex: 22-4535

Business Contacts in Hungary: Agriculture and Food

AKGER State Farms' Trading Co.
Akademia u. 1-3
H-1361 Budapest, P.O. Box 16
    Tel: 36-1-153-4444
    Telex: 22-4415, 22-4416, 22-4689

Agraria-Babolna Foreign Trade Office
H-2943 Babolna
    Tel: 34/69-111, 34/69-333
    Telex: 22-6555, 27-211

Agrex (National Institute of Agricultural Engineering)
Godollo, Tessedik S. u. 4
H-2101 Godollo, P.O. Box 103
    Tel: 28/20-644
    Telex: 22-5816

Agrikon-Kecskemet Machine Factory for Agriculture/Food Industry
Kecskemet, Kulso-Szegedi ut 136
H-6001 Kecskemet
    Tel: 76/27-666
    Fax: 76/28-182
    Telex: 26-211, 26-495
(Foreign trade office)

Agrimpex Trading Co. for Agricultural Products
Munnich F. u. 22
H-1392 Budapest, P.O. Box 278
    Tel: 36-1-111-3800, 132-9100
    Fax: 36-1-153-0658
    Telex: 22-5751

Agroper Consulting Engineers and Contractors for Agriculture and the Food
Industry
Budafoki ut 79
H-1392 Budapest, P.O. Box 93
    Tel: 36-1-162-0640
    Telex: 22-5868 agrop h

Agro-Industria Agricultural Innovation Enterprise
Szentendrei ut 17-19
H-1300 Budapest, P.O. Box 90
    Tel: 36-1-188-6945 or 188-7381
    Telex: 22-7337

Agroker Bekescsaba Sales Co. for Agricultural Equipment
Szerdah elyi u. 14
H-5601 Bekescsaba, P.O. Box 33
    Tel: 66/22-366
    Telex: 83-329, 83-605

Agroker Pecs Agricultural Machine and Equipment Trading Co.
Megyeri ut 64
H-7601 Pecs, P.O. Box 108
    Tel: 72/26-255
    Telex: 12-227

Agrotek Trading Co. for Agricultural Capital Equipment
Bajcsy-Zsilinszky ut 66
H-1038 Budapest, P.O. Box 66
    Tel: 36-1-153-0555
    Telex: 22-5651

AHSZV dbSupply Co. for the Livestock and Meat Industry
Vagohid u. 53-55
H-1725 Budapest, P.O. Box 48
Tel: 36-1-157-1144
Telex: 22-4202

AHV Hajdu-Bihar County Livestock Sales and Meat Processing Co.
Vagohid u. 9
H-4013 Debrecen, P.O. Box 13
Tel: 52/18-555
Telex: 72-256

Aliscavin Joint Wine Production Co.
H-7101 Szekszard, P.O. Box 135
Tel: 74/11-564
Telex: 14-226

Association of Grape and Wine Producers of the Northern Balaton Region
H-8241 Aszofo
Tel: 86/45-010
Telex: 32-533

Bivimpex Trading Co. of Hungarian Tanneries
Erzsebet u. 2-4
H-1325 Budapest, P.O. Box 55
Tel: 36-1-169-3965, 169-4667
Telex: 22-4279

Meat Products Plant of Budapest
Gubacsi u. 6
H-1097 Budapest
Tel: 36-1-134-3949, 113-8246, 133-9559, 113-1256
Telex: 22-4422, 22-5350

Dehydro-Coop Trading for Dehydrated Fruit and Vegetables
Raby Matyas u. 7
H-1038 Budapest
Tel: 36-1-180-3604, 180-3640
Telex: 22-7942

Delker Trading Co. for Tropical Fruit and Food
Zrinyi u. 1
H-1366 Budapest, P.O. Box 70
    Tel: 36-1-118-5888
    Fax: 36-1-118-1981
    Telex: 22-4428

Egervin Winery of the Eger-Matra Region
Szecheniyi u. 3
H-3300 Eger, P.O. Box 27
    Tel: 36-12-411
    Telex: 63-326

Monimpex Foreign Trading Co. for Food and Beverages
V. Tukory u. 4
H-1392 Budapest, P.O. Box 268
    Tel: 36-1-153-1222
    Fax: 36-1-112-2072
    Telex: 22-5371

POLAND

POLAND

In a Nutshell

		Urban Population
Population (1992)	37,928,000	61%
Main Urban Areas		Percentage of Total
Warsaw (Capital)	1,651,200	4.35
Lodz	851,500	2.25
Krakow	743,700	1.96
Wroclaw	637,400	1.68
Poznan	586,500	1.55
Gdansk	461,500	1.22
Szczecin	409,500	1.08
Bydgoszcz	377,900	1.00
Katowice	365,800	0.96
Land Area	120,725 square miles	
	304,510 square kilometers	
Comparable European State	Slightly larger than Italy	
Comparable U.S. State	Slightly smaller than New Mexico	
Language	Polish	
Common Business Language	English is prevalent	
Currency	Zloty (= 100 groszy)	
Best European Air Connection	Frankfurt (Lufthansa, Delta)	
Best Ground Connection	Frankfurt to Warsaw (1,145 kilometers)	
Best Hotel	Marriott Warsaw ($190 per night as of 1/92)	

CHAPTER CONTENTS

INTRODUCTION AND REGIONAL ORIENTATION

Geographical and Historical Background

Often referred to as the "heart" of Europe for its shape, Poland is located geographically at the center of the continent, bordering Germany on the west, the former Soviet Union on the east, and Czechoslovakia to the south, with the Baltic Sea to the north. The climate is continental with cold winters. Topography varies from mountainous regions in the south along the Czechoslovak border to forests in the northeast. The population, although highly educated and literate, is predominantly rural.

Although Poland has an ancient heritage, its existence as an independent state was terminated in the 18th century when it was partitioned between the Russian, Prussian, and Austro-Hungarian empires. Despite repeated rebellions (notably 1863), Poland regained independence only after the Treaty of Versailles, following World War I.

The interwar period was one of economic decline, heightened by the worldwide depression of the 1930s. Politically, the newly independent state began with a parliamentary orientation; however, continued failures of the government to resolve the country's problems contributed to the rise of military dictator Jozef Pilsudski, who took over in a military coup in 1926 and ruled the country with a regime called "Sanajca" until his death in 1935. The regime's policies became increasingly authoritarian and right-wing, eventually collapsing and disbanding after Hitler's troops invaded in 1939.

Probably more than any other country, Poland was devastated by World War II. A strong, well-organized resistance was unable to halt the German advances, further antagonizing the Germans, resulting in more destruction. By the war's end, the city of Warsaw was completely leveled, as were other villages (Warsaw has been meticulously reconstructed so that it resembles the prewar city).

Poland was liberated by Soviet troops, which remained in the country even after the armistice was signed, assisting with a communist takeover. Although the regime was firmly in power by 1948, and despite the backing of the Soviet Union, Poles did not accept their fate quietly. Major strikes and demonstrations by the working class and intellectuals (not necessarily together) in 1956, 1968, 1970, 1976, and 1980 led to governmental crisis. In each incident, however, the regime was able to avoid collapse, often by fragmenting the opposition and compromising on certain demands.

Most famous is the Solidarity movement of 1980, which began as a strike in a shipyard and turned into a country-wide mass movement calling for free trade union recognition, the right to a free press, and other demands. Initially, President

Throughout the 1980s, Poland's economy declined and repeated government attempts at reform failed. Eventually, the communist regime's final resort was to relegalize the Solidarity trade union movement and negotiate a compromise government with them.

The Round Table agreements of 1988 between the ruling Communist party and Solidarity opposition members launched a quick collapse of the socialist system. In 1989's free parliamentary elections, Solidarity candidates swept the available seats. However, the agreement of 1988 specified that only 35% of the seats in the Sejm would be contested, effectively guaranteeing the communists a majority in that house.

Tadeusz Mazowiecki, a leading Solidarity intellectual and journalist, was appointed Prime Minister. He set up a cabinet which included many opposition members, with the exception of Minister of the Interior and Minister of Defense, which remained in the former regime's hands. The Mazowiecki government embarked on a crash economic reform program, the Balcerowicz Plan (named for the Finance Minister), geared toward moving Poland to a market economy. Key tenets included anti-inflationary measures, price reform, privatization of state-owned enterprises, and currency convertibility.

As might be expected, the "flash cut" approach to transforming Poland's centrally-planned economy to Western market conditions gave rise to rapid inflation (Poland went into hyperinflation in 1989), rising unemployment, and increasing public discontent. By 1991, however, there were signs that the situation was stabilizing, aided by debt relief measures taken by other countries.

Along with the attempt to reform its economy, Poland has been working to democratize its political system. The first free presidential elections were held in November-December 1990, with former Solidarity Trade Union leader Lech Walesa emerging the victor, albeit only through a runoff. His victory has fueled strife between two Solidarity movement factions – those supporting faster reform and touting a "quick relief, no pain," slogan (including Walesa), and the Mazowiecki supporters, who criticize Walesa for dictatorial tendencies.

Overall, the trend in political organizations and institutions is towards the splintering of umbrella groups, formerly allied against communism. Now that they have effectively defeated that common enemy, the differences in programs are surfacing.

Expectations of a quick recovery after the demise of communism have been replaced by public apathy and discontent. Strikes and demonstrations by workers and farmers are increasing, especially against the excess wages tax (popiwek) and in support of agricultural subsidies and protectionism allowing Polish farmers to compete with Western counterparts.

By the second quarter of 1991, Poland was in a recession, due to downward pressure on demand (in part from price increases) and a trade reduction with the former Soviet Union, Poland's largest trading partner. Surprisingly, unemployment is not the critical issue that it is in some other East European countries. Rather, the focus of worker and union protests has been the control on wage levels.

Demographics

Socioeconomic Indicators and Conditions

Personal income is low, approximately US $3,733 per capita, compared with more than US $19,100 in the United States (Table 6-1).

Table 6-1: Poland's Domestic Economy

	1988	1989	1990
GNP (billion 1985 US $)	225	225	242
GNP per capita (current US $)	6,746	6,728	6,358
GNP (real percentage change)	4.1	0.1	-5.0
Hard Currency Current Account(US $ M)	-580	-1,843	-3,000
Hard Currency Debt (year-end US $ M)	39,200	40,000	43,200
Inflation (percentage)	N/A	1,266	60

Source: U.S. Department of Commerce. International Trade Association. 1991. Foreign Economic Trends and Their Implications for the United States—Poland. Washington, D.C.: Government Printing Office.

The "flash cut" program of economic transformation began under the government of former Prime Minister Tadeusz Mazowiecki and Finance Minister Leszek Balcerowicz. In January 1990, the first measures went into effect, including restricting wages and eliminating many government subsidies and price supports to reduce hyperinflation, moving toward currency convertibility, privatizing state-owned enterprises, and promoting foreign investment. By 1991, the program was receiving mixed reviews. Inflation has slowed, foreign investment has grown, and the zloty has stabilized, but at the cost of high (and rising) unemployment, reduction in industrial production, and decreases in real earnings of nearly 35%.

Political/Institutional Infrastructure

Political Organization

Poland is a parliamentary republic with a bicameral legislature. The Senate is the upper house, consisting of 100 freely-elected members, while the Sejm, the lower house, has 460 seats, 35% of which were contested in the 1990 elections.

The national government consists of a Council of Ministers, headed by the Prime Minister, who is responsible to Parliament. Prime Minister Jan Krzysztof Bielecki was appointed by President Lech Walesa and accepted by Parliament in January 1991.

The division of powers between the executive (President) and Parliament is ambiguously defined in the constitution, especially regarding the powers and limitations of the President. Thus, President Walesa has exercised great leeway, leading to criticism for taking too much power. These critics, including the faction led by Mazowiecki and other intellectuals, have also voiced fears that Walesa has dictatorial tendencies. Walesa, on the other hand, has professed a desire to work within the bounds of the Constitution in order to move Poland further toward democracy and a free market.

Since the historic Round Table agreements in 1988, Solidarity has dominated the government, winning 100% of the Senate seats contested in the first free elections since World War II. Also contested in the June 1989 elections were 35% of the seats in the Sejm, all won by Solidarity.

The leadership as of June 1991 was: President Lech Walesa; Prime Minister Jan Krzysztof Bielecki; Deputy Prime Minister and Finance Minister Jeszek Balcerowicz; Minister of Ownership Transformation Janusz Lewandowski; Foreign Minister Krzysztof Skubieszewski; Chairman Solidarity Trade Union Marian Krzaklewskii and Chairman OPZZ Trade Union Alfred Miodowicz.

Political Party

The primary parties include: Center Alliance (party of President Lech Walesa); Citizens' Movement for Democratic Action (party of ex-Prime Minister Tadeusz Mazowiecki); Liberal Democratic Congress (party of current Prime Minister J.K. Bielecki); Polish Peasant party; Democratic party; Polish Social Democratic Union; Social Democracy of the Republic of Poland (former communists); and Citizens' Parliamentary Caucus (OKP).

Federal/Regional/Municipal Organization

As on the national level, local elections in May 1990 brought new, mostly noncommunist, leaders to power. Regions are divided into districts (voivoidina).

Trade Flows

Top 10 Import/Export Trade Partners

Poland's main trading partners are the former Soviet Union, Germany, the Czech and Slovak Federal Republic, the United Kingdom, Yugoslavia, and Switzerland. Since January 1, 1991, all trade has been conducted on a hard currency basis (in contrast to the ruble-based, barter-type arrangements within CMEA prior to that). Between 1986 and 1989, U.S.-Polish trade approximately doubled CMEA countries, as 58.5% of trade was conducted with non-CMEA countries compared to only 41.5% in the communist trading bloc.

In 1989, trade conducted within CMEA consisted of 62.9% with the Soviet Union, 14.8% with Czechoslovakia, and 12% with East Germany. The largest percentage of trade with non-CMEA countries was with West Germany (22.7%), followed by Switzerland (8%), Austria (7.8%), the United Kingdom (6.8%), and Yugoslavia (5.7%). The percentage trade with the United States was approximately 3.1%.

Top 10 Import/Export Commodities

Major exports from the United States to Poland include the following: cotton textile fibers, barley, television receivers, aircraft, pulp and waste paper, alcoholic beverages, nonelectrical engines and motors, cotton fabrics, transmission shafts, and food processing equipment (Table 6-2).

Future prospects for U.S. exporters, as identified by the U.S. government, include the following:

- food packaging and processing
- commercial aircraft
- consumer items
- environmental control and antipollution devices
- hotel management and tourism-related industries
- telecommunications
- optic fiber technologies
- technology and equipment for light industry modernization
- data processing equipment and personal computers
- agricultural commodities
- medical equipment and pharmaceuticals

- agricultural commodities
- medical equipment and pharmaceuticals

Table 6-2: Major Products Traded (1989)

Exports	Percentage of Trade
Electrical engineering	38.4
Metallurgy	10.5
Chemical industry	10.5
Fuels and energy	9.6
Food products	9.6
Light industry	5.5
Agriculture	4.1
Imports	Percentage of Trade
Electrical engineering	37.0
Chemical industry	15.0
Fuels and energy	12.7
Food products	9.1
Metallurgy	8.7
Light industry	7.6
Agriculture	4.6

Source: U.S. Department of Commerce. International Trade Administration. 1991. *Foreign Economic Trends and Their Implications for the United States—Poland*. Washington, D.C.: Government Printing Office.

- chemicals
- energy technology
- construction technologies
- specialized consumer goods and services (banking, accounting, insurance, and engineering consulting)

Finance and Investment Policies

Poland has designed laws to attract foreign investment, offering benefits such as tax holidays to firms with foreign participation. Foreign entities may establish 100% ownership of a company based in Poland; however, a foreign partner's contribution must be at least 20% of the initial assets of a joint venture, but not less than US $50,000. Profits may be repatriated if they are earned from exports; repatriation of earnings from domestic sales are limited to 15%.

An investment law was proposed to Parliament in early 1991. The main features of the draft were: liberalization of entry conditions (elimination of the $50,000 and 20% participation requirements); reduction in required permits for ventures; free transfer of profits, dividends, and capital gains for foreign investors, as well as the opportunity to liquidate investment immediately; and automatic guarantees for foreign investors regarding matters such as expropriation and nationalization.

In March 1990, the U.S.-Polish Business and Economic Treaty was signed, formalizing agreements on profits and repatriation, expropriation, dispute settlement, and intellectual property rights.

Polish government guarantees are available for export-oriented enterprises, infrastructure projects, petrochemicals and gas, and "rationalization" projects (including fuel and energy, shipping and railway equipment, cement and heavy chemicals).

Policies to Attract New Business

Amendments to law on foreign investments in effect in mid-1991 included easing joint venture requirements, reducing tax holidays, and improving repatriation. In 1988, Poland passed a Law on Economic Activity significantly opening the Polish market by granting foreign investors the right to engage in business on the same terms as Polish citizens. In short, the law liberalized the foreign trade and investment regulations.

Preferred Foreign Investment Projects

Priority sectors for foreign investment or participation include the following:

- the agroprocessing industry
  - production of machinery and equipment for food processing industry and catering
  - production of baby foods and special dietary products

- production of protein concentrates, animal feed additives, and mineral pre-mixes
- potato, fruit, vegetable, and herb processing
- production of pharmaceuticals and medical equipment
  - manufacture of medical and laboratory products
  - rehabilitation equipment
  - wheelchairs
  - pharmaceutical and herbal products
  - laboratory reagents, tests, isotopes, and radioactive products
  - chemical and paper industry
  - manufacture of highly concentrated fertilizers
  - crop protection products
  - polyester
  - styrene
  - epoxy
  - polyurethane, paper, and boards
- construction materials
  - manufacture of finishing equipment for civil buildings
  - electric tools, metal plumbing, and plastic products for construction
  - finishing and insulating products
  - high quality ceramics
  - energy, water, and gas measuring equipment
  - environmental protection
  - manufacture of equipment for environmental protection
  - construction of waste treatment plants
- modern technologies
  - introduction of energy, fuel, and raw material saving technologies
  - machinery and equipment
- telecommunications, electronics, and electronic products
  - manufacture of modern telecommunications equipment, cables, computer systems, data processing systems and software
  - optical fibers, cable and equipment for their production, industrial robots, technological and measuring equipment for VLSI and LSI, equipment for surface assembly, electronic components, and materials for the electronics industry
  - quartz pipes and derivatives

- laminates for integrated circuits
- manufacture of scientific and control and measuring equipment
- printing and office automation equipment
- products of powder metallurgy
- finished products
- new generation household equipment, appliances, and metal cutting tools
  - packaging materials and package-producing equipment
- transport
  - servicing equipment for rail, road, air, and water transport
  - equipment for mechanization of loading
- tourism
  - construction of hotels, recreational and tourist facilities

Investment Incentives and Privileges

Companies with foreign investors, in addition to a three-year tax holiday, do not pay customs duty on their contribution in-kind to companies imported into Poland. They also do not pay customs duty on machinery and equipment purchased abroad if it is done within three years of the company's establishment.

Foreign investors may request the Minister of Finance to issue them guarantees of compensation payments for losses resulting from nationalization, expropriation or other measures.

Tax Incentives

Enterprises with foreign participation qualify for a three-year tax holiday; if in preferred sectors, exemptions for up to six years may be granted. The corporate tax rate is decreased 0.4% for every 1% of total sales that is exported.

Under consideration for revision are the possibility of creating a six-year tax holiday for investments exceeding $3 million in equity and exempting dividends that have been reinvested in Poland from withholding tax.

Free Trade Zones/Special Economic Zones

Thirteen Free Trade Zones have been established, allowing goods to be imported and exported freely.

APPROACHING THE MARKET

Foreign Trade and Investment Decision-Making Infrastructure

Shareholders must first obtain a permit from the President of the Foreign Investment Agency. The application should be submitted in Polish. Second, the company's founding document, in the form of a notarial act, should be completed. Third, the company should be registered in a court of law. Decisions on whether to issue a permit should be made within two months from the date of filing with the agency, provided that an application for the permit and all enclosures, a draft of the company's founding act, a feasibility study, and documentary evidence as to the legal status and financial condition of shareholders have been filed.

The application should include the following:

- names, seats, and addresses of partners
- addresses for mail delivery to the company
- name and seat of the company
- purpose of the company
- subject and scope of the company's activity
- duration of the activity
- estimated number of employees
- resources needed for the company
- shares in equity by the partners, including value of contribution by individual partners
- any other relevant information

The feasibility study should be in the form of a preinvestment study, including an analysis of the markets where the products will be sold, and a techno-organizational and financial analysis of the enterprise. The agency has published an abridged assessment form in order to simplify the process, which may be used in cases where initial investment outlays are up to 1,500 million zlotys (US $1=9500 zlotys), although full efficiency assessments should be submitted if investment is more.

Documentary evidence on the shareholders includes: passport or legal identification materials; evidence of property, bank statement or the like; statements of the partner's means of satisfying creditors and obligations; and proof of purchase against convertible currency of resources to be contributed.

Applications should be submitted to the Foreign Investment Agency (Agencja do Spraw Inwestycji Zagranicznych, P.O. Box 24, 00-950 Warszawa, Poland). They may also be submitted in person to Room 5089, 5th floor, Plac Powstancow Warszawy 1, Warsaw.

Fees incurred in the process include: stamp duty from issuing the permit (200,000 zlotys in 1990); a fee for changes in the permit (50,000 zlotys); a notarial service fee (3% of equity value); stamp duty for the notarial act (ranging from 0.1% to 2%); and court fee for registering the company (200,000 zlotys).

Further information on establishing companies is available from the agency at Plac Powstancow Warszawy 1, 5th floor, Room 501a, Warsaw. Tel: 26-90-41. Telex: 814291. Fax: 26-34-14. The agency also has a listing of consultants in Poland who can assist in the process.

Setting Up Business Operations

Forms of Business Organization

Limited liability company. A foreign investor may hold 100% of the shares in a limited liability company; however, foreign ownership of telecommunications ventures was restricted to 49% or less in 1990.

Limited liability or joint stock companies, with capital contributed jointly by other foreign and/or Polish investors are also possible, as are joint stock companies with equity raised through public subscription of the shares. Foreign investors may also acquire shares or stock in existing Polish companies.

Partnerships may be negotiated with state enterprises, the Treasury, or other companies, research institutes, foundations, universities, cooperatives and social organizations. However, the contribution of the foreign partner must be at least 20% of equity. There is no limit on the maximum share that may be held, but the authority that issues the permit to establish a company may condition the permit on a set ratio of contributions.

Both limited liability and joint stock companies have a legal personality; the partners' liability is limited to the contribution to the equity.

The founding act, in the form of a notarial deed, may restrict the right of disposal of shares of the company. Foundation of a joint stock company requires at least three founders, unless one is the Treasury.

Real estate. Companies may acquire and lease land and real estate not owned by the state; foreign parties are allowed to own property. Purchase of real estate must be approved by the Minister of Internal Affairs if the foreign party owns more than 50% of the shares of the company. State land may be given in perpetual use or leased.

INVESTMENT CLIMATE

Privatization, Investment Protection, and Dispute Settlement

Minister of Ownership and Transformation Janusz Lewandowski is heading the program to speed up the privatization process, changing the emphasis from large-scale enterprises to small- and medium-sized firms. Three strategies are being implemented simultaneously: 1) a "top down" policy, in which the Ministry of Ownership and Privatization identifies firms to be privatized; 2) an active campaign on the local level to encourage the transfer of large numbers of small shops to private ownership; and 3) the leasing of firms or selling assets piecemeal for unprofitable large-scale enterprises.

Poland is developing channels to distribute shares and methods of appraising companies to move privatization forward. Shares of five state enterprises (Exbud, Slaska Fabryka Kabli SA, Prochnik SA, Krosno Glassworks, and Tonsil) were made public, selling out within six weeks, while receiving mixed review. The Polish administration declared it a success, but the Western press was less enthused because the sale had to be extended three weeks past the initial deadline. According to Polish officials, the extension was needed because only four banks were eligible to sell the shares, state bond-owners were entitled to a 20% reduction on the price, and inflation resulted in variances of the bonds' values, which then had to be calculated.

The process was also inefficient by Western standards as Poles were forced to stand in several different lines to complete the transactions. Secretary of State in the Ministry of Ownership Transformations, Janusz Lewandowski, has been quoted as saying that in the next release of state-owned shares to the market, nearly 2,000 banks will be involved and the procedure of selling bonds will be revised. Several enterprises had been targeted for the next round of privatizations, including clothing and shoe manufacturing firms, a brewery and other factories.

Another policy accelerating the privatization process and development of small business is the establishment of new branch offices to aid local authorities. The goal is that half of the economy will be private within three years and 80% private within five years.

Economic and political differences between workers' councils, unions, and the government hinder the privatization process. Employee ownership of companies is a major issue, as workers fear that privatization will bring unemployment. The policy of issuing free vouchers to citizens to purchase shares in companies being privatized emphasizes an effort to override opposition to the process of economic adjustment.

Current information can be obtained through the East Europe Business Information Center (EEBIC), the Commerce Department office that serves as a clearing house for information on business opportunities.

Joint Ventures and Wholly Owned Subsidiaries

According to Price Waterhouse, by December 1990 there were a total of 1,900 joint ventures, 150 of which were American. U.S. investment was approximately US $16 million and the average initial investment was US $272,000, concentrated primarily in the following sectors: food processing, housing construction and production of building materials, consulting services, textile production, tourism, and machine production.

The Warsaw United Nations Industrial Development Organization (UNIDO) Industrial Cooperation and Investment Service and the Foreign Investment Agency have developed a data base with up-to-date information on Polish entrepreneurs and foreign businesses interested in setting up joint ventures. A confirmation fee of US $200 (in 1990) covers promotion, distribution, and administrative costs. Investors may be included by completing a questionnaire, available through the Agency (Pl. Powstancow Warszawy 1, 00-950 Warszawa. tel: 273265; 269041. telex: 814291-5 DLA AGENCJI. fax: 263414) or UNIDO (ul. Stawki 2, 00-950 Warszawa. tel: 6356086; 6357544. telex: 817916 unido pl. fax: 6351260). Every six months, updated catalogues are distributed in Poland (listing potential foreign partners) and abroad (listing potential Polish partners).

The U.S. Trade Development Center in Warsaw established a "Gold Key Service" program to arrange meetings, select potential joint venture partners, and schedule sessions with government officials. Contact the center for more information (ul. Wiejska 20, Warsaw. tel: 48 22 21 45 15; fax: 48 22 21 63 27).

U.S. joint ventures or business agreements that have already been established include a US $350 million deal between LOT (Polish National Airline) and McDonnell Douglas for MD-80 airliners, Ford car dealerships, $200 million telecommunications equipment contracts with engineering firms, and a $100 million telephone improvement project with AT&T.

Taxation and Regulatory Conditions

Sources of Income Liable to Taxation

A company must deposit 8% of after-tax profit in a reserve fund. After the fund reaches 4% of a company's costs in a fiscal year, the deposits may be stopped. A Value Added Tax (VAT) replaced the turnover tax on July 1, 1991.

Company Tax

Companies must pay a corporate income tax of 40% of taxable income. For the first three years of business, the company is exempted from all taxes; the tax holiday may be extended for an additional three years in certain targeted sectors of the economy. In addition, taxes are reduced 0.4% for each 1% of total sales earned from exports.

Personal Income Tax

Investment profits are subject to personal income tax, paid in zlotys. For investors domiciled in countries with which Poland has no agreement on avoidance of double taxation, the rate is 30%. In other cases, the rate varies between 5% to 15%. Poland has a tax convention with the United States, as well as: Austria, Belgium, Czechoslovakia, Denmark, Finland, France, Spain, Holland, Japan, Yugoslavia, Malaysia, Germany, Norway, Pakistan, Sweden, Sri Lanka, Thailand, Hungary, Great Britain, and Italy.

The U.S. agreement permits a 5% dividend tax for corporations with foreign holdings of at least 10% of equity; in all other cases the tax is 15%.

Personal income tax law, under revision in 1991, proposed creating a single, proportional tax not differentiating sources of income (income tax, wage taxes, the equalization tax, and part of the agricultural tax). Three proposed rates (20%, 30%, and 40%) would apply to all Polish residents and income earned by nonresidents in Poland. Also, a flat 20% withholding tax on interest and dividend income would be enacted to encourage saving.

Insurance

The primary legislation regulating insurance is the "Law of 28 July 1990 on Carrying on the Business of Insurance in Poland." Compulsory insurance include: third-party motor insurance of owners of motor vehicles against damages resulting from the vehicles, farm building insurance (against fire and other hazards), and third party insurance of farmers.

Foreign insurers may work only through a principal agent with a registered office or residence in Poland.

FINANCING AND CAPITAL MARKETS

Banking and Other Financial Institutions

The National Bank of Poland (NBP) is the central credit and clearing institution, the central foreign-exchange institution, and printer of currency.

Regulations are anticipated regarding the legal protection of money deposits, equalization of credit availability, equalization of conditions of all banks, adoption of the principle linking the extension of credit to initial capital of a bank, changes in the licensing process for banks, and the possibility of creating general reserves. Further reforms include adoption of EEC bank accountancy practices and the establishment of new commercial and specialized banks.

Foreign banks may open branches or wholly-owned subsidiaries. Details on these regulations can be found in the Finance Ministry Notice on Foreign Bank Operations from July 1990.

Payment Modalities

The Currency

Since January 1989, the Polish government devalued the zloty several times to stabilize the currency and move towards convertibility. In May 1991, the zloty was devalued from 9,500 zlotys=$1 to 11,100 zlotys=$1. The rate, previously stabilized by only the dollar, became pegged to a basket of foreign currencies, including the dollar, German mark, British pound, and Swiss franc. The devaluation continued a series of sharp increases, including December 1991 US $1=15,000 zlotys; January 1990, US $1=9,344 zlotys; December 1989, US $1−7,454 zlotys; June 1989, US $1=4,590 zlotys; January 1989, US $1=3,410 zlotys.[1]

Equity Finance and Privatization

U.S. firms may obtain short- and long-term credit assistance, loans and loan guarantees from Eximbank (202-566-8990). Loan guarantees, direct loans, and political risk insurance are available through Overseas Private Investment Corporation (OPIC) (1-800-424-6724). OPIC offers programs that include matching capital, the Small Business Loan Guarantee Program, and the Environmental Investment Fund.

The Polish-American Enterprise Fund, established through the Support for East European Democracy (SEED) Act in 1989, supports small- and medium-sized ventures assisting the development of the private sector in Poland.

Tapping International Aid Institutions

Three loans worth a total of $580 million were approved by the World Bank in June 1991. Of the total, $280 million will be applied to the privatization and stabilization program; $200 million will assist the financial sector; and $100 million will support rural development.

In March 1991, a three-year agreement with the International Monetary Fund (IMF) was approved that may result in up to $2 billion in Western aid. The World Bank provided a $715 million line of credit in 1990 to assist in the convertibility program, along with a $300 million structural adjustment loan. A program of approximately $1 billion has been planned for 1991-1992. Poland has been a member of the International Monetary Fund/International Bank for Reconstruction and Development since 1986.

Poland has also been receiving assistance from the Multilateral Investment Guarantee Agency (MIGA), an affiliate of the World Bank Group established in 1988, which is promoting foreign private investment flows into developing countries and organizing seminars to assist managers with the issues relating to foreign partnerships.

Poland is a member of GATT and also has most-favored-nation status with the United States.

The United States authorized approximately $800 million in aid in 1990 for Poland and appropriated approximately $369 million in 1991 for all of Central Europe. The United States has also appropriated $70 million in funds to the European Bank for Reconstruction and Development, combining with the Polish-American Enterprise Fund to provide start-up capital for ventures.

Poland is also a beneficiary of substantial debt reduction on the part of the West, and the short- and medium-term debt programs of the Ex-Im Bank.

A major form of assistance has been debt reduction. In April 1991, the Paris Club agreed to a 50% reduction of Poland's US $33.7 billion debt. Poland has also proposed that 10% of its debt be forgiven in exchange for Poland's application of those funds to environmental preservation programs.

Individual countries forgiving Poland's debts include the United States, reducing debt by 70% ($3.8 billion to $1.14 billion), and France canceling 50% of debt.

Financial Market Operations

The Polish stock exchange opened on April 16, 1991, when shares of the first five firms to be privatized were traded.

LICENSING, PATENTS, AND TRADEMARKS

Licensing Policy, Procedures, and Payments

Export licenses are mandatory for fuels, agricultural products and foodstuffs, butter, cheese, powdered milk, and frozen fruits. A new Customs Tariff complying with EEC regulations was introduced on July 1, 1991.

Import licenses are required only for inflammable materials, isotopes, and military equipment. Alcohol will be regulated and the import of spirits, vodka, and two-stroke car engines is prohibited.

Trademark, Patent, and Copyright Protection

The U.S.-Polish Treaty on Economic Relations passed in March 1990 protects intellectual property rights. Copyright protection covers literary works to computer programs. Product and process protection is guaranteed in the fields of pharmaceuticals and chemicals. Protection from unfair competition and for integrated circuit layout designs was also emphasized.

VISITING AND LOCATING

General Travel Checklist

Visas

Visas are not required for Americans staying fewer than 90 days, except for those planning to work in Poland. More information on visa regulations can be obtained from the Polish embassy in Washington, DC (202/232-4517).

Currency

The currency is the zloty (in May 1991, US $1 = 11,100 zlotys). The zloty is pegged to a basket of currencies, as of May 1991.

Getting Around

Taxis are relatively cheap and abundant in the larger cities. Nonstop express trains are recommended and rental cars are available for traveling between cities.

Accommodations and Housing

The official Polish tourist agency is Orbis (800/223-6073); it can assist with travel arrangements, as can many private travel agents.

There are a number of major hotels in Warsaw, Gdansk, Szczecin, Poznan, Wroclaw, Krakow, and Katowice. Some of these include the following:

Warsaw

- Mariott (Al. Jeorzolimskie 65/79; tel: 306306; fax: 300852; telex: 816515 marbc tl)
- Inter Continental Victoria (ul. Krolewska 11; tel: 278011; telex: 2516)
- Holiday Inn (ul. Zlota 2; tel: 200341; telex: 817418, 817778)
- Forum (ul. Nowogrodzka 24/26; tel: 280364; telex: 2521, 4704)
- Europejski (ul. Krakowskie Przedmiescie 13; tel: 265051; telex: 3615, 3587)
- Novotel (ul. 1 Sierpnia 1; tel: 464051; telex: 2525)

Gdansk

- Hevelius (ul. Heweliusza 22; tel: 315631; telex: 0512458)
- Marina (ul. Jelitkowska 20; tel: 532079; telex: 0512458)
- Novotel (ul. Pszenna 1; tel: 315611; telex: 0512724).

Szczecin

- Neptun (ul. Matejki 18; tel: 240111; telex: 0422732)
- Reda (ul. Cukrowa 2; tel: 822461; telex: 0425265)

Poznan

- Merkury (ul. Roosvelta 15/20; tel: 40801; telex: 0441-343435)
- Novotel (ul. Warszawska 64/66; tel: 70041; telex: 041-3519)
- Poznan (pl. Gen. H. Dabrowskiego 1; tel. 332081; telex: 041-3519)
- Polonez (al. Stalingradzka 56/68; tel: 699141; telex: 041-3491)

Wroclaw

- Wroclaw (ul. Powstancow Slaskich 7; tel: 614651; telex: 071-5252)
- Novotel (ul. Wyscigowa 35; tel: 675051; telex: 071-5198)

Krakow

- Cracovia (al. Puszkina 11; tel: 228666; telex: 0322341)

- Holiday Inn (ul. Koniewa 7; tel: 375044; telex: 0325356)
- Forum (ul. Marii Konopnickiej 28; tel: 669500; telex: 0325356)

Katowice

- Silesia (ul. Piotra Skargi 2; tel: 596211; telex: 0315674)
- Warszawa (ul. Rozdzienskiego 16; tel: 596011; telex: 0315747)

Telecom, Postal, and Courier Services

The telephone system is poor, and telephones are not abundant in Poland. Both local and international calls may not get through because it is easier to call into Poland than to call the United States from Poland. Business travelers should arrange contact times and set up appointments in advance because of the difficulty in making last minute telephone calls.

Shopping

Some stores accept major credit cards. Polish specialties include silver and amber jewelry, hand-embroidered garments, and crystal.

Dining

Major hotels usually have nice restaurants, with reservations taken by telephone. A recommended lunch can be found in the Intraco building in Warsaw, in where many foreign firms have offices.

Sightseeing and Tourist Information

The official Polish tourist agency is Orbis (see section on accommodations in this chapter).

The Short-Term Business Visitor

Airlines Serving

Airlines with service to Warsaw include American, LOT, Austrian Airlines, Sabena, KLM, and Lufthansa.

The Short-Term Business Visitor

Airlines Serving

Airlines with service to Warsaw include American, LOT, Austrian Airlines, Sabena, KLM, and Lufthansa.

Availability of Temporary Services

Translation. Polish business people, especially those who are younger, may know English. Other common second languages include German and French.

The Expatriate

Hourly/Annual Mean Wages

In May 1990, the average wage was estimated to be $0.40 per hour. Subsequently, however, wages have been indexed to inflation, although a tax on excess wage increases has also been initiated to prevent a wage spiral.

Immigration and Work Permits

Foreign employees must obtain a work permit by the appropriate local authority. They have the right to purchase foreign currency in an exchange bank with their pay, after taxes have been deducted.

Labor Force

Employment and labor relations. Companies with foreign participation must comply with Polish labor law.

In general, trade unions are powerful and organized. Legislation on trade unions, organizations of employers, and resolving collective disputes are planned.

ENDNOTES

1   U.S. Department of Commerce, International Trade Administration. 1991. *Foreign Economic Trends and Their Implications for the United States—Poland.* Washington, D.C.: Government Printing Office.

POLAND

KEY CONTACTS FOR BUSINESS

Key Officials of the Government of Poland

Foreign Investment Agency
00-950
ul. Postancow Warsawy 1
    Tel: 26-90-41, 26-20-31, 26-10-31
    Telex: 814501
President: Zbigniew Piatrovsky
Vice President: Hurbert Janiszewski

Ministry of Foreign Economic Relations
00-507 Warsaw
pl. Trzech Krzyzy 5
    Tel: 69-35-000
    Fax: 29-06-17, 28-68-08
    Telex: 814501 MHZ PL
Minister: Marcin Swiecicki
Director of Department: Andrzej Olechowski
(GATT, EC, UN, Developed Western Countries)

Ministry of Finance
00-916 Warsaw
ul. Swietokrzyska 12
    Tel: 20-03-11
    Telex: 815592 MINFIN PL
Foreign Dept: Tel: 26-65-44
Minister: Leszek Balcerowicz

Ministry of Industry
00-926 Warsaw
ul. Wspolna 4
    Tel: 28-21-41 (Foreign Dept.)
    Telex: 814267, 814261
    Fax: 21-25-50
Minister: Tadeusz Syryjczyk

Ministry of Health and Social Welfare
00-923 Warsaw
ul. Miodowa 15
  Tel: 31-34-41
  Telex: 81-38-64 MZIOS PL
Minister Andrzej Kosiniak-Kamysz

Ministry of Environment
00-920 Warsaw
ul. wawelski 52/54
  Tel: 25-00-01, 25-40-01
  Telex: 81-28-16
Minister: Bornislaw Kaminiski

Polish Chamber of Foreign Trade
00-950 Warsaw
ul. Trebacka 4
  Tel: 26-02-21
  Telex: 81-43-61 PIHZ PL
President: Tadeus Zylkowski
Legal Expert on Joint-Venture Law: Andrzej Burzynski

Polish Commercial Office
820 Second Street 17th Floor
New York, NY 10017
  Tel: 212/370-5300
  Telex: 595657 POLCOMER NYC
Commercial Counselle: Jerzy Kapuscinski

U.S. Embassy — Republic of Poland (May 1991)

WARSAW

Aleje Ujazdowskle 29/31
American Embassy Warsaw
c/o Am ConGen (WAW)
APO, NY 09213
   Tel: 48-22-283-0419
   Telex: 813304 AMEMB PL

Ambassador: John R. Davis, Jr.
Deputy Chief of Mission: Karryl Johnson
Political: Terry R. Snell
Economic: Howard H. Lange
Commercial: M. Spillsbury
Congressional: Phyllis Villegoureix-Ritaud
Administrative: Mark J. Lijek
Military: Thomas J. Comiskey
SCI: Gary R. Waxmansky
Agriculture: John Harrison
PRESS/CULT: Stephen M. Dubrow
Military: Col. Glen A. Bailey USA

U.S. Trade Center (Warsaw)

Ulica Wiejska 20;
   Tel: 48-22-214515
   Telex: 813934 USTDO PL

KRAKOW

Ulica Stolarska 9
31043 Krakow
c/o Am ConGen (KRK)
APO, NY 09213
   Tel: 48-12-229764, 221400, 226040, 227793
   Telex: 0325350

CG: Michael T. Barry
Political/Economic: Steven L. Blanke
Congressional: Michael D. Kirby
Administrative: Daniel F. Romano
Military: John H. Brown

POZNAN

Ulica Chopina 4
c/o Am ConGen (POZ)
APO, NY 09213
   Tel: 48-61-529586, 529587, 529874
   Telex: 041-34-74 USA PL
Political: Peter S. Perenyi
Congressional: Robert O. Tatge
Administrative: Wiliam A. Heidt

Republic of Poland Government Institutions

Ministry of Foreign Economic Relations
Plac Trzech Krzyzy 3
00-507 Warsaw
   Tel: 69-34-0000
   Fax: 290617

Polish Chamber of Foreign Trade
ul. Trebacka 4
00-950 Warsaw
   Tel: 26-02-21
   Telex: 814361 PHZ PL

Polish Commercial Officer (USA)
820 Second Ave., 17th Floor
New York, NY 10017
   Tel: (212) 370-5300
   Telex: 595657 POLCOMER NYC

Ministry of Finance
ul. Swietokrzyska 12
00-926 Warsaw
   Tel: 26-65-44
   Telex: 815592 MINFIN PL

Ministry of Industry
ul. Wspolna 4
Foreign Department
00-926 Warsaw
   Tel: 28-21-41
   Telex: 814267

Other Government Institutions

UNIDO Industrial Cooperation & Investment Promotion Service
ul. Stawki 2
00-959 Warsaw
  Tel: 635-71-12, 635-60-86
  Fax: 635-12-60
  Telex: 817916 UNIDO PL

National Bank Poland
ul. Swietokrsyska 11/21
Warsaw
  Tel: 26-56-41
  Telex: 814681 NBPPI

Private Sector in Poland-Chamber and Associations

Zwiazek Rzemiosla Polskiego
ul. Miodowa 14
00-950 Warsaw
  Tel: 311-461 Ext. 317, 215, 312, 126

Polska Izba Gospodareza
Prywatnego Przemyslu i Handlu
ul. spokojna 7
00-950 Warsaw
  Tel: 385-683, 382-231
Secretary: Mr. R. Wojnarowski
  Tel: 261-510

Izba Przemyslowo-Handlowa
Inwestorow Zagranicznych
Krakowski Przedmiescie
00-950 Warsaw
Mr. Stefan Lewandowski, Chairman
  Tel: 391-903
Mr. Ciszewski, Director
  Tel: 271-231

Polska Isba Innowaacyjna
ul. Wspolna 1/3
00-950 Waraw
Mr. Jan Konarzewski, Chairman
  Tel: 212-336

Slaska Izva Przemyslowo-Handlowa
ul. Rodziewiczowny 18
41-503 Chorzow
Mr. Adolf Gebara, Chairman
    Tel: 415-964

Towarzystwo Gospodarcze
ul. Pabryczna 27 m. 27
Warsaw
    Tel: 294-110
Dr. Zbigniew Warzesinski, Chairman
    Tel: 340-559

Krakowskie Towarzystwo Przemyslowe
Krakow
Mr. Andrzej Baranski
    Tel: 012-219-853

Wielkopolskie Towarystwo Przemyslowe
Poznan
Mr. Maciej Puk
    Tel: 061-660-700

Staropolskie Towaezystwo Przemyslowe
Kieslce
Mr. Jozef Plokoka
    Tel: 310-616

Republic of Poland Foreign Trade Enterprises

AGPOL—Foreign Relations
ul. Kierbedzia 4
00-7228 Warsaw
    Tel: 41-60-61
    Telex: 813364 AGPOL PL
General Director: Mieczyslaw Kroker
    Tel: 41-59-81

AGRICOOP—Food
Al. Jerozolimskie 27
00-508 Warszawa
    Tel: 21-33-17
    Telex: 81708
Director: Jan Szerszen
    Tel: 29-65-15

AGROMET-MOTOIMPORT
ul. Prezemyslowa 26
P.O. Box 990
00-950 Warsaw
    Tel: 28-50-71
    Telex: 813665 MOTO PL or 813511 MOTO PL
General Director: Andrezej Michejda
    Tel: 21-39-88, 21-58-34

AGROS—Foodstuffs, Farm Machinery
ul. Chalubinskiego 8
P.O. Box 41
00-613 Warsaw
    Tel: 30-10-00
    Telex: 814391 PL
General Director: Zofia Gaber
    Tel: 30-06-14

ANIMEX—Animal Products
ul. Chalubinskiego 8
00-613 Warsaw
    Tel: 30-10-00
    Telex: 814431 AX PL
General Director: Witold Pereta
    Tel: 30-26-39

BALTONA—Duty-free Items
ul. Pulaskiego 6
P.O. Box 365
81-963 Gdynia
    Tel: (0-58) 20-23-50
    Telex: 054361 balt pl
General Director: Jerzy Mrozowicki
    Tel: (0-58) 20-01-06

BALTONA—Warsaw Branch Office
ul. Partyzantow 6
P.O. Box 6
00-950 Warsaw
    Tel: 25-40-31
    Telex: 813758 balwa pl
Director: Tadeusz Gorecki
    Tel: 25-91-49

BEFAMA—Textile Machinery
Export Office
ul. Powstancow Slaskich 6
  Tel: (830) 230-61
  Telex: 035333 bmwf pl
Director: Piotr Tyran
  Tel: (830) 274-23

BUDIMEX—Building Trades
ul. Zurawia 3/5
00-503 Warsaw
  Tel: 21-03-51
  Telex: 813473 chzb pl
General Director: Grzegorz Tuderek
  Tel: 29-23-97

BUMAR—Construction Machinery
ul. Marchlewskiego 11
P.O. Box 85
00-828 Warsaw
  Tel: 20-46-61
  Telex: 814805 bmar pl
General Director: Boguslaw Jarzynski
  Tel: 20-76-61

H. CEGIELSKI—Marine Engines
ul. 28 Czerwca 1956 r. 223-229
P.O. Box 41
60-965 Pozan
  Tel: (0-61) 31-12-00
  Telex: 0413451 hcp pl
General Director: Ryszard Solowiej
  Tel: (0-61) 31-11-04

CENTROMOR—Ships and Marine Equipment
ul. Okopowa 7
P.O. Box 384
80-819 Gdansk
  Tel: (0-58) 31-22-71
  Telex: 0512376 pl
          0512161 pl
General Director: Aleksy Latra
  Tel: (0-58) 31-21-34

CENTROMOR S.A.—Warsaw Branch Office
ul. Wspolna 65
P.O. Box 729
00-950 Warsaw
    Tel: 21-64-45
    Telex: 813303 pl
Manager: Ryszard Erbel
    Tel: 28-84-60

CENTROMOR S.A.—Szczecin Branch Office
ul. Firlika 43
P.O. Box 105
71-637 Szczecin
    Tel: (0-91) 43-318
    Telex: 0422231 cmor pl
Manager: Jan Weldzinski
    Tel: (0-91) 21-13-16

CENTROZAP—Metallurgical Equipment
ul. Mickiewicza 29
P.O. Box 825
40-085 Katowice
    Tel: (832) 51-34-01
    Telex: 0315771 czap pl
General Director: Henryk Kalita
    Tel: (832) 51-25-44

CENTROZAP—Warsaw Branch Office
ul. Koszykowa 6a
00-564 Warsaw
    Tel: 28-97-03
Manager: Wojciech Grunwald
    Tel: 21-54-46

CEPELIA—Handicrafts
ul. Lucka II, P.O. Box 1041
00-950 Warsaw
    Tel: 20-50-01
    Telex: 813671
General Director: Wieslaw Winiarski
    Tel: 20-97-94

CIECH—Chemicals
ul. Jasna 12
P.O. Box 271
00-950 Warsaw
Tel: 26-90-31
Telex: 814561 cie pl
General Director: Wladyslaw Szczepankowski
Tel: 26-98-68

CONFEXIM—Apparel
Al. Kosciuszki 123
P.O. Box 130
90-950 Lodz
Tel: (0-42) 36-35-22
Telex: 886877 conf pl
886878 conf pl
General Director: Dr. Tadeusz Kaminski

COOPEXIM—Handicrafts
ul. Pulawska 14
P.O. Box 215
00-975 Warsaw
Tel: 49-48-51
Telex: 814211 cox pl
General Director: Przemyslaw Delatkiewicz
Tel: 49-18-07

DAL—Countertrade
ul. Marszalkowska 82
00-683 Warsaw
Tel: 28-42-51, 29-82-41
Telex: 814831 dal pl
General Director: Marek Pietkiewicz

DROMEX—Road and Bridge Construction
ul. Trojanska 7
02-105 Warsaw
Tel: 46-20-45
Telex: 816527 dromex pl
General Director: Jerzy Trepinski
Tel: 46-39-01

ENERGOPOL—Gas and Oil Equipment
Al. Jerozolimskie 53
P.O. Box 367
00-950 Warsaw
    Tel: 29-80-81
    Telex: 813663 epol pl
General Director: Bogdan Wos
    Tel: 21-62-39

FILM POLSKI—Movies
ul. Mazowiecka 6/8
P.O. Box 161
00-950 Warsaw
    Tel: 26-04-41
    Telex: 813640 film pl
General Director: Adam Zawistowski
    Tel: 26-84-55

HORTEX—Food Products
ul. Warecka IIa
00-034 Warsaw
    Tel: 26-52-81
    Telex: 816606 hor pl
General Director: Ludwik Olejarz
    Tel: 27-71-74

IMPEXMETAL—Ball Bearings
ul Lucka 7/9
P.O. Box 62
    Tel: 20-02-01
    Telex: 814371 imp pl
813372 imp pl
General Director: Wojciech Opalko
    Tel: 20-77-36

INTERPEGRO—Small Agricultural Equipment
ul. B. Brechta 3
03-472 Warsaw
    Tel: 19-93-91
    Telex: 815764 ipgr pl
President: Zbigniew Hryniewicz
    Tel: 19-93-91

INTER-VIS—Machine Tools
ul. Kasprzaka 29/31
P.O. Box 55
00-961 Warsaw
Tel: 36-88-21, 36-31-49
Telex: 812482 m x v pl
General Director: Slawian Krzywinski
Tel: 36-85-31

KOLMEX—Railroad Equipment
ul. Mokotowska 49
P.O. Box 236
00-950 Warsaw
Tel: 28-22-91
Telex: 813270 kolx pl
813714 kolx pl
General Director: Aleksander Gudzowaty
Tel: 28-39-06

KOPEX—Overseas Mine Construction
ul. Grabowa 1
P.O. Box 245
40-952 Katowice
Tel: (832) 58-00-45
Telex: 0315681 kopx pl
031682 kopx pl
General Director: Jozef Garlej
Tel: (832) 58-53-06

LABIMEX—Laboratory Equipment
ul. Krakowskie Przedmiescie 79
P.O. Box 261
00-950 Warsaw
Tel: 26-64-31
Telex: 814349 lbmex pl
814349 lbmex pl
General Director: Jerzy Rychter
Tel: 26-85-96

LOCUM—Housing
ul Marchlewskiego 13
P.O. Box 31
00-828 Warsaw
    Tel: 20-03-51
    Telex: 816237 zsm pl
General Director: Wojciech Cymbala
    Tel: 20-15-99

MERA-ELWRO—Computers
ul. Ostrowskiego 9
53-238 Wroclaw
    Tel: (0-71) 61-68-33
    Telex: 0715518 elwro pl
General Director: Andrzej Musielak
Director of Foreign Trade Office: Boleslaw Wos
    Tel: 61-53-47

METALEXPORT—Machine Tools
ul. Mokotowska 49
P.O. Box 442 and 642
00-950 Warsaw
    Tel: 28-22-91
    Telex: 814241 mex pl
General Director: Dr. Inz Zbigniew Pawlik
    Tel: 28-18-23

METRONEX—Electronics
ul. Mysia 2
P.O. Box 198
00-950 Warsaw
    Tel: 21-03-71
    Telex: 814471 mtx pl
General Director: Andrzej Ziaja
    Tel: 21-94-19

MINEX—Glass, Crystal, China
ul. Chalubinskiego 8
P.O. Box 1002
00-950 Warsaw
    Tel: 30-10-00
    Telex: 814401 min pl
General Director: Jerzy Mitoraj
    Tel: 30-23-05

NAVIMOR—Small Boats, Docks
ul. Heweliusza II
P.O. Box 423
90-980 Gdansk
    Tel: (0-58) 31-68-21
    Telex: 0512453 na pl
General Director: Dr. Stanislaw Laskowski

NAVIMOR—Szczecin Branch Office
ul. Ludowa 13
P.O. Box 51
71-700 Szczecin
    Tel: (0-91) 24-27-27
    Telex: 0422379 navi pl
Manager: Wieslaw Gryczka

NAVIMOR—Warsaw Branch Office
ul. Hoza 20
00-950 Warsaw
    Tel: 28-37-21
Manager: Bogdan Baranowski

ORBIS—Travel
ul. Very Kostrzewy 16
P.O. Box 195
00-366 Warsaw
    Tel: 22-74-21
    Telex: 816017 hzorb pl
General Director: Marek Manowiecki
    Tel: 27-27-02

PAGED—Furniture, Wood, and Paper Products
Pl. Trzech Krzyzy 18
P.O. Box 991
00-950 Warsaw
    Tel: 29-52-41/9
    Telex: 814221 pgd pl
General Director: Miron Trzeciak
    Tel: 28-11-01

PEWEX—Internal Export
Intraco Bldg.
ul. Stawki 2, P.O. Box 240
00-950 Warsaw
    Tel: 635-91-11
    Telex: 815404 pewx pl
General Director: Tadeusz Bielski
    Tel: 635-77-43

PEZETEL—Aircraft
Al. Stanow Zjednoczonych 61
P.O. Box 199
00-950 Warsaw
    Tel: 10-80-01
    Telex: 813314 pzl pl
    812815 pzl pl
General Director: Jerzy Krezlewicz
    Tel: 13-52-65

POLCOOP—Food Processing
ul. Kopernika 30
P.O. Box 199
00-950 Warsaw
    Tel: 26-10-81
    Telex: 814451 polc pl
General Director: Kazimierz Pracki
    Tel: 26-23-63

POLCOTEX—Export of Clothing
ul. Kujawska 1
00-957 Warsaw
    Tel: 43-38-51
    Telex: 813406 pl
General Director: Zygmunt Karpinski
    Tel: 21-92-40

POLIMEX-CEKOP—Turnkey Plants
ul. Czackiego 7/9
P.O. Box 815
00-950 Warsaw
    Tel: 26-80-01
    Telex: 814271 poli pl
General Director: Kazimierz Zaczek
    Tel: 26-87-24

POL-MOT—Cars, Trucks, Buses
ul. Stalingradzka 23
P.O. Box 16
00-983 Warsaw
    Tel: 11-00-01
    Telex: 813621 pomo pl
           813901 pomo pl
General Director: Manager Roman Grzzywacz
    Tel: 11-10-93

POLSERVICE—Patents, Licenses, Legal Services
ul. Chalubinskiego 8
P.O. Box 335
00-950 Warsaw
    Tel: 30-20-00
    Telex: 813538 upol pl
           816321 upol pl
General Director: Jerzy Fijalkowski
    Tel: 30-05-22

POLTEL—Television Films, Programs
ul. Woronicza 17
P.O. Box 211
00-950 Warsaw
    Tel: 43-81-91
    Telex: 815331 rtv pl
General Director: Lew Rywin
    Tel: 47-81-91

PRACOWNIE KONSERWACJI ZABYTKOW—Monument Preservation Workshop
ul. Jazdow 2
00-467 Warsaw
    Tel: 29-30-78
    Telex: 812387 pkzex pl
General Director: Andrzej Orczykowski
    Tel: 28-83-80

RADWAR—Professional Electronics
ul. Poligonwa 30
04-051 Warsawa
    Tel: 10-40-61
    Telex: 813401 wzr pl
           816061 wzr pl
General Director: Marian Migdalski
    Tel: 10-11-53

REMEX—Handicrafts
ul. Bracka 25
P.O. Box 408
00-950 Warsaw
    Tel: 27-60-21
    Telex: 816656 remex pl
General Director: Lech Wojcik
    Tel: 27-93-75

ROLIMPEX—Grains, Feed Stocks
ul. Chalubinskiego 8
P.O. Box 364
00-950 Warsaw
    Tel: 30-10-00
    Telex: 814341 rolx pl
General Director: Roman Mlyniec
    Tel: 30-27-99

ROLIMPEX—Gdynia Branch Office
ul. Dokerow 9
P.O. Box 245
81-336 Gdynia 1
    Tel: 058 20-19-50
    Telex: 054228 rol pl

RYBEX—Fish
ul. Odrowaza 1
71-420 Szczecin
    Tel: (0-91) 22-08-11/9
    Telex: 0422326 brk pl
General Director: Wojciech Polaczek
Warsaw Office: ul. Hoza 20
    Tel: (0-91) 22-46-29

SKORIMPEX—Leather
ul. Piotrkowska 148/150
P.O. Box 133
90-950 Warsaw
    Tel: (0-42) 36-38-33
    Telex: 885251 sim pl
General Director: Ireneusz Mintus
    Tel: (0-42) 36-25-29

STALEXPORT—Steel
ul. Mickiewicza 29
P.O. Box 401
40-992 Kato ice
    Tel: (832) 51-34-41
    Telex: 0315751 stex pl
General Director: Ryszard Harhala
    Tel: (832) 51-19-41

TEXTILEIMPEX—Textiles, Clothing
ul. Traugutta 25
P.O. Box 320
90-950 Lodz
    Tel: (0-42) 32-51-80
    Telex: 8864719 texim pl
General Director: Stanislaw Jaros
    Tel: 36-16-38

TRICOT—Apparel
ul. Piotrkowska 270
P.O. Box 278
90-361 Lodz
    Tel: (0-42) 84-02-60
    Telex: 884545 phz pl
General Director: Andrzej Moryc

TORIMEX—Consumer Goods
ul. Nowogrodzka 35/41
P.O. Box 394
00-691 Warsaw
    Tel: 21-66-52
    Telex: 816751 tor pl
General Director: Leslaw Skibinski
    Tel: 21-66-82

UNITRA—Radios, TVs
ul. Nowogrodzka 50
P.O. Box 66
00-950 Warsaw
    Tel: 28-94-11
    Telex: 814878 eluni pl
            815491 eluni pl
General Director: Jan Brukszo
    Tel: 21-33-82

UNIVERSAL—Consumer Products
Al. Jerozolimskie 44
P.O. Box 370
00-950 Warsaw
    Tel: 26-74-41
    Telex: 814431 univ pl
General Director: Dariusz Przywiecerski
    Tel: 27-07-48

VARIMEX—Hospital, Restaurant Equipment
ul. Wilcza 50/52
P.O. Box 263
00-950 Warsaw
    Tel: 28-80-41
    Telex: 814311 pl
General Director: Andrzej Sobczyk
    Tel: 28-68-02

VARIMEX-WIFAMA—Hospital Equipment
ul. A. Struga 16
90-513 Lodz
    Tel: (0-42) 36-00-40
    Telex: 885413 vawi pl
           886335 prema pl
General Director: Longin Matras
    Tel: (0-42) 36-00-40

WEGLOKOKS—Coal
ul. Mickiewicza 29
40-085 Katowice
    Tel: (832) 51-22-11
    Telex: 0132384 weks pl
General Director: Andrzej Poreebski
    Tel: (832) 58-13-18

WEGLOKOKS
ul. Piwna 1/2
P.O. Box 172
80-831 Gdansk
    Tel: (0-58) 31-62-81
    Telex: 0512303 pl
General Director: Eugenuisz Chorzelski

WEGLOKOKS—Maritime Branch Office
ul. Gdansk 21
7Direct

or: Andrzej Jagus
Tel: (0-91) 35-850

WEGLOKOKS—Warsaw Branch Office
ul. Krucza 6/14
00-496 Warsaw
Tel: 28-76-60
Telex: 813490 pl
General Director: Ryszard Pludowski

U.S. Business Offices in Poland

AIRCO-HELEK
Supervisory Office
ul. Krotoszynska ZOG
63-430 Odolanow
woj. Ostrow Wlkp.
Tel: z(0-641) 64-441, 65-897
Telex: 462441
Director: Mr. Janusz Golebiowski
Deputy Director: Mr. Tomasz Golbiewski

AMERICAN TRAVEL ABROAD, INC.
Branch Office
ul. Armil Ludowej 12
00-638 Warszawa
Tel: 25-30-74, 25-35-17
Telex: 816649
Director: Mr. Piotr Jaslowski

BECKMAN INSTRUMENTS
Branch Office
ul. Marconich 11/1
02-954 Warszawa
Tel: 40-88-22, 40-88-33
Telex: 816767 beck pl
Administrative Manager: Mr. Marian Kawczynski

BOEING
c/o LOT, Polish Airlines
ul. 17 stycznia 39
00-006 Warszawa
    Tel/Fax: 46-75-80
    Telex: 816200
Customer Support Rep: Mr. Stanley Golanka

CARGILL
ul. Szpitalna 1/7
Warszawa
    Tel: 26-55-23
Director: Mr. Edward Hazar

CURTIS INTERNATIONAL, LTD.
Branch Office
ul. Marchlewskiego 34, apts. 5 & 6
00-141 Warszawa
    Tel: 24-72-81, 24-72-82
    Fax: 247068-451
    Telex: 817548 curtis pl
Director: Mr. Zbigniew Niemczycki

DONAO TRADING CORP.
Technicial Information Office
Al. Na Skarpie 21
00-488 Warszawa
    Tel: 28-18-31
Director: Mr. George Osypowicz

THE DOW CHEMICAL COMPANY
Branch Office
ul. Smolenskiego 1, apts. 11/12
01-698 Warszawa
    Tel: 33-22-22, 33-22-62
    Telex: 816466 dow pl
District Sales Manager: Dr. Grzegorz Rytko

DRESSER INDUSTRIES, INC.
Technical Information Office
Al. Jerozolimskie 51, apt. 3
00-697 Warszawa
    Tel: 28-48-74
    Telex: 814594 in pl
Manager: Mr. Bogdan Kryca

E.I. DUPONT DE NEMOURS & CO., INC.
Branch Office
Intraco Bldg., 21st floor
ul. Strwki 2
    Tel: 635-04-01
    Telex: 812376 dup pl
Administrative Manager: Mr. Jerzy Kalinowski

ELI LILLY INTERNATIONAL CORPORATION - ELANCO
Technical Information Office
Intraco Bldg., 6th floor
ul. Stawki 2
00-193 Warszawa
    Tel: 635-00-45, 635-00-48
    Telex: 815640 lilly pl
Office Manager: Mr. Andrzej Wrobel

FOUNDATION FOR THE DEVELOPMENT OF POLISH AGRICULTURE (FDPA)
ul. Saska 74A
03-958 Warszawa
    Tel: 17-19-17
    Fax: 17-59-39
    Telex: 816994 fdpa pl
Executive Director: Mr. Gregory A. Vaut

GENERAL ELECTRIC
c/o LOT, Polish Arlines
ul. 17 stycznia 39
02-954 Warszawa
    Tel: 46-59-59
    Fax: 46-75-80
    Telex: 816200
Manager for Poland: Mr. Clide Griffith

HBB, LTD.
(Budget Rent a Car)
Al. Jerozolimskie 245
00-222 Warszawa
    Tel: 662-1784
    Telex: 817888
Director: Ms. Ewa Maczynska

HEWLETT PACKARD
ZOTPAN (Zaklad Obslugi Techniczne)
ul. Newelska 6
01-447 Warszawa
    Tel: 36-83-00
Representative: Mr. Adam Kowalski

IBM Branch Office
ul. Wawelska 56
02-067 Warszawa
    Tel: 25-48-65, 25-12-81 x337
    Telex: 812552 ingra pl
Branch Manager: Mr. Janusz Uscinski

JOHNSON & JOHNSON
Branch Office
ul. Krolowej Marysienki 13/1
02-954 Warszawa
    Tel: 42-05-76
Director: Mr. Jon Bachman

MARRIOT
Branch Office
Alege Jerozolimskie 65/79
00-697 Warszawa
    Tel: 306-306, 300-030
    Telex: 815622
Director: Mr. Haile Aguiler

MONSANTO POLAND, INC.
Technical Information Office
Intraco Bldg., 26th Floor
ul. Stawki 2
00-193 Warszawa
    Tel: 635-14-71
    Telex: 812747 mons pl
Office Supervisor: Ms. Ewa Szaniawska

MRS. PAUL'S KITCHENS, INC.
Branch Office
ul. Studencka 50
02-735 Warszawa
    Tel: 43-68-15
    Telex: 816326 pauls pl
Director: Mr. Stranislaw Moszuk

MULTI INVESTMENT INTERNATIONAL MARKETING, INC.
ul. Boya Zelenskiego 6, suite 46
Warszawa
Tel: 25-26-17
Fax: 25-12-64
Telex: 813593B txcb pl
President: Mr. Jacque Tourel

PFIZER CORPORATION
Branch Office
ul. Lektykarska 9 m., apts. 7/8
01-687 Warszawa
Tel: 33-17-13, 33-18-66
Telex: 816469 pfiwa
Director: Mr. Andrej Zarebski

PHILLIP MORRIS
ul. Szpitalna 6
00-031 Warszawa
Tel: 27-71-39
Fax: 27-96-27
Telex: 8160011 pinor pl
Manager for Poland: Mr. Krzysztof Sokolik

3M
Branch Office
ul. Lektykarska 5, apt. 21
01-687 Warszawa
Tel: 33-18-34
Telex: 817459 mmm pl
Manager for Poland: Mr. Peter Krapf

UNITRONEX
ul. Dabrowki 9/3
03-909 Warszawa
Tel: 17-95-24
Fax: 17-00-64
Telex: 812488
Director: Mr. Bogdan Bitowski

UPJOHN
Branch Office
ul. Kubickiego 17, apt. 27
00-979 Warszawa
    Tel: 42-05-46, 40-95-88
    Fax: 4205-46
    Telex: 817074 upj pl
Branch Manager: Mr. Jerzy Surowiecki

WANG
Service Office
ul. Goraszewska 3
02-910 Warszawa
    Tel: 42-08-91
    Telex: 817513
Office Manager: Mr. Zbszko Celga

Polish Trade Firms and Institutes: Computer-Related

Baltona Foreign Trade Company
ulitsa Pulaskiego 6, POB 365
81-963 Gydnia
    Telex: 054361 balt pl
(Distribution of computers through hard-currency shops in Poland)

Pewex Foreign Trade Company
ulitsa Stawki 2, POW 240
00-950 Warszawa
    Telex: 812688, 815404 pewex pl
(similar to above)

Centrum Informatyki Gospodarki Morskie
Maritime Economy Computer Centre
Foreign Trade Division
ulitsa Heweliusza II
80-958 Gdansk 50
    Telex: -715518
(Export-import of computers and related equipment)

Elwro
Foreign Trade Office
ulitsa Ostrowskiego 9
53-238 Wroclaw
    Telex: 0715518
(Export-import of computers and related equipment)

Metronex
ulitsa Mysia 2, POB 198
00-950 Warszawa
    Telex: 814471 mtx pl
(Export-import of computers, software, automatic control systems)

Uniwersytet Warszawski
(University of Warsaw)
Export Office
Ulitsa Karakowskie Przedmiescie 26/28
00-297 Warszawa
    Telex: 812274 pl

Akademia Gorniczo-Hutnicza
Academy of Mining and Metallurgy
Centre for Servicing Scientific Research and Export
u. ulitsa Mickiewicza 30
30-059 Krakow
    Telex: 0322203 agh pl

Akedemia Tecniczno-Rolnicza
Academy of Agriculture and Technology
Department of Foreign Relations
Ulitsa Oldzewskiego 20
85-225 Bydgosxcz
    Telex: 0562292

Bistyp
Research and Design Center for Industrial Building
Foreign Trade Office
Ulitsa Parkingowa 1
00-518 Warszawa
    Telex: 813473

Budimex (Contractor for industrial, engineering projects)
Building Foreign Trade Enterprise Ltd.
Ulitsa Marszalkowska 82
00-517 Warszawa
    Telex: 813473 chzb pl

Dom Handlowy Nauki
Science Trading House Ltd.
00-950 Warszawa POB 410
    Telex: 817529 dshn pl

Elektrim
Polish Foreign Trade Company for Electrical Equipment
ulitsa Chalubinskiego 8, POB 638
00-927 Warszawa
    Telex: 814351 hzem pl

Infoterminal
Computer Center for Data Base and Processing
ulitsa Krakowskie Przedmiescie 26/28
00-927 Warszawa
    Telex: 817520

Polish Economic Association
Economic Expertise Establishment (economic consulting)
ulitsa Nowy Swiat 49
00-042 Warszawa
    Telex: 817451 pte zg pl

Politechnika Gdanska
Gdansk Technical University
Implementation and Export Team
ulitsa Majakowskiego 11/12
80-952 Gdansk
    Telex: 0512302 plg pl

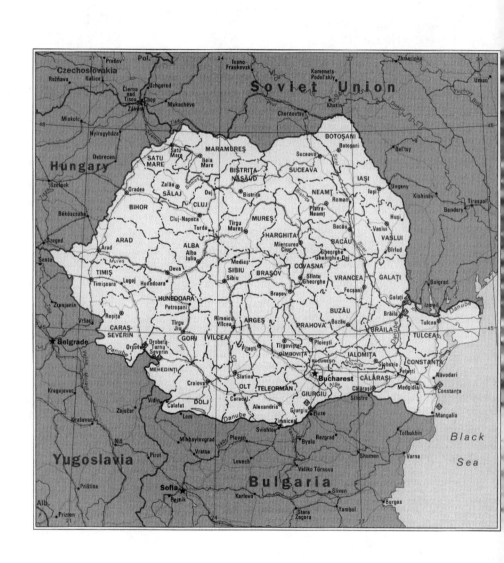

ROMANIA

ROMANIA
In a Nutshell

		Urban Population
Population (1992)	22,828,000	49%

Main Urban Areas		Percentage of Total
Bucharest (Capital)	1,989,823	8.72
Brasov	351,493	1.54
Constanta	327,676	1.44
Timisoara	325,272	1.42
Iasi	313,060	1.37
Cluj-Napoca	310,017	1.36
Galati	295,372	1.29

Land Area	91,699 square miles
	230,340 square kilometers

Comparable European State	Slightly smaller than the U. K.
Comparable U.S. State	Slightly smaller than Oregon

Language	Romanian

Common Business Language	German and French are common

Currency	Lev (= 100 Bani)

Best European Air Connection	Frankfurt (Lufthansa, Delta)

Best Ground Connection	Vienna (1,151 kilometers)

Best Hotel	Intercontinental Bucharest
	($225 per night as of 1/92)

CHAPTER CONTENTS

INTRODUCTION AND REGIONAL ORIENTATION

Geographical and Historical Background

Romania's area measures 237,500 square kilometers. It is bordered by the Soviet Union to the east and north, Hungary on the west, Yugoslavia on the southwest, Bulgaria on the south, and the Black Sea on the east.

There are several climatic zones, ranging from mediterranean mild temperatures in the southeast to a harsher continental climate in the north and west. Differences in the altitude due to a rugged topography, which include mountain and submountain chains, also produce variations.

The average annual temperature is 52 degrees Fahrenheit, 11 degrees Celsius. Extremes are 111 degrees Fahrenheit in the south to -36 degrees Fahrenheit in the mountains. Average annual rainfall is 26 inches, but varies by region with heavy rainfall in the Carpathian region and light rainfall in the southeast. It is often humid in summer, and harsh icy winds make the country chilling in winter.

The state officially became Romania in 1862. It was declared a constitutional principality in the Constitution of 1866 under Prince Carol of Hohenzollern-Sigmaringen. In 1881, he became king. Independence was declared on May 9, 1877, and Romania fought with the Russians against Turkey in the 1877-1878 war. The Romanian state was officially recognized in the Treaty of San Stefano and the Treaty of Berlin in 1878.

In World War I, Romania joined the Entente hoping to gain territories it considered part of its nation, including Bassarabia, Bukovina, and Transylvania. December 1, 1918 has been recognized and celebrated as the day of independence and union when the last of those territories chose unification with Romania.

Between the wars, the government was based on a liberal constitutional system, dominated by the land-owning aristocracy. The Social Democratic party was a small, but active, labor party. The Communists worked primarily underground. Throughout this period, Romania's government and population became increasingly right-wing and authoritarian. A popular fascist movement, the Iron Guard, threatened the government of King Carol. In 1940-1941, it took power in a coup led by General Ion Antonescu.

Initially, Romania declared neutrality in World War II, but after losing territories to the Soviet Union (Bassarabia and Bukovina), Hungary (northern Transylvania), and Bulgaria (southern Dobruja), it joined the Axis powers in June 1941. In 1944, Antonescu was deposed by a coup led by King Michael. Shortly afterwards, Romania switched to join the Allies. Under the peace treaty, Romania regained the Transylvanian territories, but those territories annexed by the Soviets remained under Soviet control. Romania was also required to pay war reparations to the Soviet Union, as well as other allied states.

The end of the war also brought about Soviet occupation, which supported Communist rule in Romania. In 1947, King Michael was forced to abdicate and the People's Republic was declared. Romania soon became one of the most repressive regimes, at least domestically, in all spheres of life — including economic, political, and social aspects. The rule of Nicolae Ceausescu from 1964 until 1989 was especially rigid. Although Stalinist policies dominated the domestic atmosphere, the foreign policy of Romania was extremely independent from the Soviet Union and other bloc countries.

In December 1989, Ceausescu was suddenly overthrown in a bloody, violent coup. The opposition was primarily made up of Communist party members, since there was no organized opposition tolerated under the Communist regime. The National Salvation Front, accused by some of being Communists under a different name, took power. The government has committed itself to economic and political restructuring, although the process has been difficult.

Demographics

Socioeconomic Indicators and Conditions

Romania has had a particularly high population growth rate in the past few years, attributable in part to restrictive abortion and birth control laws. The 1989 birth rate (per 1,000) was 16.0. The urban population has also grown significantly from 20.6% in 1930 to 53.2% in 1989.

The population is overwhelmingly Romanian (88.1% in 1989), but there are significant minority groups, including Hungarian (7.9%), German (1.6%) and other, such as Gypsy (2.4%). Official government policy towards minorities provides for autonomy, but also integration into the economy and compulsory study of Romanian.

The official language is Romanian. The most common foreign languages spoken are French, English, German, and Russian.

Approximately 80% of Romanians are Romanian Orthodox Church members, approximately 6% are Roman Catholic and about 4% are Calvinist, Jewish, Baptist, or Lutheran.

The economy was nationalized when the Communists took power. Industrial production was emphasized during this period and increased at an annual average rate of 16%. The rigid centralization of the industrial activity resulted in inefficient industries, often financed and supported without reference to the market. There was also an emphasis on heavy industry, at the expense of consumer goods. At the same time, despite domestic shortages, a priority was given to eliminate international debt, so imports were cut and products were exported. This was especially the case in agricultural products. By the 1980s, standards of living had decreased significantly.

Today, the result is not only an inefficient structure and a lack of well-trained management, but also a high demand for nearly any consumer goods. Industrial production was approximately 60% of national income in 1976, with the largest growth in the electronics, machine building, chemical, and metallurgical sectors.

Estimates set GDP at $US 37.8 billion in 1989. Per capita GDP was approximately $US 1,632. Investment was concentrated in industry (approximately 60%), especially electric power, metallurgy, machine building, chemicals, and, more recently, the energy and light industry.

Political/Institutional Infrastructure

The Parliament, elected in May 1990, has been drafted a new constitution. The 396-seat House of Deputies (lower house) and 190-seat Senate (upper house) were elected to two-year terms. The government has been consumed with repealing restrictions adopted under the Ceausescu regime. Some of these include: dismantling the Security Police, guaranteeing free expression, releasing political prisoners, abolishing travel restrictions, abolishing the death penalty, allowing the formation of political parties, abolishing food rationing and export policies, and dismantling the centralized economy.

Political Organization

There is a multiparty provisional government (Table 7-1). The executive branch, consisting of president, vice president, prime minister, and council of ministers, was appointed by the provisional government. The Chief of State is President Ion Iliescu (appointed December 23, 1989). Head of government is Prime Minister Petre Roman (appointed December 23, 1989). Minister of Reforms and Parliamentary Relations is Adrian Severin. Minister of Foreign Affairs is Theodor Dumitru Stolojan. The Minister of Economic Orientation is Eugen Dijmarescu.

Table 7-1: Political Parties

Party	Percentage of Votes	Seats
National Salvation Front	66	335
Democratic Hungarian Union	7	41
National Liberal Party (center-right)	6	38
Greens	3	13
National Peasants	3	13
Alliance Unity From Romania	11	-
Democratic Agriculture Party	9	-
Ecologists Party	9	-
Socialists Democratic Party	5	-
Other	28	-

Source: U.S. Department of Commerce. International Trade Administration. 1991. *Foreign Economic Trends and Their Implications for the United States—Romania*. Washington, D.C.: Government Printing Office.

Federal/Regional/Municipal Organization

There are 40 counties and one municipality within Romania.

Trade Flows

Top 10 Import/Export Trade Partners

Romania's trade is still oriented towards the Soviet Union and Eastern Europe, but it is making efforts to focus more on the West (Table 7-2). In 1987, major export partners (percentage of total) included the following: U.S.S.R. 27%; Eastern Europe 23%; the European Community (EC) 15%; the United States 5%; and China 4%. Import balance between East and West was approximately 60% to communist countries and 40% to noncommunist countries in 1987.[1]

Table 7-2: Romania's Chief Import and Export Partners in 1989 (Percentage of total)

Export Partners			
Socialist Countries		*Convertible Currency*	
U.S.S.R.	51.9	Italy	16.7
GDR	12.2	Germany	11.4
Czechoslovakia	7.2	United States	9.5
Poland	7.0	Iran	5.2
Hungary	6.1	Turkey	5.2
		United Kingdom	4.2
		France	4.2
Import Partners			
Socialist Countries		*Convertible Currency*	
U.S.S.R.	52.4	Iran	29.2
East Germany	12.5	Saudi Arabia	15.2
Czechoslovakia	7.7	West Germany	5.3
Poland	6.7	United States	4.9
Hungary	5.5	Egypt	4.4
		Syria	4.1

Source: Donald E. deKeiffer, *Doing Business with the New Romania*. (Portsmouth: Peter E. Randall, 1990), 81-82.

Romania has adopted the Harmonized System of tariffs, but implementation will take years. The Romanian Ministry of Trade and Tourism can provide information on duty rates for various products. All imports and exports are subject to licensing.

Temporary imports, such as items for personal use, are exempt from customs duties.

As of May 1991, Romania did not have most-favored-nation status with the United States.

Top 10 Import/Export Commodities

Romania under Ceausescu pursued an "export at all costs" policy, which placed strict restrictions on importing of goods. Romania is currently developing a trading system based on Western approaches, but recovery from the earlier structural damages will take some time.

Principal exports in 1989 included roller bearings, tractors, passenger cars, gasolines, gas and fuel oil, ferrous metal rollings, aluminum, chemical fertilizers, cement, timber, paper, rayon, meat and meat preparations, fruits, refined sugar, cotton and fabrics, leather goods, and wood furniture.

Principal imports in 1989 included metal cutting machines, power equipment, cranes, motor transport equipment, textile industry equipment, chemical equipment, excavators, pit coal and coke, crude oil, fuel gas, electricity, iron ore, apatite concentrate, ferroalloys, cotton fiber, raw hides, and raw sugar.

Romania has a large agrarian base and is currently emphasizing a program that will modernize agricultural production and lead to export sales of agricultural commodities.

The U.S. Department of Commerce has identified the following as the best export prospects: coal, consumer goods, commercial aircraft, high-technology goods, energy-related equipment, automation and manufacturing equipment, replacement parts, chemicals, and food processing.

Finance and Investment Policies

Since the 1989 revolution, Romania has been rewriting its foreign investment laws to encourage and attract foreign capital. Previous restrictions, such as allowing investment only on a state-controlled basis and subordinating business interests to the five-year plans, have been eliminated in favor of allowing capital to enter Romania more easily. The legal structure, however, is still largely untested.

Unlike most of the Central and East European countries, Romania had no external debt in 1989. This was due primarily to harsh austerity conditions imposed by the Ceausescu regime. Unlike many of its neighbors, the new government may have more time in which to implement new finance and investment policies because the population is accustomed to little or no increases in the standard of living. However, the converse may also prove to be true. Economic reforms in other East European countries have also brought with them rising expectations of the populations. On the other hand, Ceausescu issued a number of credits to countries (often for political reasons) which the country may now be unable to pay. Those outstanding loans may have to be written off.

Policies to Attract New Business

Preferred Foreign Investment Projects

Areas of investment in which foreign capital is sought include industry, agriculture, construction, tourism, scientific and technological research, foreign trade, and banking services. Foreign firms are prohibited from investing in the munitions industry or in industries involving narcotics or drugs. Ventures that will produce goods for export are preferred.

Tax Incentives

Companies with foreign partners are exempt from tax for two years after profits are realized. After that period, companies can apply to the Ministry of Finance for a 50% reduction of tax on profits for an additional three years. If profits are reinvested in a Romanian company, the tax on profits is automatically reduced by 50%.

Free Trade Zones/Special Economic Zones

There is a foreign trade zone at a free port at Sulina.

APPROACHING THE MARKET

Foreign Trade and Investment Decision-Making Infrastructure

Romania is in transition from a centralized economic decision-making structure to decentralizing the process. Foreign firms no longer deal exclusively with the government, which formerly held monopoly control over all trade. However, the decentralization and privatization processes are far from complete. Romanian companies and business people have had little experience in international trade or negotiating contracts. Until 1989, the ministries and state-run foreign trade organizations controlled all international transactions. Now some independent trade organizations exist.

A number of governmental organizations are still playing major roles in foreign trade. Some of these include the Ministry of Foreign Trade, technical-production ministries, industrial centrals, foreign trade organizations, research and design institutes, and the Goods Control Organization (ROMCONTROL). A brief discussion of each is listed below.

The Ministry of Foreign Trade is responsible for developing and administering the trade policy of the government. It also issues licenses as required for products entering or exported from Romania, in a fairly bureaucratic manner, and is responsible for customs regulation.

Technical-production ministries were formerly responsible for implementing economic policies and directly controlling the production and delivery of products. Those duties are now being spread to independent entities as well. The role of these ministries now varies depending on the ministry—from actively seeking foreign partners for projects to serving as "caretakers" for their products.

Industrial centers were the production units, most of which are now independent units. They are permitted to deal directly with foreign investors, buyers, and sellers. It is projected that all will be privatized by 1993. Joint ventures with these organizations are being encouraged by the government to speed privatization and improve technology transfers. The Chamber of Commerce and Industry can provide a list of industrial centers.

Foreign trade organizations were the government's arm that negotiated and implemented import and export policies. They are being slowly replaced by independent trading companies, but it is expected that the process will take until at least 1995 to complete.

Research and design was also formerly under government control. A program of decentralization is planned.

ROMCONTROL is the inspection organization; it checks for quality and quantity control.

Nongovernmental agencies include factories and enterprises, which are now allowed to work directly with foreign firms. The Chamber of Commerce and Industry provides information about the economy, foreign trade system, laws, and regulations. It also arranges contracts between Romanian and foreign firms and works to assist foreign business people to invest in Romania.

The Center for Economic Information and Documentation (CIDE) was set up in December 1989 to assist in the transition to a market-oriented economy. It provides assistance in establishing new enterprises in Romania, helps provide business contacts, legal assistance, advertising and publicity, and economic and trade statistics.

State and Private Services

Incorporation/Registration

Parties prepare a Memorandum of Association, which is in essence a study of technical and economic efficiency stating how the company will pursue its objectives. It also includes the Contract of Association and statutes.

Government approval is required to establish firms wholly owned by foreign investors. Joint ventures need nominal approval of the ministry in the field of activity. Commercial companies in the production field require the advice of the Ministry of the National Economy. The registration fee in 1990 was the lei equivalent of $US 500.

Legal Services

There is an absence of independent legal counselors in Romania; most counselors are actually state employees. Consulting with Western attorneys is advised to ensure that contracts will be drafted that will hold up in countries other than Romania. Litigation may be brought before Romanian courts, but the parties may agree to arbitration, usually through the Arbitration Commission of the Chamber of Commerce and Industry of Romania.

Setting Up Business Operations

Forms of Business Organization

Either joint ventures with Romanian firms or firms with 100% foreign ownership may be established. Terms of joint ventures are stated in a Contract of Association. It must include the following: the name of the corporation, object of the corporation, registered office, duration of the company, capital and means for subscription of shares and for transfer of shares or capital, the number in value of shares or capital, and the rights and obligations of the parties and any other obligations mutually agreed upon by the parties. Statutes or bylaws included in the contract should state provisions on the organization and operation of the company, such as the following: general meeting, organization, exercise of voting rights, organization of the board of directors, method by which the board adopts decisions, appointment of arbitrators, responsibilities of managing directors, methods for writing off profit and loss accounts, calculation and distribution of profits, methods for settling disputes between partners and company, and methods for winding up the company. Amendments to the contract need the approval of the Romanian government.

Accounting may be done in either lei or foreign currency. Depreciation must be included in fixed costs. At least one delegate from the Ministry of Finance of Romania must belong to the organization in the company which controls the accounting activities.

Reserve funds must be allocated from the profits of the company as specified in the contract. Five percent must be set aside until the fund totals 20% of foundation capital. The remainder of the after-tax profits can be distributed to the investors.

Partners have the right to see information about the company's activities, state of assets, profits and losses, and the like, as established in the statutes.

Dissolution procedures should be established in the statutes. A deed of dismemberment and liquidation must be registered with the Ministry of Finance and published in the *Official Monitor*.

Limited liability company. Either stock or limited liability companies may be established. Specifics on the organization of the firm are usually detailed in the

Contract of Association. In February 1991, a law went into effect limiting the transfer of hard-currency profits to 50% for new joint ventures. Joint ventures set up under the March 1990 legislation may transfer all profits abroad after taxes, social insurance, and other obligations are paid.

Sales Promotion, Fairs, Conferences, and Advertising

The most important trade fair is the Bucharest International Fair, held in the spring for consumer goods and in the fall for technical goods. There are also a number of industrial exhibitions held each year. Information about fairs and exhibitions can be obtained through: PUBLICOM, 22 N. Balcescu Boulevard, Bucharest; telex: 11374. The organization that organizes Romania's participation in international affairs, as well as international fairs in Romania is ROMEXPO. ROMEXPO can be reached at telex: 11108 TIBR.

Commercial advertising in the media is rare, but there are billboards, signs, and some types of advertising possible. More difficulty may be encountered when trying to market Romanian goods abroad, because packaging is generally less appealing to Western markets.

PUBLICOM can assist foreign firms with advertising services in Romania. It is responsible for publicizing Romanian exports abroad, as well as organizing trade shows.

Setting Up Offices, Retail Stores, and Service Facilities

Real Estate. Foreigners may not own land or real estate. Joint ventures may lease land owned by a Romanian partner.

Transportation and Freight (Air/Sea)

Romania has 234 kilometers of coastline on the Black Sea. Water transport was facilitated with the 1983 completion of the Cernavoda and Constanta-Danube-Black Sea canal. The Danube River winds through Romania. Major Romanian ports serve Yugoslavia, Hungary, Austria, Czechoslovakia, and Switzerland. They include: Constanta, Mangalia and Sulina on the Black Sea; and Orsova, Drobeta-Turmu Severin, Turnu Magurele, Giurgiu, Oltenita, Calarasi, Hirsova, Braila, Galati, and Tulcea on the Danube.

Air transport is run by TAROM (Transportul Aerian Romana) and LAR (Limiile Aerience Romene). There are 16 airports for domestic traffic and three international airports at Bucharest, Constanta, and Timisoara.

The rail system reaches all major population centers; it was approximately 11,343 kilometers in 1980. In the country, railways are the main form of transportation for people and goods. Thirty-two percent of the lines are electrified. However, by Western standards, they are unreliable, due to low levels of maintenance.

The total length of public roads in 1989 was 72,816 kilometers, 34,893 of which was paved. They have been poorly maintained and the lack of high speed expressways makes road transport of goods difficult, if not impossible, especially in winter. However, improvements to the road system has been one of the government's priorities.

INVESTMENT CLIMATE

Privatization, Investment Protection, and Dispute Settlement

The privatization strategy is generally the demonopolization of state entities, price liberalization, and currency convertibility. Initial steps toward convertibility have been taken, such as allowing the Romanian Foreign Trade Bank to buy and sell foreign exchange at market prices to exporters.

A National Agency for Privatization has been created to promote private enterprises. As of January 1991, approximately 50,000 private companies had been registered, most of which were small service or trade organizations. Small private enterprises have been legal since March 7, 1990. Banks will lend start-up capital to small businesses.

Joint Ventures and Wholly Owned Subsidiaries

One hundred percent foreign ownership is allowed, but approval must be obtained from the Romanian government.

Taxation and Regulatory Conditions

Sources of Income Liable to Taxation

There is a company tax and a dividend tax of 10%, which applies to all profits repatriated as dividends. There is also a personal income tax.

Company Tax

Foreign companies in Romania are subject to an annual tax of 30% on profits, as computed prior to distribution to shareholders. Reserve funds may be used as deductions against computed profits, but contributions of reserve funds are limited to 5% of the profits each year until the total reserve fund accounts for 5% of invested capital. A tax holiday of two years is allowed to companies established with foreign partners. The ministry can approve a 50% reduction of tax on profits for up to three years beyond that. The tax is automatically reduced by 50% if profits are reinvested by the foreign participant in Romania.

Provisional taxes are filed with a written statement and a copy of the balance sheet with the financial department of the City Hall in Bucharest or the district in which the business is registered. They are to be paid in quarterly installments through the bank where the company keeps its account. Differences between the account and final tax must be paid within ten days of the date of receipt of notification from the financial authorities. Funds paid above the amount will be credited to the account or returned.

Tax assessments may be appealed within 20 days of receipt of notification; they must be filed with the financial department that established the difference. Decisions will be taken within 30 days. Those decisions can be appealed to the Ministry of Finance, which will resolve cases by a committee process.

Penalties for tax evasion include a 25% fine of the tax. Late payments may be fined up to 0.05% per day, but not more than double the tax due. The Ministry of Finance has the authority to garnish a company's funds for unpaid taxes. The statute of limitations is two years.

An export surtax of 10% is applicable if profits are transferred abroad.

Personal Income Tax

Taxes on wages and social security payments for Romanian personnel are paid in the currency as established in the Contract of Association.

Insurance

Insurance is in the process of being privatized. It was formerly under the administration of the state monopoly the State Insurance Administration (ADAS). It provides compulsory and voluntary insurance for companies and individuals. In 1990, it was allowed to participate in joint ventures with foreigners and to invest in any project in Romania, although its ability to underwrite projects has been questioned. Information can be obtained at: Administratia Asigurarilor De Stat (ADAS), 5 Smirdan, Bucharest 70406. Tel: 14 77 48. Telex: 11209. Fax: 13 91 06. ADAS began the privatization process in 1990. Foreign insurance companies are now permitted to offer policies in Romania.

Automobile insurance can be obtained through the State Insurance Agency (ADAS).

FINANCING AND CAPITAL MARKETS

Banking and Other Financial Institutions

In the past Romania has opened its banking system to competition with the passage of legislation. Financial markets are expected to diversify in the next few years. Existing banks include: The National Bank of Romania, The Romanian Bank for Foreign Trade, The Investments Bank, The Bank for Agriculture and Food Industry, and The Loans and Savings Bank. A brief discussion of each bank follows.

The National Bank of Romania serves as the central bank. With the Ministry of Finance, it sets the foreign exchange rate, establishes foreign exchange budgets, and decides on the distribution of exchange balances among currencies and depositories. It issues and circulates currency, executes the state budget, supervises the implementation of the financial credit and currency policy, and provides discounts and loans to government operations. As of 1991, the bank has been restricted to the functions of a central bank.

The Romanian Bank for Foreign Trade is responsible for payments in foreign trade and service transactions. This bank provides letters of credit, endorsement of bills of exchange, credit guarantees, the buying and selling of currencies, and concluding agreements with foreign banks. A new function of the bank is to provide credits to the Romanian private sector, especially for joint ventures with foreign investors. The hope is that the bank will come to play the role of an international merchant bank and discuss the financing of any investment in Romania.

The Investments Bank finances, credits, and discounts investments of state-owned enterprises and various cooperatives. The bank provides local capital to the private sector.

The Bank for Agriculture and Food Industry finances and discounts production, investment, and goods in the agricultural sector, food industry, and water management. Because these are sectors targeted for development and foreign investment, the bank will probably play a large role in the future for financing projects and lending funds to the food processing industries.

The Loans and Savings Bank was theoretically similar to a Western savings and loan bank, although in actuality its primary role was as a depositary for consumer savings. The bank will probably develop into a more consumer-oriented segment of the banking and financial sector.

Foreign banks, including Societe Generale, Manufacturers Hanover, Misir Bank, and Frenkfurter A.G., had been established in Romania as of 1990.

Financing of imports and exports to Romania may be obtained through United States, Japan, and European banks, although they generally extend only short- and medium-term financing. Long-term financing was not yet available in May 1991 from the Export-Import Bank. U.S. commercial banks may arrange long-term financing through syndication with European banks or financial entities.

Payment Modalities

The Currency

The currency was not convertible as of December 1991. Changing to a convertible system would probably result in inflation and a reduction in living standards. However, the emergence of an unofficial transactions market may be undermining the government's general reform attempts.

Enforcement of currency controls has been relaxed, and the black market flourished in 1990. The reported difference between official and black market rates range between 3-7 (on the black market) to 1 on the official exchange rate. This is in sharp contrast to other former bloc countries who have taken steps to move towards convertible currencies on a more realistic market level, thus significantly reducing black market transactions.

Any amount of foreign currency is allowed into the country, but the export of lei is prohibited. Currency is to be exchanged only at the foreign trade bank or authorized bodies. An exchange voucher should be obtained that will allow lei to be reconverted to hard currency. In 1990, there was a requirement that the equivalent of $10 in hard currency be spent each day, unless traveling on a prepaid tour.

Tapping International Aid Institutions

Romania is a member of the International Monetary Fund and the International Bank for Reconstruction and Development. It is not eligible for U.S. export-import bank loans.

LICENSING, PATENTS, AND TRADEMARKS

Licensing Policy, Procedures, and Payments

Licensing agreements are negotiated through foreign trade organizations and independent enterprises. Royalty payments without a counterpurchase agreement are now allowed, although Romania prefers to tie the purchase of a license to a cooperation in which the purchase is paid for in part by the resulting product.

Trademark, Patent, and Copyright Protection

Romania subscribes to the International Convention for Protection of Industrial Property. Foreign citizens are entitled to treatment as Romanian citizens under Romanian patent law. Therefore, to preserve patent priority, one must file a corresponding application in Romania within one year of the filing of the original application in his or her home country. Full protection for foreign technical processes is provided. Applications are filed with the State Office for Inventions and Trademarks (OSIM). Foreign inventors generally must use a power of attorney and go through ROMINVENT, the Agency of Patents and Inventions of the Chamber of Commerce and Industry, to apply. If granted, patents are valid for 15 years from the date of registration. It must be utilized within three years from date of issue or four years from the filing date, whichever is later, or it will become subject to compulsory license. Patents provide exclusive rights to the use of the invention in Romania.

Trademark applications are also filed with OSIM through ROMINVENT. They do not require prior registration in the home country. Trademarks are valid for ten years from the date of application and may be renewed for an additional ten-year period. There are 34 classes of goods and eight classes of services for registration. A registered trademark gives exclusive rights to the owner and is enforceable against unauthorized use.

The U.S. has a reciprocal copyright agreement with Romania. Romania is a member of the Berne Convention on Copyrights.

VISITING AND LOCATING

General Travel Checklist

Visas

As of August 1990, visas were still required for most travelers from the United States or the United Kingdom. Visas may be obtained at the entry point, but delays can be avoided by obtaining one in advance through any Romanian embassy. Multiple entry visas are now available.

Currency

The currency is the leu/lei ($1=35 lei at the official 1990 rate). 1 leu=100 bani. Denominations are issued in 10, 25, 50 and 100 lei bills and 5, 15, and 25 bani and

1, 3 and 5 lei coins. The official exchange rate is fixed, with rates determined by the national bank.

Any amount of foreign currency is allowed into the country. The export of lei is prohibited. Currency is to be exchanged only at the foreign trade bank or authorized bodies. An exchange voucher should be obtained that will allow lei to be reconverted to hard currency.

Getting Around

There are taxis, public transport (which is inexpensive but often crowded), and car rentals.

Accommodations and Housing

The International Agency of the Tourist Office can assist in finding temporary housing for foreigners. Apartment rentals range from $10 to $100 per day, depending on size and location.

Foreigners are expected to pay bills in hard currency. Deluxe hotels accept major credit cards. Reservations may be guaranteed by the Intercontinental Hotel chain or by the Chamber of Commerce and Industry of Romania, as well as by the National Travel Office.

Electricity Supply

Electricity is 220 volt, 50 cycle. Romania uses continental style plugs.

Telecom, Postal, and Courier Services

There were 4,596 post offices in 1989 that handled all surface and air mail deliveries and cables.

Local telephone service is fairly dependable. Delays may be experienced when making international calls, but the connections for both telephone and telegraph are considered good. Telephone, telex, and fax facilities are available at most major hotels. Some hotels add service charges to overseas calls. Foreign businesses can obtain telephones, telexes, and faxes through the International Agency of the National Tourist Office.

The majority of the population does not have phones, although they seem to be accessible for the visiting business person. There is a lack of phone lines, which has resulted in saturation. In general, the telecommunications sector is well behind international standards.

Business Cards

Business cards are almost always given, and foreign business people should reciprocate.

Business Hours

Normal business hours are from 8:00 a.m. to 4:30 p.m., Monday through Thursday and from 8:00 a.m. to 2:00 p.m. on Friday. A lunch break is frequently taken around noon. Department stores are open from 8:00 a.m. to 7:00 p.m. Food stores are open from 6:00 a.m. to 9:00 p.m.

Official holidays in Romania are: January 1, New Year's day, May 1, worker's day, and December 1, national holiday. The day following each of these is also a national holiday.

Tipping

Tips are discouraged but usually appreciated. For exceptional service, 10% is usually adequate. Some restaurants include a 12% gratuity, so additional tipping is not necessary.

What to Wear

The climate is temperate. Business people often dress casually, and government officials tend to dress slightly more formal.

Health Care

Drug names often vary from Western counterparts, so it is advised that an adequate amount of any prescription be brought. Emergency prescriptions can be purchased 24 hours a day at Chemists #5, 18, Magheru Blvd., Bucharest. Tel: 14 61 16.

The Media

There are a number of local Romanian stations, and Radio Free Europe and Voice of America broadcasts can also be heard. Romanian television broadcasts in black and white and color. There are some English language newspapers, but foreign newspapers and periodicals are not easily available. Romanian newspapers can usually be obtained in different languages at hotels.

Availability of Foreign Products

Foreign products are available in the hard currency shops, often found in hotels. They are most often found in COMTURIST shops.

Shopping

Deluxe hotels have convertible currencies, where goods not available in regular Romanian stores can be bought. Best buys on the regular market are crystal, handicrafts, lambskin, sweaters, carvings, and fox. Diner's Club, American Express, MasterCard, Access Card, Barclaycard, Carte Blanche, Eurocard, Visa, and Inter-bank are valid in Romania, but visitors are advised to check if accepted at particular places.

Dining Out

There are numerous restaurants, brasseries, and self-service restaurants throughout the city.

Entertainment

Western quality entertainment is scarce.

Sightseeing and Tourist Information

The main tourist organization is Carpati-Bucharest National Tourist Office (7, Magheru Blvd., Tel: 14 51 60. Telex: 11270 CarpatR). It provides reservations at hotels, currency exchange, sightseeing tours of Budapest, booking of tickets for cultural and sporting events, rent-a-car, multilingual guides, and travel arrangements. Tours of the outlying regions can also be arranged. Most major hotels can also arrange for these services.

Popular areas for tourists include the Black Sea coast, the Transylvanian Alps and the Carpathians and the Danube Delta. There are ski resorts in the mountains and numerous resorts and spas in the Moldavian region.

The Short-Term Business Visitor

Airlines Serving

Airlines with regularly scheduled flights to Romania include: Aeroflot, Air France, Alitalia, AUA, British Airways, CSA, El Al, Interflug, JAT, KLM, LOT, Lufthansa, Malev, Sabena, SAS, SwissAir, and Tapso.

Limousine

Cars may be rented with or without a driver. The rate in 1990 was $5 to $6 per hour for a minimum of four hours with a driver; $19 per day plus $.25 per kilometer without a driver. Taxis are metered and may be ordered through the hotel. It is advised that "gypsy cabs" be avoided because they are illegal and frequently expensive.

The Expatriate

Hourly/Annual Mean Wages

Wages of both Romanian and foreign personnel are established by the individual parties.

Labor Force

The labor force in 1990 was approximately 11.4 million, with 34% employed in industry, 28% in agriculture, and 38% elsewhere.

Employment and labor relations. The board of directors or management committee may establish the rights and obligations of foreign personnel. Foreigners may hold management positions. Wages may be transferred abroad using the Bank of Foreign Trade.

Employment and medical insurance. Contributions to social insurance for foreign personnel must be made in foreign currency. Companies may deduct the contribution for social insurance as a quarterly payment that goes to a "super-annuation fund" for foreign personnel normally resident in another country. Companies can avoid making the social insurance payments if the foreign personnel waives coverage under the Romanian insurance services.

ENDNOTES

1 Central Intelligency Agency. Directorate of Intelligence. September 1990. *Handbook of Economic Statistics, 1990*. Washington, D.C.: Government Printing Office.

ROMANIA

KEY CONTACTS FOR BUSINESS

Foreign Trade Organizations and their Directors (By Institutional Subordination and Fields of Activity) (May 1991)

Ministry of Foreign Trade (MFT)

Dunarea: Constantin Gavril
Mercur: Marin Paris
Mineral Import/Export: Basile Zama
Navlomar: Viorel Covrig
Petrol Export/Import: Florian Stoica
Rom Consult: Florin Burada
Romania Transport: Ion Mirica
Sulina Free Port Administration: Mihai Micu
Terra: Ionel Dumitrescu

MFT & Ministry of Heavy Equipment

Industrial Export/Import: Nicolae Constantin
Mecano Export/Import: Stelian Postelnicu
Romenergo: Alexandru Pirvescu
Uzin Export/Import: Vasile Stevoiu

MFT & Ministry of Machine Building

Auto Dacia: Ion Stamatescu
National Aeronautical Center: Dumitru Stanescu
Techno Import/Export: Mircea Bortes
Universal Auto/Tractor: Ovidiu Barbu

MFT & Ministry of Electrical Engineering

Electro Export/Import: Mircea Ionescu
Electronum: Anghel Stan
Masin Export/Import: Ion Balanuta

MFT & Ministry of Metallurgy

Metal Export/Import: Constantin Ghita

MFT & Ministry of Chemical and Petrochemical Industry

Chimica: Virgil Popescu
Danubiana: Mircea Negoescu

MFT & Ministry of Light Industry

Arpimex: Misu Negritoiu
Confex: Neculai Popirlan
Romano Export: Petre Crisan

MFT & Ministry of Wood Processing and Building Materials

Exportlemn: Eduard Vasiliu
Romsit: George Lungurean
Tehnoforest Export: Mihalache Neacsu

MFT & Ministry of Agriculture

Romafgrimex: Doru Tirpea

MFT & Ministry of Food Industry

Prodexport: Consdtantin Iancu

MFT & Ministry of Agricultural Produce Procurement

Fructexporet-Agroexport: Victor Stoiculescu

MFT & Handicraft Cooperatives (UCECOM)

Icecoop-Ilexim: Bujor Ursulescu

MFT & Ministry of Petroleum

Rompetrol-Geomin: Stelian Tanasescu

MFT & Ministry of Electrical Power

Romelectro: Corneliu Lazar

MFT & Ministry of Transport and Telecommunications

Contransimex: Gheorghe Tudor
Rompresfilatelia: Alexandru Lache

Ministry of National Defense

Romtehnica: Nicolae Popescu

Department of Constructions Abroad

Arcif: Vasile Berbeci
Arcom: Ionel Mocanu
Romproject: Ion Mititelu

Chamber of Commerce and Industry

Trade Fair Authority: Octavian Moarcas
Romcontrol: Viorel Paul

Ministry of Tourism

Conturist: Ilie Moraru
International Tourism & Publicity Company: Pompiliu Matei

Radio-TV Board

Export-Import Department: Ion Todan, Head of Dept.

Consumer Cooperatives

Eximcoop: Dumitru Fainis

Council of Socialist Culture and Education

Artexim: Constantin Voiculescu

"Carpati" Central Economic Office

Carpati: Alexandru Nitulescu

YUGOSLAVIA

YUGOSLAVIA

In a Nutshell

		Urban Population
Population (1992)	23,814,000	46%
Regional Population		Percentage of Total
Serbia	9,830,000	41.28
Croatia	4,683,000	19.66
Herzegovina, Bosnia	4,479,000	18.80
Macedonia	2,110,000	8.86
Slovenia	1,948,000	8.18
Montenegro	639,000	2.68
Main Urban Areas		Percentage of Total
Belgrade (Capital, Serbia)	1,470,073	6.17
Zagreb (Croatia)	768,700	3.23
Skopje (Macedonia)	505,547	2.12
Sarajevo (Bosnia)	448,519	1.88
Ljubljana (Slovenia)	305,211	1.28

Land Area	98,766 square miles
	255,400 square kilometers
Comparable European State	Slightly larger than West Germany
Comparable U.S. State	Slightly larger than Wyoming
Language	Serbo-Croat, Slovenian, Macedonian and several other minor Slavonic, Romance and Magyar dialects
Common Business Language	English
Currency	Dinar
Best European Air Connection	Frankfurt (Lufthansa, Delta)
Best Ground Connection	Vienna to Belgrade (660 kilometers)
Best Hotel	Hyatt Belgrade ($235 per night as of 5/91)

CHAPTER CONTENTS

INTRODUCTION AND REGIONAL ORIENTATION

Geographical and Historical Background

Yugoslavia, officially named the Socialist Federal Republic of Yugoslavia, is located on the Adriatic Sea. It is bounded by Italy to the northwest, Austria and Hungary to the north, Romania and Bulgaria to the east, and Albania and Greece to the south. The Yugoslav region is mostly mountainous, covering 255,400 square kilometers.

After a long domination by the Ottoman and Hapsburg empires, the peoples of the region formed a unified state in 1918 known as the Kingdom of the Serbs, Croats, and Slovenes, which became Yugoslavia in 1929. The Serbs dominated the highly centralized state, much to the dissatisfaction of the Croats. Under Nazi occupation during World War II, the country was torn by internal strife. Some Croats were allied to the Axis powers while the resistance was split into pro-royalist Chetniks and the Communist-inspired Partisans. The more effective Partisans, led by Josip Broz Tito, won Allied recognition and aid. In 1945, they formed a government of national unity which a few months later became the People's Republic of Yugoslavia.

With Western support, Yugoslavia maintained its independence through the Stalin period and Tito imposed himself as a leader of the Nonaligned Movement. Since Tito's death in 1980, the country has been plagued by worsening political rivalries between Serbia, the largest republic, and Croatia and Slovenia, the more prosperous, as well as by Serbian repression of the Albanian minority.

In March 1989, Ante Markovic, a Croat, was installed as Yugoslavia's ninth Communist prime minister since 1946. He replaced Branko Mikulic, a Bosnian Croat who resigned with his cabinet in December 1988 — the first Yugoslavian government to resign in the post-war period. Markovic, who is 66 years old, is described as an experienced economist and politician favoring extensive market-oriented reforms and radical political changes. He has called for a "new socialism for a modern Yugoslavia with a self-managing market economy." Such an economy will supposedly be free of political interference and will guarantee political pluralism. A multiparty system, however, has not been guaranteed, and the League of Communists remains the only legal political party.

Markovic's reform program calls for more control over macroeconomic policy by the federal government and the creation of the legal basis for a single, united market economy with "pluralism of ownership," i.e., competition. Establishment of a uniform code of taxation, centralization of the state security force, and reform of the criminal code are also desired. The Slovenian republic has voiced objections to centralization of economic policy on the grounds that, in general, it is an encroachment on the sovereignty of the federal units of the country. Furthermore, Slovenia has been critical of the government for avoiding the issue of Serbia's boycott of Slovenia that began in November 1989. Serbia has consistently opposed the new program claiming that the poorer republics in the South will have to bear a disproportionate share of the burdens and sacrifices entailed by the reforms.

Ethnic feuds, the historical North-South disparity in wealth, and the resurgence of nationalism — particularly in Serbia — continue to muddle the political waters in Yugoslavia. As these factors combine with powerful forces demanding greater political reforms throughout Eastern Europe, the monopoly on the power of the League of Communists may be challenged or, possibly, even taken away altogether, thus calling into question the continued existence of the current Yugoslav republic.

Violent upheavals throughout 1991 have resulted in the dissolution of Yugoslavia into much smaller republics with very volatile political and economic foundations. Table 8-1 shows the land area of these republics.

Slovenia was the first republic to declare independence on June 25, 1991. Representing approximately 8% of the territory and population of Yugoslavia, yet producing 19% of the gross national product (Table 8-2), Slovenia ceded from the federation primarily on economic grounds. Its leadership was dissatisfied with the heavy-handed communist central planning in Belgrade. Slovenia's per capita income is close to double its neighboring republic, Croatia and almost three times the value for Serbia (Table 8-3). By the end of 1991, Slovenia had introduced its own flag and national currency and adopted a new constitution.

Croatia's parliament also declared its independence on June 25, 1991. Unlike Slovenia's secession, which went relatively calmly, Croatia's declaration immediately sparked violent rebellion from its Serbian minorities. Within six months, close to 10,000 lives were lost in the ensuing civil war with Serbia, the republic whose capital is Belgrade.

On January 15, 1992, bowing to pressure from member state Germany, the European Community formally recognized both Slovenia and Croatia as independent states.

Serbia is Yugoslavia's largest republic and has remained the bastion for continued communist control of the federation. Serbia has backed its political posture with military intervention; federal forces throughout Yugoslavia had always been under central control from Belgrade. It was the December 1990 re-election of hard-line communist Serbian President Slobodan Milosevic which ignited the disintegration of Yugoslavia. His 4-to-1 victory over his closest rival was a clear indication that Serbs took heart to his impassioned appeals to Serbian nationalism — largely at the cost of other ethnic minorities. By the end of 1991, Serbian government officials had proposed the formation of a smaller Yugoslavia, incorporating any smaller republics or national groups that may wish to join. To date, only the tiny Montenegro offered any hope for such a new union — neither it nor Serbia have requested recognition by the European Community.

Macedonia, Yugoslavia's poorest republic, voted for independence in September 1991. It was denied its request for recognition by the European Community, as EC-member Greece opposes Macedonian independence. Greece still asserts territorial claims over Macedonia, dating back to well before World War I.

Citizens in Bosnia-Hercegovina voted for independence in a referendum in October 1991. The new government petitioned the European Community for recognition but was denied. It is uncertain whether the EC will reconsider at any time in the near future.

Table 8-1: Land Area

Republic	Square Kilometers	Percentage of Total
Serbia	88,361	34.54
Serbia without Kosovo and Vojvodina	55,968	21.88
Kosovo	10,887	4.26
Vojvodina	21,506	8.41
Croatia	56,538	22.10
Bosnia and Herzegovina	51,129	19.99
Macedonia	25,713	10.05
Slovenia	20,251	8.10
Montenegro	13,812	5.40
Total	255,804	

Note: Percentages exceed 100% due to rounding.
Source: Yugoslavian Federal Statistical Office, 1989

Table 8-2: Social Product and National Income (1987)

Republic	Social Product Value	Social Product Percentage	National Income Value	National Income Percentage
Serbia	17,126	35	15,168	35
Serbia without Kosovo and Vojvodina	10,884	22	9,645	22
Kosovo	1,111	2	956	2
Vojvodina	5,131	10	4,567	10
Croatia	12,628	26	11,306	26
Slovenia	9,352	19	8,323	19
Bosnia and Herzegovina	6,503	13	5,634	13
Macedonia	2,667	5	2,360	5
Montenegro	936	2	787	2
Total	49,212		43,578	

Note: 1989 prices in billion dinars. Percentages exceed 100% due to rounding.
Source: Yugoslavian Federal Statistical Office, 1989

Table 8-3: Per Capita National Income

Republic	GNP	Population	Per Capita
Slovenia	8,323	1.9	3,520
Croatia	11,306	4.7	1,934
Serbia	15,168	9.8	1,244
Serbia without Kosovo and Vojvodina	9,645		
Kosovo	956		
Vojvodina	4,567		
Montenegro	787	0.6	1,054
Bosnia and Herzegovina	5,634	4.5	1,006
Macedonia	2,360	2.1	903
Total	43,578	23.8	1,472

Note: GNP is for 1987 at 1989 prices in billion dinars. Population is for 1990, in millions. Per capita GNP is in U.S. dollars (US $1 = 1,244 dinar). Percentages exceed 100% due to rounding.
Source: Yugoslavian Federal Statistical Office, 1989

Demographics

Socioeconomic Indicators and Conditions

With an annual growth rate of 0.6%, the 23.8 million Yugoslavs include a number of distinct nationalities. The primary groups include Serbs (37%), Croats (20%), Bosnians (9%), Slovenes and Albanians (each 8%), Macedonians (6%), Montenegrins (3%), and Hungarians (2%).

Only 14% of Yugoslavia's economy, including fisheries and forestry, is based on agriculture. More than 80% of the agricultural land is privately owned. Industry accounts for half of the economy, with socialized enterprise dominating. Inflation and unemployment remain among the highest in Europe.

Economic Outlook

Today, after outperforming most of its Eastern European neighbors a decade ago, Yugoslavia's economy is showing signs of fatigue. Liberal spending on ill-advised projects while ignoring the rules of the marketplace has taken its toll. Bureaucrats with little understanding of free enterprise have weakened the economic system by making poor decisions about the allocation of resources. The result has been reduced output, lackluster labor productivity, declining real personal income, and soaring inflation in the 1980s. The lesson of the Yugoslavian example, experts say, is that there is no middle path between a market economy and a centrally planned economy.

In January 1990, the government enacted a tough austerity plan to halt economic decline and curb inflation. Wage and price controls have been proposed. Its currency, the dinar, has been made convertible into U.S. dollars and West German D-marks.

Wages under Markovic's plan will be pegged to rates 18% and 32% higher than wages paid on December 15, 1989. Wages will be adjusted according to fluctuations in the new dinar versus the D-mark.

The new program will also remove price controls on nearly 85% of all commodities, thus allowing the market to determine most prices. Prices of essential items and services, such as electricity, gasoline, oil, coal for power plants, certain minerals, railroad, postal, and telephone services, will be controlled until June 30, 1991, after which time they will be adjusted according to changes in industrial production.

Implementations also associated with the new program include tighter monetary and budgetary controls, the freeing of interest rates, elimination of state subsidies to inefficient enterprises, and strict application of bankruptcy laws.

Western sales to Yugoslavia were estimated to be $8.4 billion in 1989. Sales projections in 1990 were expected to reach approximately $9.7 billion. Despite the opening of other Eastern European markets, Yugoslavia should retain its number two position behind the former Soviet Union in terms of Organization for Economic Cooperation and Development (OECD) sales. Yugoslav exports to the OECD should grow at more modest rates, perhaps around 8%. Exports to the OECD for 1989 were approximately $7.2 billion. Yugoslav exports still represent a good value.

Sales of consumer goods, computers, and enterprises which perform value-added operations for export represent excellent opportunities for sales. The market for heavy capital equipment looks hazy due to financial weaknesses and systematic problems that prevent adequate long-term investment planning.

The reformist government of Markovic views Western imports favorably, hoping that they will serve to break up local monopolies and combat inflation. Increased trade with the West and stronger implementation of market mechanisms form the foundation of Markovic's economic program. Ninety percent of all import categories fall under the title "free imports."

Banking reform laws envisage the appearance of new commercial banks and the modification of existing banks. Many banks will register in the hope of engaging in foreign transactions and will be set up according to the needs of their particular region. Banks in the more developed northern areas will undoubtedly be rated higher than their counterparts to the south. In all, banking in Yugoslavia may be quite confusing in the foreseeable future.

Foreign debt will remain a concern; however, support from the IMF will reassure most Western creditor banks and governments.

Current accounts should continue to show a surplus. Records for 1989 showed an estimated $2.5 billion surplus.

Real wages will likely drop under the new austerity measures, as will total industrial output.

The anti-inflation program and currency convertibility may attract more interest in joint ventures. Repatriation of profits seems to have been made simple, and existing joint venture laws are relatively uncomplicated.

Political/Institutional Infrastructure

Yugoslavia is a federation of six republics and two autonomous provinces. It has a collective presidency comprised of one representative from each of the republics and autonomous provinces, with the positions of president and vice-president rotating annually. The republics and provinces also send representatives to the Federal Assembly, which consists of two houses, a Federal Chamber, and a Chamber of Republics and Provinces.

The 1974 constitution gives broad powers to the republics and provinces, but until early 1990 the country was a one-party state with political control exercised at every level by the Communist party. Various non-Communist opposition groups have since been formed in all the republics, and nationalist rivalries have heightened to the point where the Federation appears close to collapse.

Trade Flows

In 1987, exports totaled $11.4 billion. Exports included raw materials and semi-manufactured goods (50%), consumer goods (31%), and capital goods and equipment (19%). Major markets are the European Community, Council for Mutual Economic Assistance (CMEA) countries, and the United States.

Imports in 1987 totaled $12.6 billion and included raw materials and semi-manufactured goods (79%), capital goods and equipment (15%), and consumer goods (6%). Major suppliers are the European Community, CMEA countries, and the United States.

Policies to Attract New Business

Free Trade Zones/Special Economic Zones

The purpose for setting up free trade zones in Yugoslavia is the promotion of manufacture and export products, not trade. The newly enacted Law on the Free Trade Zones and Customs Zones provides for requirements for setting up and developing the free trade zones. The law stipulates that new systematic solutions treat the free trade zones as an instrument of economic policy and an element of external economic relations. The solutions provided for in the law have brought about some major qualitative changes as follows:

- Differentiation between the free trade zones and the customs zones.
- An obligation specifying that the free trade zone must be a legal entity.
- The free trade zone must be set up in areas near harbors, ports, airports, or commodity-transportation centers.
- Conditions required to achieve a status of the free trade zone, such as space and premises available; power supply, technical, and other conditions for performing activities inside the free trade zone; and staff and personnel for carrying out operations of common interest for businesses using the free trade zone.

- Economic activities including manufacturing, warehousing, and/or providing services that do not endanger the country's security or environment
- Establishment of the free trade zone to be socially and economically justified.
- Operations and activities performed inside the zone defined as those generating foreign exchange (inflow).
- Users of the free trade zone to be the legal persons or natural persons, domestic or foreign, who have the funds invested in the zone. The founder of the zone can also be a foreign person investing in the construction of infrastructural projects inside the zone.
- Continuance of operations of existing customs zones with adjustment of their business activities accordingly within a period of three years and to reregister as the free trade zones.

These conditions of the law enable the ports, the harbors, the airports and the goods transportation centers to carry out their business activities. These activities include: warehousing, loading, unloading, reloading (transshipment), distribution of goods, construction of needed facilities, etc.

Several laws, such as the Customs Law, the Law on Foreign Trade Transactions, and the Law on Foreign Exchange Transactions also help to determine the conditions for carrying out economic activities inside the free trade zone.

Customs Zone

A customs zone is a part of the customs area of the Social Federal Republic of Yugoslavia in which there are applied special measures of customs surveillance and special concessions given in respect of customs procedure. A customs zone can be established in a seaport, an airport, or a riverport open to international public traffic and in a goods-transport center. The following operations can be performed in a customs zone:

1. Unloading, loading, reloading (transshipment), and storing of uncleared goods intended for export and goods to be transported.

2. Usual preparation of goods for market: sorting, measuring (weighing), marking, packing, equalization, assembling, dismantling, and sample taking.

APPROACHING THE MARKET

Setting Up Business Operations

Forms of Business Organization

According to the Foreign Investments Law, foreign investments in any forms have national status, i.e., an enterprise with foreign capital participation (joint venture) and foreign person's wholly owned enterprise (alien's enterprise), have a status of a Yugoslav legal entity, established and operating in accordance with Yugoslav regulations. According to the law, a foreign legal or individual entity or natural person may do the following:

1. Invest his or her resources in the existing socially owned enterprise — called in practice "joint venture organization." (This is a socially owned enterprise which does not provide for the co-ownership title or the foreign investor.)

2. Buy a socially owned enterprise or a part of the socially owned enterprise at a public competitive bidding, according to the law. The funds are paid by the foreign investor — buyer in favor of the Republican Fund for Development (Public Enterprise). By buying the socially owned enterprise the foreign investor becomes the owner, and by buying a part of the enterprise he or she becomes a co-owner of the enterprise.

3. Establish a mixed enterprise together with social-legal and/or civil-legal entities and/or natural persons, in the following forms: limited liability society, public limited society (joint-stock society), limited partnership, or unlimited partnership (unlimited joint and several liabilities society). This is an equity joint venture which provides for the co-ownership title over the resources invested by the foreign investor. On this basis, it provides his or her right to manage and control the enterprise, as well as other rights stipulated by joint venture incorporation contract and rules (by-laws) of enterprise.

4. Establish a shop, contractual enterprise, small-scale enterprise, agricultural holdings, etc., together with civil-legal entities and/or natural persons.

5. Establish his or her wholly owned enterprise (alien's enterprise) anywhere within the Yugoslav territory, excluding specific areas and specific activities (private enterprise).

6. Obtain a concession for the exploitation of certain renewable natural resources or goods in common use.

7. Obtain a permission for the construction, management, and exploitation of certain economic facilities, installation or plant for a limited period of time (System B.O.T. — build, operate, transfer).

Representative Offices

Conditions for the establishment and performance of activities of foreign persons in Yugoslavia have been liberalized as concerning the number of representative offices to be established by the foreign person in Yugoslavia, as well as conditions to be met by the foreign person on the establishment of the representative office. The foreign person is entitled to establish several representative offices and operating units, thus contributing to the development of economic relations and promotion of business relations between foreign persons and Yugoslav enterprises. The foreign person, in addition to general requirements, should meet the specific conditions referred to in Article 4 of the Regulation on Precise Conditions for Establishment and Performance of Activities by Foreign Representative Offices in Yugoslavia.

Agents and Distributors

Sale of goods and services in Yugoslavia were affected by the foreign persons engaging exclusively in Yugoslav socially owned enterprises by transferring to them the authorization to perform agency operations and organization of sale of goods from the consignment stock. The law provides the founding of mixed and private enterprises in Yugoslavia, thus creating different conditions for further promotion of agency operations and sale of goods from the consignment stock. The Law on Foreign Trade Transactions and the Provision on Agency operations in Yugoslavia stipulate rules and regulations for agency operations. The requirements include the following:

- Obligatory written contract on agency operations;
- Duration of the contract at least for the period of one year;
- Obligatory contractual clause on validity of the agency operations contract concerning representing foreign principal on the whole territory of the Socialist Federal Republic of Yugoslavia;
- Strict observance of the general agency provisions covering the entire production program by the foreign principal and exclusive agency operations; and
- Obligatory presentation for evidencing the contract with the Federal Secretariat for Economic Relations Abroad.

There are also prescribed conditions to be fulfilled at the conclusion of the contract on agency operations representing simultaneously valid text of the contract, such as personal information of the contractual parties, the subject of the contract, rights, and obligations of the parties.

INVESTMENT CLIMATE

Joint Ventures and Wholly Owned Subsidiaries

A foreign investor can establish a joint venture by investing his or her resources in an existing socially owned enterprise. Regulations on foreign investments are described in the Foreign Investments Law, Enterprises Law, and other Yugoslav regulations. According to the law, an enterprise with foreign capital participation shall have the same status, rights, and obligations on the market as other Yugoslav enterprises in terms of price formation, import, export, customs duties, taxation, etc. The law provides for no limits as to the foreign party's share; his or her stake in nominal capital may exceed 50%. Also, the foreign parties can be all legal entities with a seat in a foreign country, as well as foreign natural persons. Under the provision of the Yugoslav law, foreign persons may invest their resources in all economic (production, trade, and services) and social activities. There are also requirements for a foreign shareholder's contributions as specified in the law.

Taxation and Regulatory Conditions

Yugoslavia has been carrying out reform of the tax system in stages. The Law on the Basis of Taxation System refers to the state's regulation of the basis of taxation systems which are of interest for the functioning of the unified Yugoslav market and for state budgetary revenue. The law determines the following: taxpayers, sources, kinds of taxes, and tax basis. Other elements of the system — tax rates, tax exemptions, and tax facilities, as well as the system of other taxes which are not of an importance for the functioning of the unified Yugoslav markets — are regulated by the republics and provincial laws.

Sources of Income Liable to Taxation

According to the Law on the Basis of Taxation System, enterprises with foreign capital participation (joint ventures), as well as alien's enterprises are liable for the following taxes:

- Personal income tax of the employed workers
- Personal income tax of the foreign persons employed in the enterprise
- Tax on enterprise profits
- Tax on foreign persons revenue realized through their engagement in international transport activities

Company Tax

Tax on enterprise profits is paid on the account of a base which represents a difference between gross income and gross expenditures accepted for the purpose of taxation, including the following: (1) material costs; (2) depreciation costs as stipulated by the law; (3) cost of labor (gross personal incomes based on current labor); and (4) other expenditures.

Personal Income Tax

Personal income tax of the employed workers is in the competence of the state and will be determined by the federal regulation. This tax is included in the gross personal income of the workers employed in a joint venture or alien's enterprise and represents the enterprise expenditures.

The tax on foreign persons personal income is in the competence of the state and will be uniformly regulated by a separate federal law. This tax is paid by foreign persons employed in a joint venture or alien's enterprise. Taxpayer is a foreign person realizing revenue by providing transportation services (without having a representative office in Yugoslavia) under the condition that his or her residential country applies the same tax on Yugoslav persons engaged in transportation on a reciprocal basis.

Tax on Goods and Services

In addition to these taxes, the Law on Turnover Tax for Goods and Service envisages basic and specific tax on goods and services turnover. Tax basis for a turnover tax is a retail price of products and services sold. The tax is incorporated in a price of these products and services and is payable by consumers (consumption taxation). Basic turnover tax applies to the entire Yugoslav territory, whereas the specific turnover tax applies for the republics and provinces, in accordance to their regulations.

FINANCIAL MARKETS

Payment Modalities

The Currency

The monetary reforms of Markovic created the convertible dinar. The "new" dinar was pegged to the West German D-mark at the rate of D7 = Dm1 until the end of June 1990 and was declared convertible. The national bank has promised to intervene when necessary to maintain this rate. Officials have stated that the new dinar will allow enterprises and individuals to convert Yugoslav currency to Western currency on demand, thus greatly enhancing Yugoslavia's market attraction for foreign suppliers.

Financial Market Operations

Money Market and Capital Market

The Law on Money Market and Capital Market regulates the establishment of money markets and capital markets, their status, and intermediation in money and securities trading. Certain guidelines are offered regarding the regulation of these markets they include the following:

1. As organizations of financial intermediation, money markets and capital markets are founded to link the supply and demand of money and securities.

2. These markets are founded by banks and other financial institutions.

3. The money market and capital market are founded at the constituent assembly of the market, which comprises representatives of the founders. In addition, it adopts the by-laws and rules of procedure for the work of the market and appoints the managing board of the market.

4. The National Bank of Yugoslavia gives approval for the start-up work of the money market and supervises the operations thereof. The National Bank of Yugoslavia is also a participant in the work of the money market on the basis of regulating the volume of supply and demand of money and short-term securities.

5. The by-laws of the market determine:

   - the internal organization of the market;
   - the functions of the managing board and other bodies;

- criteria to be fulfilled by its participants;
- the type of securities traded on the market;
- the rights and duties of the participants;
- the manner of supervision regarding transactions by the managing board;
- the manner of resolving disputes relative to the market's affairs; and
- other questions relative to the work of the market.

6. Money markets and capital markets are legal entities.

7. Banks and other financial organizations may be participants in the work of the money market. In capital markets, on the other hand, participants may be banks and other financial institutions as well as social funds and enterprises and other legal entities through their duly authorized participants.

8. Participants in the markets act on the markets in their own name and for their own account, in their own name and for the account of other persons and in the name and for the account of other persons. Participants must also pay a commission on concluded transactions with money and securities.

9. Intermediation in transactions with money and short-term securities are carried out on the money market. Intermediation with long-term securities, on the other hand, shall be carried out on the capital market.

Securities Market

The Law on Securities prescribes the terms and modes of issuance and transfer of shares, bonds, treasury bills, certificates, and commercial notes (hereinafter securities). As a definition, a security is a written document issued to bearer or as a registered security. Securities may be issued by enterprise, banks and other financial organizations, insurance organizations, sociopolitical communities and other legal persons (hereinafter issuer). Securities may be denominated in dinars and in foreign currency. The Federal Executive Council appoints the members of the commission which approves the issuance of securities. The council also prescribes the composition, methods of work, and scope of activity of the commission. The law also defines the rights and duties of the issuer and bearer.

A share of a security is a document on ownership of resources invested in an enterprise, bank, or other issuers as stipulated by the law. The shareholder is entitled to a part of the profits and, depending on the kind of share, may also have the right to participate in management. Shares may be denominated in dinars or in foreign currency, but are bought and sold on the Yugoslav market for dinars.

The Law on Securities defines the different types of securities traded on the market. They are as follows:

1. A bond is a document in writing whereby the issuer undertakes to pay the person designated in the bond, or by his or her order, or to the bearer of the bond, on the specified day the amount designated on the bond or the sum of the annuity coupon. Participants in this market include banks, enterprises, and other issuers as stipulated above.

2. A Treasury bill is a security denominated in a specific sum, with a specified maturity period and specified interest rate. Treasury bills are issued by the National Bank of Yugoslavia, banks, other financial institutions, and sociopolitical communities.

3. A certificate is a document regarding resources deposited in a bank or other financial organization with a maturity date of over one year.

4. A commercial note is a written security which is sold for the purpose of procuring short-term resources. Notes are issued by enterprises, cooperatives, and other forms of associations with the status of legal entities.

Gold Market

Gold may be exported and taken abroad, in unprocessed or forged form, by the National Bank of Yugoslavia, gold manufacturers (only in unprocessed form), and banks authorized to perform international activities (only in forged form).Other domestic persons may take out gold in unprocessed or forged form only with approval by the National Bank of Yugoslavia.

Gold to be imported is paid freely under the approval issued by the Federal Secretariat for Foreign Economic Relations.

In the case that payment liquidity and foreign exchange reserves and their structure request it, the Federal Executive Council may restrict or prohibit export and taking of gold abroad, as well as restrict the gold trading in the country.

LICENSING, PATENTS, AND TRADEMARKS

Trademark, Patent, and Copyright Protection

Protection of inventions and origin identification marks in Yugoslavia is made in compliance with The Law on the Protection of Inventions, Technical Improvements, and Trademark (Patent Law). Amendments to the law were made attempting to stimulate both the Yugoslav and foreign inventors to protect their inventions in Yugoslavia, as well as to enable Yugoslav patent right to comply with the international conventions to which Yugoslavia has already entered. The essential provisions of the amended patent law are as follows:

1. Duration of the patent is extended to a 20 year term. Models and designs are protected for ten years from the day of the patent application date. Trademark is protected for ten years from the application date, provided that its validity may be extended to unlimited duration for several times. The origin identification mark is protected in unlimited duration.

2. The patent protection has been extended to (1) all matters created either by physical or chemical processes and (2) application of matter for any purposes, as well as for medical treatment of people and animals.

3. The patent cannot protect: (1) innovations, the announcement and application of which, is not consistent with the law or is contrary to the moral and (2) selected plants and animal breeds.

The amended law stipulates the main elements which should be included in the patent application. These include the following: (1) description of the innovative product, (2) indication of essentially new elements in the innovative product, (3) what the patent applicant wants to protect, and (4) stating, at least, one manner for application of the innovative product.

VISITING AND LOCATING

General Travel Checklist

Visas

A valid U.S. passport is required and no entry visa is currently required. Visas were available at all border crossings, airports, and Yugoslav embassies and consulates. There was no charge for a visa in the past and no photograph was required.

Currency

The Yugoslav currency is the New Yugoslav Dinar (NYD). One U.S. dollar is equivalent to 10 NYD. Credit cards, such as American Express, Visa, MasterCard, and Diners Club, are readily accepted as are all traveler's checks. Traveler's checks can be exchanged at all hotels, banks, and currency exchange offices throughout

Yugoslavia. Dollars can be purchased at banks, and the local currency is convertible o dollars.

Getting Around

Yugoslavia has six international airports: Belgrade, 12 miles west of the city; Dubrovnik, 13 miles from the city; Ljubljana, 21 miles from the city; Split, 15.5 miles from town; Zagreb, 10 miles southwest of the city; and Sarajevo, 10 miles from the city. Coaches and taxis are available from all airports except Sarajevo. JAT Yugoslav Airlines, the country's flag-carrier, has a network of internal flights between major cities and most other major towns. The best way to see all the country has to offer, with limited time, is to fly from city to city.

Rail service is also an option. The main line runs from Ljubljana to Zagreb, Belgrade and Skopje, with four branches to the coast. Children under the age of four travel free; children up to the age of 12 travel at a 50% discount. Supplements are charged for express and "fast" trains.

Most travelers will want to visit one or more of the many picturesque islands off the country's Adriatic coastline. Regular ferry services run to the following islands: Cres, Krk, Rab, Pag, Ugljan, Pasman, Solta, Brac, Hvar, Korcula, Mljet, and the peninsula of Peljesac.

Car rentals are another option. A variety of firms, including Hertz and Avis, have offices located in nearly all major towns and all tourist resorts. Drivers of foreign-registered cars can use foreign currency at all frontier crossings to buy gasoline coupons. Gas stations are widely available, easily accessible, and many sell lead-free gasoline. The speed limits are 120 km/hour on motorways, 100 km/hour on most highways except the coast, and 60 km/hour unless otherwise posted. The condition of major roads is excellent. The Adriatic highway is a fine motoring network.

Accommodations and Housing

Yugoslavia has a wide variety of accommodations to meet the budgetary and luxury requirements of every traveler. Visitors can select from deluxe, first, second, third, and fourth class hotels, vacation apartments, guest houses, or campgrounds for tents and trailers. Accommodation rates tend to be higher in the main cities and resorts and lower in the smaller resorts and inland regions. Costs are highest in the peak tourist season of July and August.

Electricity Supply

Electricity is supplied at 220 Volts AC. Most outlets are of the two-pin plug, round variety. Americans and Canadians should bring a transformer/adapter or dual-voltage appliances.

Telecom, Postal, and Courier Services

Regarding telephone services, international calls can be made from certain pay phones in all areas. International direct dial service is available. Yugoslavia's country code is 38.

Telex facilities are available in the main international hotels and central post offices. Fax machines are also available throughout Yugoslavia.

Airmail to the United States takes approximately one week. Stamps are available at bookstores nationwide.

Business Hours

Banks are open from 7:30 a.m. to 12:00 p.m. Monday through Friday. Currency exchange offices are open from 7:00 a.m. to 11:00 p.m.

Public holidays include the following: New Year's Day, January 1st and 2nd; Labor Day, May 1st and 2nd; July 4th; Veterans Day; and Republic Day, November 29th and 30th.

Tipping

Ten percent is the normal tipping in hotels, restaurants, and taxis.

What to Wear

The type of clothing required will depend on location and time of year. Yugoslavia has two main climatic regions. The north of the country has a continental climate with hot summer and cold winters, while the Adriatic Coast is Mediterranean in climate with warm summers and mild winters. Inland temperatures range from a low of 37 degrees in January to a high of 84 degrees in July, while coastal temperatures range from a low of 50 degrees in January to a high of 80 degrees in July.

A general guideline for winter is layered medium-weight clothing and an overcoat. A heavier overcoat, gloves, and a scarf are usually required inland. During summer, lightweight clothing and a raincoat will be all you require. A sun hat is advisable, especially on the coast.

Health Care

As for all Western Europe, no special inoculations are necessary. Tap water is chlorinated and is completely safe to drink. Charges are made for prescribed medicine and proof of nationality is required before treatment is given.

Shopping

Shops are generally open Monday to Friday from 8:00 a.m. to 12:00 p.m. and then reopen from 4:00 p.m. to 8:00 p.m. On Saturdays, shops are open from 8:00 a.m. to 3:00 p.m.

Large department stores and self-service shops in major towns generally stay open throughout the day. Items to look for include embroidery, lace, crystal, leatherwork, handicrafts, and designer clothing.

Sightseeing and Tourist Information

For further information on any aspect of traveling to or within Yugoslavia, contact the Yugoslav National Tourist Office, 630 Fifth Avenue, New York, NY 10111, or call 212/757-2801.

JAT Yugoslav Airlines also has offices in New York. Tel: 212/246-6401 or 1-800-PLAN JAT.

The American Embassy in Yugoslavia is located at Kneza Milosa 50, Belgrade, Yugoslavia 11000. Tel: 11-645-655.

Sporting Activities

Yugoslavia is ideal for all types of land and water-based sports. Among the more popular are hunting, fishing, sailing , and skiing.

Hunting is popular in the mountains. A permit from the Belgrade National Hunting Association is required.

Permits are available from hotels, travel agencies, or local authorities for fishing. Fishing on the Adriatic Coast is unrestricted, but freshwater angling and fishing with equipment need a permit. The best way to learn of the country's prime fishing areas and associated rules and regulations is when applying for a fishing permit.

Sailing and boating are popular all along the coastline and on major lakes. Renting and chartering (both bare-boat and with crew) are widely available. Excellent marinas and facilities are also widely provided along the coast and on most of the islands.

Yugoslavia boasts some of the finest ski areas in all of Europe.

Languages

The official language of Yugoslavia is Serbo-Croatian or Croato-Serbian. Latin and Cyrillic are the two alphabets used. The Macedonians and Slovenians have their own language: Macedonian and Slovene. English is widely spoken in the major towns and resort areas.

The Short-Term Business Visitor

Airlines Serving

JAT is the Yugoslavian national airline. Lufthansa, Olimpic, British Air and a host of other major airlines serve Belgrade and a few smaller cities.

Rent-an-Office Facilities

Several services are offered as a part of a business center. Some of these include full secretarial services, photocopying, typewriters, dictation equipment, personal computer, video cassette recorder, and film sound projector.

YUGOSLAVIA

KEY CONTACTS FOR BUSINESS

The Republic of Slovenia
1300 19th Street, NW 4th Floor
Washington, DC 20036
  Tel: 202/828-1650
  Fax: 202/828-1654

Slovenian National Home
6411 St. Clair Avenue #8
Cleveland, OH 44103
  Tel: 216/391-4000
  Fax: 216/391-4001
Chairmanl: Edmund J. Turk

U.S.-Yugoslav Trade/Economic Council
818 18th Street, NW #230
Washington, DC 20006
  Tel: 202/857-0170
Contactl: Richard Johnson

U.S. Department of Commerce
14th & Constitution Avenue, NW
Washington, DC 20030
  Tel: 202/377-5373
Yugoslavia Desk Officer: Jeremy Keller

Yugoslav Chamber of Economy
767 Third Avenue 24th Floor
New York, NY 10017
  Tel: 212/355-7117
Contact: Cedomil Stanicic
  Tel: 415/391-2499
Contact: Zarko Petkov (San Francisco)

Yugoslav Press & Cultural Center
767 Third Avenue 18th Floor
New York, NY 10017
  Tel: 212/838-2306
Contact: Damir Grubisa

UNIDO Investment Promotion Service
1660 L Street, NW #215
Washington, DC 20036
    Tel: 202/659-5165
    Fax: 202/659-7674
    Telexl: 3730475 IPS WSH

Progres-Beograd Trading Company
Knez Mihajlova 27
11000 Beograd
    Tel: 38-11-623-766
    Fax: 38-11-632-984
635 Madison Avenue
New York, NY 10022
    Tel: 212/758-2315 or 758-3070
    Fax: 212/755-6014 or 486-0804
President: Ratomir Zivkovic

LBS Bank (Ljubljanska Banka)
101 East 52nd Street
New York, NY 10022
    Tel: 212/980-8600
    Fax: 212/593-1967

Yugoslav Chamber of Economy
Terazije 23
11000 Beograd
    Tel: 38-11-336-251 or 339-461

Chamber of Economy of Bosnia & Herzegovina
Mis Irbina 13
71000 Sarajevo
    Tel: 38-71-31-777

Chamber of Economy of Croatia
Roosweltov trg 2
41000 Zagreb
    Tel: 38-41-443-422

Chamber of Economy of Kosovo
Marsala Tita 28
38000 Pristina
    Tel: 38-38-24-055 or 24-683

Chamber of Economy of Macedonia
Ivo Lola Ribar 25
91000 Skopje
    Tel: 38-91-33-210 or 33-230

Chamber of Economy of Montenegro
Novaka Miloseva 11
81000 Titograd
    Tel: 38-81-22-311 or 22-316

Chamber of Economy of Serbia
Generala Zdanova 15
11000 Beograd
    Tel: 38-11-240-611

Chamber of Economy of Slovenia
Titova 19
61000 Ljubljana
    Tel: 38-61-23-951

Chamber of Economy of Vojvodina
Bul. Marsala Tita 23
21000 Novi Sad
    Tel: 38-21-57-022

EASTERN EUROPE KEY CONTACTS

EASTERN EUROPE BUSINESS INFORMATION CENTER (EEBIC)

To meet business needs for information on new trade and investment opportunities in Eastern Europe, (former) Secretary of Commerce Robert A. Mosbacher opened the Commerce Department's Eastern Europe Business Information Center (EEBIC) on January 23, 1990. The center was mandated by Congress under the Support for East European Democracy (SEED) Act, enacted in late 1989.

EEBIC serves as a central clearinghouse for information on business opportunities in Eastern Europe and on U.S. government programs supporting expanded private enterprise, trade, and investment. EEBIC is also a referral point for programs of voluntary assistance to the region. It encourages development of economically sound proposals for the Polish-American, Hungarian-American, and Czechoslovak-American Enterprise Funds. During his visit to Hungary and Poland in July 1989, President Bush announced establishment of these funds to assist the growth of private enterprise.

EEBIC works closely with other U.S. government agencies with programs in Eastern Europe, including the Agency for International Development, the Overseas Private Investment Corporation, and the U.S. Trade and Development Program. Staff members include representatives of the Commerce Department, the Small Business Administration, and other government agencies.

Correspondence with the Center may be directed to the following address:

Eastern Europe Business Information Center
U.S. Department of Commerce
14th and Constitution Avenue, NW
Washington, DC 20230
Tel: 202/377-2645

U.S. DEPARTMENT OF COMMERCE
EASTERN EUROPEAN INFORMATION RESOURCES

1. International Trade Administration

    A. Support for Eastern European Democracy (SEED) Information
       Susan Blackman, Director
       Tel: 202/377-2645

    B. Country Desk Officers (Tel: 202/377-4915)

Director, Eastern Europe	Jay Burgess
Poland	Will Winter
Hungary	Russ Johnson
Bulgaria	Russ Johnson
Czechoslovakia	Russ Johnson
Yugoslavia	Jeremy Keller
Romania	Mary Moscaluk

    C. Office of Telecommunications
       Richard Paddock, Director for Major Projects
           Tel: 202/377-1304

2. National Telecommunications and Information Administration
   Jack Gleason, Director
       Tel: 202/377-1304

3. Office of Technology Policy Assessment
   William Clements, Director
       Tel: 202/377-4188

4. Bureau of Export Administration
   Joe Westlake, Director
       Tel: 202/377-0730

U.S. TRADE AND DEVELOPMENT PROGRAM (TDP)

The Trade and Development Program (TDP), is an independent U.S. government agency of the International Development Cooperation Agency (IDCA), which promotes economic development in middle income and developing countries by funding feasibility studies and other project planning services. In Eastern Europe, TDP assists U.S. firms by identifying major development projects which offer large export potential and by funding U.S. private sector involvement in project planning.

This, in turn, helps position U.S. firms for following on contracts when these projects are implemented.

TDP currently has activities in Bulgaria, Czechoslovakia, Hungary, Poland, and Romania. Yugoslavia has been temporarily placed on hold due to U.S. government travel restrictions, and Albania is expected to commence program activities shortly after the American embassy is activated in Tirana. In January 1992, activities commenced in the Baltic states of Lithuania, Latvia, and Estonia.

TDP activities cover a wide range of sectors of high priority to host governments and international development efforts. Additionally, TDP has statutory authority to facilitate access to natural resources of interest to the United States. U.S. technological expertise can help accelerate the development process in all these sectors. They include, but are not limited to telecommunications, industry, energy development, transportation, educational technology, minerals development, and waste treatment.

Since 1985, TDP has had an ongoing program in Yugoslavia and had funded a number of studies in that country, particularly in the energy and industrial sectors. TDP initiated its program in Hungary in July 1989 with a grant for a study of a project to down-size an inefficient metallurgical complex at Miskolc, Borsod County.

TDP has channeled its initial efforts using the $2 million of appropriated 1990 SEED funds in Poland and Hungary to the telecommunications sector. In Hungary, a grant to the Ministry of Transport, Communications, and Construction was awarded for a master plan for a new digital overlay network and for a technical orientation visit of Hungarian telecommunications officials to the United States. In Poland, TDP provided a grant to the Ministry of Communications for a planning study for the modernization of the Polish telecommunications system.

Other areas of expressed interest which TDP will pursue subject to availability of funds will include power sector modernization, transportation, and selected industrial priorities.

For more information on the TDP program in Eastern Europe, inquiries may be addressed to Geoffrey Jackson, Regional Director for Eastern Europe, SA-16, Room 309, Washington, D.C. 20523-1602, Tel: 703/875-4357; Fax: 703/875-4009.

OVERSEAS PRIVATE INVESTMENT CORPORATION (OPIC)

The Overseas Private Investment Corporation (OPIC) is a self-sustaining U.S. government agency whose purpose is to promote economic growth in developing countries by encouraging U.S. private investment in those nations.

In April 1989, President Bush announced the framework of American policy towards Eastern Europe. Congress then authorized OPIC to operate in Poland and Hungary. In October 1990, OPIC signed bilateral agreements with those governments and in November 1990 led a mission of 29 U.S. companies to Warsaw to look at investment opportunities. By the end of fiscal year 1990, 110 Americans firms had applied for OPIC investment insurance or financing for projects in Eastern Europe. Investor demand remained so great that OPIC organized back-to-back investment missions for Hungary and Poland in April 1990.

OPIC's key programs are its loan guaranties, direct loans, and political risk insurance. For example, OPIC recently approved its first project in Eastern Europe: insurance for the General Electric Company's $150 million investment to purchase a Hungarian electric lighting products company. OPIC professionals are now working with American companies and Hungarian and Polish counterparts to structure scores of additional investment projects in Hungary and Poland.

Other OPIC programs applicable to Eastern Europe include: the Eastern European Growth Fund, designed to match OPIC funds with private venture capital to finance new business enterprises; the Small Business Loan Guaranty Program for Poland which will provide loans to U.S. small business investors; and an Environmental Investment Fund which will invest in environmentally sound natural resource enterprises.

In 1990, Congress also authorized OPIC programs in Bulgaria, Romania, East Germany, Czechoslovakia, and any other East European or Baltic state which the president might designate.

For additional information on OPIC programs in Eastern Europe, please address your inquires to James V. Hall, Director of Public Affairs, Telephone: 202/457-7093; Fax: 202/223-3514.

PRIVATE CAPITAL INSTITUTIONS ACTIVE IN EAST/WEST BUSINESS

Dan McGovern, Senior Economist
Bank of America
555 California Street
San Francisco, CA 94104
Tel: 415/622-2073

Natasha Gurfinkel
Bank of New York
One Wall Street
New York, New York 10017
Tel: 212/635-8130

Prudencio L. Vieira
Bankers Trust
280 Park Avenue
New York, NY 10017
    Tel: 212/850-4882

Barclays Bank PLC
75 Wall Street
New York, NY 10017
    Tel: 212/412-3661

Brian Murray, Manager/Director
Bears, Stearns & Co., Inc.
245 Park Avenue
New York, NY 10167
    Tel: 212/272-3596

CAWT - Creditanstalt
245 Park Avenue
New York, NY 10167
    Tel: 212/559-8577

Gail Buyske, Vice President
Chase Manhattan
One Chase Manhattan Plaza
14th Floor
New York, NY 10081
    Tel: 212/552-4676

Mauri Kutila, Vice President
Chemical Bank
277 Park Ave.
New York, NY 10172
    Tel: 212/310-5370

Miljenko Horvat
Citibank
399 Park Avenue
New York, NY 10043
    Tel: 212/559-8577

Robert I. Thomas,
    Assistant Vice President
International Structured Finance
    Group
First National Bank of Chicago
One First National Plaza -
    Mail Suite 0040
Chicago, IL 60670
    Tel: 312/732-6796

Kristyan Schellander, Manager
Girozentrale Vienna
Schwarzenbergplatz 2
Vienna, AUSTRIA
    Tel: 43-1-71-194-2837

Stephen Xavier Graham, President
Graham, Rogers & Company, Inc.
1730 K Street, NW #900
Washington, DC 20006
    Tel: 202/296-1789
    Fax: 202/296-7783

Daniel Kazdan,
Product Manager - Eastern Europe
ICD
641 Lexington Avenue
11th Floor
New York, NY 10022
    Tel: 212/644-1509

Ian Clark, Managing Director
J.P. Morgan & Company
60 Wall Street
New York, NY 10260
    Tel: 212/648-7597
    Fax: 212/837-5053

Manufacturer's Hanover
270 Park Avenue
New York, NY 10022
    Tel: 212/286-3314

Roger Kodat, Vice President
MG Trade Finance Corporation
520 Madison Avenue
New York, NY 10022
    Tel: 212/826-2120

Donna Gavin
National Westminister
175 Water Street
New York, NY 10038
    Tel: 212/826-2120

Phillip Brothers, Inc.
1221 Avenue of Americas
New York, NY 10020
    Tel: 212/790-5127

Henry Owen, Director - Eastern Europe
Salomon Brothers, Inc.
1616 H Street, NW 4th Floor
Washington, DC 20006
    Tel: 202/783-7000
    Fax: 202/393-4655

Jeffery Malakoff, Vice President
Security Pacific Trade Finance
595 Madison Avenue
New York, NY 10022
    Tel: 212/644-0020

COMMERCIAL OFFICES OF EAST EUROPEAN COUNTRIES IN THE UNITED STATES

Albania

Sazan Bejo
Charge D'Affairs
Albanian Mission to U.N.
320 E 79th Street
New York, NY 10021
   Tel: 212/249-2059
   Tel: 301/649-4562 (DC metro)

Bulgaria

Dimiter Karamfilov
Commercial Counselor
Bulgaria Commercial Office
121 East 62nd Street
New York, NY 10021
   Tel: 212/935-4646

Czech & Slovak Federal Republic

Richard Hlavaty
Commercial Counselor
Czechoslovak Commercial Office
292 Madison Ave, 18th Floor
New York, NY 10017
   Tel: 212/532-2662

Igor Snobl
Second Secretary
Czech & Slovak Federal Republic
3900 Linnean Avenue
Washington, DC 20008
   Tel: 202/363-6315
   Fax: 202/966-8540

Republic of Hungary

Dr. Jazsef Heiszig
Commercial Counselor
Embassy of Hungary
150 East 58th St, 33rd Floor
New York, NY 10022
   Tel: 212/752-3060

Ivan Nowak
Commercial Attache
Hungarian Commercial Office
1930 East Prudential Plaza
130 East Randolph Drive
Chicago, IL 60601
   Tel: 312/856-0274

Republic of Poland

Bazyli Samojlik
Commercial Counselor
Embassy of Poland
2224 Wyoming Ave, NW
Washington, D.C. 20008
   Tel: 202/232-4528

Jerzy Kapuscinski
Commercial Counselor
Commercial Office
820 Second Ave, 17th Floor
New York, NY 10017
   Tel: 212/370-5300

Romania

Vamfir Moise
Economic Counselor
Romanian Commercial Office
573 Third Avenue
New York, NY 10016
Tel: 212/682-9120

Yugoslavia

Lililjana Milojevic-Borovcanin
First Secretary
Embassy of SFR Yugoslavia
2410 California Street, NW
Washington, DC 20008
Tel: 202/462-6566

U.S. COMMERCIAL OFFICERS IN EASTERN EUROPE

Albania

Rich Muller
Economic/Commercial Counsel
American Embassy Tirana
Box A, PSC 59, APO, AE 09624
Tel: 355-42-32-874 or 875
Tel: 355-42-33-520
Fax: 355-42-32-222

Bulgaria

Michael Gelner
Economic/Commercial Officer
American Embassy Sofia (SOF)
APO, NY 09213
Tel: 359-1-884801
Fax: none
Telex: 22690 BG

Czech and Slovak Federal Republic

Janet Speck
Commercial Attache
American Embassy Prague (PRG)
APO, NY 09213
Tel: 42-2-536641
Fax: 42-2-532457
Telex: 121196 AMEMBC

Republic of Hungary

Patrick Hughes
Senior Commercial Officer
American Embassy Budapest (BUD)
APO, NY 09213
Tel: 36-1-1126450
Fax: 36-1-1328934
Telex: 227136 USCDC H

Republic of Poland

Edgar Fulton
Senior Commercial Officer
U.S. Trade Center/American
   Embassy Poland
APO, NY 09213
48-22-214515
Fax: 48-22-216327
Telex: 813934 USTDO PL

Romania

Kay Kuhlman
Senior Commercial Officer
American Embassy Bucharest
   (BUH)
APO, NY 09213
40-0-104040
Fax: None
Telex: 11416

Yugoslavia

David K. Katz
Commercial Counselor
American Embassy Belgrade
Kneza Milosa 50
APO, NY 09213
    Tel: 38-11-645-655
    Telex: 11529

VALUABLE PHONE NUMBERS FOR COMMERCIAL ASSISTANCE IN THE UNITED STATES

U.S. Department of Commerce

East European Business Information Center (EEBIC)
Room 7412
14th & Constitution Avenue, NW
Washington, DC 20030
    Tel: 202/377-2645
    Fax: 202/377-4473
    (The "one-stop shop" for all business information regarding the region, including information on U.S. government funding of programs for the region, market research, publications, directories, and expertise/referrals.)

Office of Domestic Service
Export Counseling Center: Room 10066
    (Export counseling and marketing assistance) 202/377-3181

Export Promotion Services
Office of Information Product Development & Distribution:
Washington, DC 20044
(Reports on markets and trade leads) 202/377-2432

Office of Marketing Programs
    (Trade shows and trade missions)..202/377-4231
Information on *Commercial News USA* and other
    Commerce export-related publications 202/377-5367

Trade Development: Product Service Specialists

Aerospace: Room 6877..202/377-8228
Automotive Affairs and Consumer Goods: Room 4324...................202/377-0823
Basic Industries: Room 4045..202/377-0614
Capital Goods & Construction: Room 2001B.............................202/377-5023
Export Trading Company Affairs: Room 5618.............................202/377-5131
International Major Projects: Room 2007....................................202/377-5225
Science & Electronics: Room 1001A...202/377-4466
Services: Room 1128..202/377-5261
Textiles & Apparel: Room 3100..202/377-4466
Trade Information & Analysis: Room 3814B................................202/377-1316

Trade Administration: Office of Export Administration

Exporter's Service Staff: (Export Licensing,
    controls, etc.) Room 1099...202/377-4811

U.S. Department of Treasury

U.S. Department of Treasury
15th & Pennsylvania Avenue, NW
Washington, DC 20220

U.S. Customs Strategic Investigation Division 202/566-9464
    (Exodus Command Center)

Office of the United States Trade Representative

Winder Building
600 17th Street, NW
Washington, DC 20506

General Counsel..202/395-3150
Private Sector Liaison..202/395-6120
Agriculture Affairs & Commodity Policy....................................202/395-6127
The Americas Trade Policy 202/395-6135
East-West & Non-Market Economies...202/395-4543
Europe & Japan 202/395-4620

General Agreement on Tariff and Trade (GATT)..............................202/395-6843
Industrial & Energy Trade Policy..202/395-7320
Investment Policy..202/395-3510
Pacific, Asia, Africa & North-South Trade Policy..........................202/395-3430

Small Business Administration (SBA)

All export programs administered through SBA are available through SBA field offices. More information about the programs can be obtained through:

Small Business Administration (SBA)..202/653-7794
Office of International Trade
1441 L Street, NW
Washington, DC 20416

FINANCIAL INSTITUTIONS ACTIVE IN EAST/WEST BUSINESS (March 1991)

Bank of America
555 California Street
San Francisco, CA 94104
   Tel: 415/622-2073
Contact: Dan McGovern,
   Sr. Economist

Bank of New York
One Wall Street
New York, NY 10017
   Tel: 212/635-8130
Contact: Natasha Gurfinkel

Bankers Trust
280 Park Avenue
New York, NY 10017
   Tel: 212/850-4882
Contact: Prudencio L. Vieira

Girozentrale Vienna
Schwarzenbergplatz 2
Vienna, Austria
   Tel: 011/431-71194-2837
Contact: Kristyan Schellander,
   Manager

CAWT- Creditanstalt
245 Park Avenue
New York, NY 10167
   Tel: 212/559-8577

ICD
641 Lexington Ave.
11th Floor
   Tel: 212/644-1509
New York, NY 10022
Contact: Daniel Kazdan,
   Product Manager, Eastern Europe

Barclays Bank PLC
75 Wall Street
New York, NY 10265
    Tel: 212/412-3661

Bear, Stearns & Co., Inc.
245 Park Ave.
New York, NY 10167
    Tel: 212/272-3596
Contact: Brian Murray,
    Managing Director

Chase Manhattan
One Chase Manhattan Plaza
14th Floor
New York, NY 10081
    Tel: 212/552-4676
Contact: Gail Buyske, VP

Chemical Bank
277 Park Ave.
New York, NY 10172
    Tel: 212/310-5370
Contact: Mauri Kutila, VP

Citibank
399 Park Avenue
New York, NY 10043
    Tel: 212/559-8577
Contact: Miljenko Horvat

First National Bank of Chicago
Mail Suite 0040
One First National Plaza
Chicago, IL 60670
    Tel: 312/732-6796
Contact: Robert I. Thomas,
AVP, International Structured Finance Group

Manufacturer's Hanover
270 Park Avenue
New York, NY 10022
    Tel: 212/286-3314

MG Trade Finance Corp.
520 Madison Ave.
New York, NY 10022
    Tel: 212/826-5506
Contact: Roger Kodat,
    Vice President

National Westminster
175 Water Street
New York, NY 10038
    Tel: 212/826-2120
Contact: Donna Gavin

Phillip Brothers, Inc.
1221 Avenue of Americas
New York, NY 10020
    Tel: 212/790-5127
Contact: Gary Marcus,
    Director

Security Pacific Trade Finance
595 Madison Ave.
New York, NY 10022
    Tel: 212/644-0020
Contact: Jeffrey Malakoff, VP

EASTERN EUROPE KEY RESOURCES

MAJOR SOURCES OF NEWS AND INFORMATION

AmCham Newsletter
Newsletter of the American Chamber of Commerce in Poland.
American Chamber of Commerce
ul. Wiejska 20
00-490 Warsaw
POLAND
Tel: 48-22-214515
Fax: 48-22-216327
Telex: 813954

AmCham Today
Newsletter of the American Chamber of Commerce in Hungary.
American Chamber of Commerce
Budapest VI
Dozsa Gyorgy u. 84/a
Room 412
H-1068 HUNGARY
Tel: 36-1-142-8752

Bilateral Economic Councils Information
Free listing of key trade promotion groups and affiliate chambers of commerce in
Eastern Europe.
Thad Kopinski, Director for International Affairs
U.S. Chamber of Commerce
1615 H Street, NW
Washington, DC 20062
Tel: 202/463-5460
Fax: 202/463-3114

Bloc Magazine
Bimonthly on business and economic news.
Bloc Magazine
350 Broadway # 1205
New York, NY 10013
Tel: 212/966-0655
Fax: 212/966-0898

Business Czechoslovakia

Monthly newsletter on economic and political events and business opportunities.
The Rendon Group, Inc.
1802 T Street, NW
Washington, DC 20009
Tel: 202/745-4900

Business Directory of Eastern Europe

Listing of over 3,000 Eastern European companies still in business and interested in international trade.
American Business Press
P.O. Box 623
Lewiston, NY 14092-0623

Business Eastern Europe

Weekly newsletter on market opportunities and business information.
Business International Ltd.
40 Duke Street
London W1A 1DW
GREAT BRITAIN
Tel: 44-71-493-6711
Fax: 44-71-491-2107

Business Opportunities in Eastern Europe

Bimonthly newsletter on investment leads by country and sector.
Atlantic Information Services, Inc.
1050 17th Street, NW #480
Washington, D.C. 20036
Tel: 800/521-4323
Fax: 202/331-9542

Countertrade Outlook

Weekly intelligence on reciprocal international trade and unconventional trade finance.
Suzanne O. Payne
DP Publications
P.O. Box 3141 Park Fairfax Station
Fairfax, VA 22039
Tel: 703/425-1322
Fax: 703/425-7188

Czechoslovak Update

Monthly update on legal, economic, and political events in the CSFR. Typically eight-page edition with feature-length articles on timely topics such as CSFR's first bankruptcy.

Colleen Mihailovich, Editor
Central Europe Institute
1100 Connecticut Avenue, NW #500
Washington, DC 20036
 Tel: 202/296-9141
 Fax: 202/296-9153

Daily Report — Eastern Europe

Daily reports based on foreign radio and television broadcasts and news publications.

Foreign Broadcast Information Service
c/o National Technical Information Service
5285 Port Royal Road
Springfield, VA 22161
 Tel: 703/487-4630
 Fax: 703/321-8547

Directory of Consultants & Contractors Active in Eastern Europe

Lists consultants and contractors in the areas of architecture and interior design, consulting engineers, consultants in urban and rural planning, and construction contractors.

Projects Research, Inc.
P.O. Box 2558
Falls Church, VA 22042
 Tel: 703/698-9330
 Fax: 703/698-9837

Directory of Contacts for Central-Eastern Europe & Soviet Union

A 33-page list of key trade contacts.

Ingrid McKensie
U.S. Chamber of Commerce
1615 H Street, NW
Washington, DC 20062
 Tel: 202/463-5460
 Fax: 202/463-3114

Directory of Foreign Trade Organizations in Eastern Europe

Over 450 pages of export/import companies and supporting organizations engaged in foreign trade as well as related companies in Eastern Europe.

Vance T. Petrunoff, Publisher
2 Townsend Street #2-304
San Francisco, CA 94107
Tel: 415/979-0260
Fax: 415/495-5843
Telex: 640/419-2419
MCIMail: 419-2419

Directory of U.S. Companies Doing Business in the Soviet Union and Eastern Europe

Lists American firms with established business activities in the region and identifies essential sources of assistance for pursuing trade and investment there.

Wetherby International Company
P.O. Box 5393
Arlington, VA 22205
Tel: 703/241-0586

East European Construction

Biweekly newsletter on construction and real estate development in Eastern Europe and the Soviet Union.

Finnexus International Company
2140 Partridge Berry Road
Birmingham, AL 35244
Tel: 205/987-2948
Fax: 205/987-1812

East European Industrial Monitoring Service

Monthly publication on key industries, including a clipping service with translation and analysis of Eastern European publications.

Business International
214 Park Avenue South
New York, NY 10003
Tel: 212/460-0600
Fax: 212/985-8837

East European Markets

Weekly publication on economic reform, legislation, business opportunities, statistics, and EC-Comecon news.
Financial Times Business Information, Ltd.
European Business Publications
P.O. Box 891
Darien, CT 06820
   Tel: 203/656-2701
   Fax: 203/655-8332

Eastern Europe: An Energy Report

Monthly publication on energy and environmental issues and markets in Eastern Europe.
Eastern Europe Marketing Group
Strategic Marketing, Inc.
171 Madison Avenue Suite 401
New York, NY 10016
   Tel: 212/213-8044

Eastern Europe Business Briefing

Bimonthly newsletter on western interests in Eastern European markets.
Eurospan, Ltd.
Publications Group
P.O. Box 3045
Barrington, IL 60010-3045
   Tel: 708/202-0099
   Fax: 708/705-6575

Eastern Europe Business Bulletin

Bimonthly bulletin on business information and opportunities.
Eastern Europe Business Information Center (EEBIC)
U.S. Department of Commerce
14th & Constitution Avenue, NW Room 6037
Washington, DC 20230
   Tel: 202/377-2645
   Fax: 202/377-4473

Eastern Europe Demographics & Business Opportunities

Quarterly, updated set of reports on business opportunities in Eastern Europe, including the telecommunications, computer, and energy/environmental sectors.
Enterprise Development International, Inc. (EDI)
5619 Bradley Boulevard
Bethesda, MD 20814
Tel: 301/652-0141
Fax: 301/652-0177

Eastern Europe Finance

Biweekly newsletter on sources of financing for projects in Eastern Europe.
Mr. Michael Morrison
DP Publications
P.O. Box 7188
Fairfax Station, VA 22039
Tel: 703/425-1322
Fax: 703/425-7911

Eastern Europe Finance Update

Quarterly update on banking and finance in Eastern Europe, including sources of finance and strategies for countertrade.
Business International
215 Park Avenue South
New York, NY 10003
Tel: 212/460-0600
Fax: 212/995-8837

Eastern Europe Looks for Partners

Monthly newsletter listing East European firms seeking Western partners. Available free of charge. Compiled by the East European Business Information Center (EEBIC) from U.S. embassy sources, the Agency for International Development, and referrals.
East European Business Information Center (EEBIC)
Room 7412
14th & Constitution Avenue, NW
Washington, DC 20030
Tel: 202/377-2645

Eastern Europe Newsletter

Bimonthly publication on political and economic policy forecasts and assessments on Eastern Europe and the Soviet Union.

Eastern Europe Newsletter, Ltd.
67 Duke Street
London W4 2BW
GREAT BRITAIN
    Tel: 44-081-995-3860
    Fax: 44-081-747-8802

Eastern Europe Report

Weekly newsletter on opportunities in trade and investment.

American Banker
P.O. Box 30240
Bethesda, MD 20824
    Tel: 301/654-5580
    Fax: 301/654-1678

Eastern Europe Strategist

Private publication on political, economic, and social developments in Eastern Europe.

T.G. Cutler, Editor
31 Headley Road
Morristown, NJ 07960
Tel: 201/538-5672

Eastern European Business Monitor

Monthly newsletter on business and legal developments.

I.A. Ernst & Company, Inc.
5328 Saratoga Avenue
Chevy Chase, MD 20815
    Tel: 301/656-6767
    Fax: 202/686-1897

Eastern European & Soviet Telecom Report

Authoritative monthly newsletter highlighting country and company profiles in the telecom, information processing, and broadcasting sectors.

Blake Swensrud, Editor-in-Chief
International Technology Consultants
2940 28th Street, NW
Washington, DC 20008-3413
Tel: 202/234-2138
Fax: 202/483-7922

East-West Report

Monthly publication with financial advisory, market research, and legal topics.

Health & Sciences Communication
Circulation Director
1090 Vermont Avenue, NW
Washington, DC 20005
Tel: 800/842-3482

Euro Access

Weekly newsletter on business and economic news briefs, and trade events abroad, including Eastern Europe.

Europamerica, Inc.
1401 Wilson Boulevard #505
Arlington, VA 22209
Tel: 703/939-9800
Fax: 703/939-7126

(The) European

Weekly large-format newspaper covering events across Europe, including regular in-depth news coverage of Eastern Europe.

Headington Hill Hall
Oxford OX3 OBW
GREAT BRITAIN
Tel: 865-813372
Fax: 865-60285
In USA (US $115/year):
P.O. Box 860 Canal Street Station
New York, NY 10013
Tel: 800/927-6477
212/966-6245

European Marketing and Data Statistics

Annual statistical compendium covering Eastern and Western Europe. Superb reference volume for marketing staff.

EUROMONITOR
87-88 Turnmill Street
London EC1M 5QU
GREAT BRITAIN
Tel: (071)251-8024
Fax: (071)608-3149
Distributed in North America by:
Gale Research Company
Penobscot Building
Detroit, MI 48226

Europe Now

Covers events in the EC and opportunities being created by changes in Eastern Europe.

Single Internal Market Information Service
U.S. Department of Commerce
14th & Constitution Avenue, NW Room 3036
Washington, DC 20230
Tel: 202/377-5276
Fax: 202/377-2155

Eye on the East

Biweekly publication on events in Eastern Europe and the Soviet Union.

Pacific-Sierra Research Corporation
1401 Wilson Boulevard #1100
Arlington, VA 22209
Tel: 703/527-4975

General Trade Index & Business Guide

Over 700 pages detailing the intricacies of the Polish legal and tax systems and listing potential Polish trade partners.

Business Foundation
Warzsawa, ul. Wspolna 1/3
POLAND
Tel: 48-22-28-40-71 do 87 wew. 438
Fax: 48-22-28-05-49

Gazeta International
Weekly publication on Poland.
Gazeta Wyborcza
P.O. Box 348
New York, NY 10040
Tel: 212/956-4040

Hungary International
A guide to companies and individuals interested in doing business in Hungary
and other newly liberated East European countries.
Szablya Consultants
4416 - 134th Place, SE
Bellevue, WA 98006
Tel: 206/643-1023
Fax: 206/562-6381

(The) Insider
Weekly tabloid-newspaper published in English covering business and social
news in the region (primarily Poland).
Jane Dobija, Editor-in-Chief
The Insider
Dzielna 11A/21
01-023 Warsaw, Poland
Tel: 48-22-383344
Fax: 48-22-383344 (ask for fax extension)

Newsletter International — Focus on Hungary and Eastern Europe
Weekly newsletter on political, economic, social, cultural, and other develop-
ments in Eastern Europe.
Liberty Media, Inc.
5842 Mayfield Road
Cleveland, OH 44124-2934
Tel: 216/449-0800

PlanEcon Report
Weekly publication on economic situations in Eastern Europe.
PlanEcon
1111 14th Street, NW # 801
Washington, DC 20005-5603
Tel: 202/898-0471
Fax: 202/898-0455

PlanEcon Business Report
Biweekly newsletter that reports on business developments in the Soviet Union and Eastern Europe.
> PlanEcon Europe Ltd.
> Wimbledon Bridge House
> 1 Harthouse Road
> Wimbledon SW19 3RU
> GREAT BRITAIN
>> Tel: 081/545-6206
>> Fax: 081/545-6233

PEER — Poland and Eastern Europe Report
Monthly issue briefing on public and private sector political and economic issues and programs implemented in Eastern Europe.
> W.M.C. Public Affairs Group
> 3000 K Street, NW Penthouse 3-A
> Washington, DC 20007
>> Tel: 202/944-4920
>> Fax: 202/944-4924

Polish Business Voice
Monthly publication devoted to current political and economic changes in Poland and Eastern Europe.
> Krystyna Stachowiak, Managing Editor
> Richard Cottrell & Associates International
> 655 15th Street, NW #300
> Washington, DC 20005
>> Tel: 202/639-4082
>> Fax: 202/347-6109

Rel-EAST
Quarterly newsletter of computer-related activities throughout Eastern Europe and the Soviet Union.
> Esther Dyson, Publisher
> East-West High-Tech Information Service
> EDventure Holdings, Inc.
> 375 Park Avenue
> New York, NY 10152
>> Tel: 212/758-3434
>> Fax: 212/832-1720
>> MCIMail: 443-1400

Socialist Economies in Transition

Monthly publication from the World Bank on research, conferences, and workshops concerning the transitions of the socialist economies.

Matyas Vince, Editor
The World Bank
1818 H Street, NW Room N-6027
Washington, DC 20433
Tel: 202/473-6982

Tracking Eastern Europe

Weekly newsletter on headline news in Eastern Europe.

A.M.F. International Consultants
812 North Wood Ave.
Linden, NJ 07036
Tel: 201/486-3534
Fax: 201/486-4084

(The) U.S.-Eastern European Trade Directory

Reference book for conducting business, consisting of lists and rosters of key trade officials.

William S. Loiry, Editor
Global Trading Associates, Inc.
Washington, DC 20007

U.S. Department of Commerce - NTIS

The U.S. government produces a wide range of excellent materials on Eastern Europe, and NTIS is the designated clearinghouse for much of the reports and analyses. NTIS acts as agent for Commerce, State, and the Central Intelligence Agency, and orders may be placed over the telephone and charged to major credit cards. A complete listing of current releases can be obtained by calling 800/553-NTIS or 703/487-4650. Two representative publications lists, available free of charge include:

- Central & Eastern Europe Business Information
  - Listing of reports covering trade, markets, finance, investment, and joint venture leads. Compiled by the East European Business Information Center (EEBIC) of the Department of Commerce.
- Central & Eastern Europe Legal Texts
  - List of recently enacted commercial laws and regulations. Compiled by the Office of the General Counsel, Department of Commerce.

CABEE GRANT RECIPIENTS

In October 1991, the U.S. Department of Commerce awarded $2.5 million in grants to assist American firms establish a commercial presence in Eastern Europe. The Consortia of American Businesses in Eastern Europe (CABEE) program provides the five recipient organizations with "seed" money to set up offices in one or more cities, provide education and training, organize trade shows, and conduct market research.

Telecommunications & Electronics (Consortium in Eastern Europe)
Ms. Allyn Enderlyn, Project Manager/Membership
Telecommunications Industry Association
In cooperation with the American Electronics Association (AEA)
2001 Pennsylvania Avenue, NW #800
Washington, DC 20006-1813
  Tel: 301/652-0141 or 202/457-7737
  Fax: 301/652-0177

Housing & Construction (Consortium of American Housing Industries in Eastern Europe)
Mr. Robert Erwin, Executive Director
American Building Products Export/Import Council
1090 Vermont Avenue, NW
Washington, DC 20005
  Tel: 202/289-4558

Central European Food Industries Consortium (CEFIC)
Mr. George Melynkovich, President
Food Processing Machinery & Supplies Association
200 Daingerfield Road
Alexandria, VA 22314-2800
  Tel: 703/684-1080

Agriculture
Mr. Terry J. Albertson, International Sales Associates
Sun-Diamond Growers of California
5568 Gibraltar Drive
Pleasanton, CA 94566
  Tel: 510/463-7533

Eastern European Environmental Business Consortium
Mr. Conrad O. Kleveno, Project Director
Water Environment Federation
601 Wythe Street
Alexandria, VA 22314-1994
  Tel: 703/684-2424

MAJOR TRADE SHOWS

MAJOR TRADE SHOWS*

Central-Eastern Europe and Soviet Union: Trade Events

DATE	LOCATION	DESCRIPTION
January 9-12	Frankfurt	HEIMTEXTIL — Apparel
January 22-25	Warsaw	Computers
January 28-30	Stockholm	MACWORLD Expo/Stockholm
January 29-February 2	Zabreb, Yugoslavia	Textiles
February 4-8	Sarajevo, Yugoslavia	Textiles/Fashion
February 9-16	Helsinki & Moscow	Assessing Business Opportunities in the Soviet Union I
February 14-16	Helsinki	MACWORLD Expo/Helsinki
February 19-22	Zabreb	Leather, Footwear, and Clothing Week
February 23-March 2	Sarajevo	Civil Engineering
March 1-8	Sarajevo	Consumer Goods
March 4-6	Budapest	1991 East-West Telecommunications Forum
March 5-8	Warsaw	Consumer Goods
March 12-14	Birmingham, England	MACWORLD Expo/Birmingham
March 12-15	Poznan, Poland	Domestic Fair (Spring)
March 13-20	Hannover, Germany	CeBIT '91 — Data and Communications Technology
March 16-23	Helsinki & Moscow	Assessing Business Opportunities in the Soviet Union II
March 18-21	Sarajevo	Tourism and Sports
March 19-21	Paris	MACWORLD Expo/Paris
March 19-23	Zabreb	Printing and Paper Industry
March 22-26	Budapest	Tourism
March 25-29	Leningrad	First International Soviet Fiber Optics Conference
April 4-5	San Diego, California	Investing in Central and Eastern Europe
April 8-12	Moscow	COMTEK '91
April 8-14	Moscow	Meditech '91 — Medical Techniques and Equipment

* Dates given are taken from the year 1991

DATE	LOCATION	DESCRIPTION
April 9-12	Budapest	East EuroComm '91
April 9-12	Budapest	MIPEL
April 9-12	Budapest	Agriculture & Food Processing
April 9-12	Budapest	Rubber
April 9-12	Budapest	Light Industrial Machinery
April 16-20	Poznan	Infosystem
April 16-20	Poznan	Printing Machines
April 16-20	Poznan	Electronics and Computer Engineering
April 16-21	Zagreb	Zabreb Spring Fair
April 23-26	Birmingham	Communications '91
April 23-27	Vienna	IFABO — Office and Communications Technology
April 26	Amsterdam	Electronics '91
April 26-29	Budapest	East-European International Telecom, Computer and Office Exhibition
May 2-6	Poznan	Furniture
May 7-10	Budapest	IFABO — Office and Communication Technology Exhibition
May 7-10	Bucharest	ROMCONTROLA — Computers Office Equipment
May 7-10	Bucharest	Medical Equipment
May 7-10	Bucharest	Pharmaceutical Products
May 7-10	Bucharest	Measurement and Control Equipment
May 7-11	Erfurt, Germany	Computer Com '91
May 7-11	Zagreb	Furniture and Interior Decoration
May 7-12	Zagreb	Travel and Tourism
May 15-17	Amsterdam	MACWORLD Expo/Amsterdam
May 15-19	Prague	Computerworld Forum/Prague
May 15-19	Zagreb	Aircraft and Airport Equipment
May 15-20	Prague	Computerworld/Forum Prague '91
May 15-30	Budapest	Air and Water Pollution Control Trade Mission to Czechoslovakia and Hungary
May 19-22	Lugano, Switzerland	International Markup '91 — Graphic Communications

DATE	LOCATION	DESCRIPTION
May 20-24	Sarajevo	Art and Craft
May 21-25	Zagreb	Medical Equipment, Pharmaceuticals, and Laboratory Equipment
May 22-24	Paris	Teleconference Europe '91
May 22-30	Budapest	Budapest Spring Fair — Capital Goods
May 22-31	Moscow	Communication Tech
May 30-June 6	Bucharest	Consumer Goods, Chemicals
June 3-6	Berlin	MACWORLD Expo/Berlin
June 5-10	Moscow	ExpoComm Moscow '91 — Telecommunications and Computers
June 9-15	Frankfurt	Achema '91 — Chemical Engineering and Biotechnology
June 9-16	Poznan	Poznan International Trade Fair — Capital Goods
June 10-14	Vienna	Vinova Wine Equipment, Supplies
June 10-14	Brussels	Matchmaker Trade Delegation — Telecommunications Lasers and Fiber Opti
June 10-16	Perm, USSR	Technology '91 — Mechanical Engineering
June 11-15	Zagreb	Heating, Cooling, Water Treatment, and Power Supply Equipment
June 13-18	Montreaux, Switzerland	17th International TV Symposium and Exhibition
June 17-21	Amsterdam	Matchmaker Trade Delegation — Telecommunications Equipment
June 18-20	Birmingham	RoSPA — Occupational Health and Safety Products
June 20-25	Zurich and Vienna	Matchmaker Trade Delegation — Process Controls
June 25-27	Karlsruhe, Germany	DATASAFE — Computer Hardware, Software, etc.
July 2-7	Amsterdam	Internation Broadcasting Convention
July 8-12	Brussels	Society for Clinical Trials Annual (Medical Packaging and Software)
July 9-14	Moscow	PC World Forum/Moscow
July 11-14	Zurich	EXPO CSI — General Merchandise
August 18-22	Amsterdam	XIII Congress of the European Society of Cardiology

DATE	LOCATION	DESCRIPTION
August 30-September 9	Berlin	International Funkausstellung (International Audio and Video Fair)
September	Warsaw	ComExpo Poland
September 1-4	Amsterdam	EuroComNet
September 1-4	Gdansk, Poland	Maritime Exhibition
September 2-6	Sarajevo	Textiles/Fashion, Autumn
September 3-6	Poznan	Domestic Fair (Fall)
September 11-18	Brno, Czechoslovakia	Brno International Engineering Fair
September 14-18	Katowice, Poland	Mining
September 16-22	Zagreb	Zagreb International Autumn Fair
September 20-29	Budapest	Consumer Goods
September 20-29	Budapest	Toys and Educational Appliances
September 23-27	Stockholm	Matchmaker Trade Delegation — Pollution Control Equipment
September 23-29	Plovdiv, Bulgaria	Plovdiv Fair
October	Budapest	ComExpo Hungary
October	Prague	ComExpo Czechoslovakia
October 3-8	Poznan	Polagra, Agribusiness Trade Fair
October 3-8	Poznan	Industrial Fair
October 3-8	Poznan	Packaging, Storage, and Handling
October 8-15	Geneva	Telecom '91 — International Telecommunications
October 10-17	Bucharest	Bucharest International Fair
October 10-17	Bucharest	Industrial and Consumer Goods
October 14-18	Sarajevo	Wood
October 17-21	Budapest	USA Showcase '91 — Industrial/Bussiness Technology and Consumer Products
October 22-25	Warsaw	Video and Audio Equipment
October 22-25	Poznan	Small Industry and Handicrafts
October 22-26	Zagreb	Information, Telecommunications, and Office Equipment
November 4-8	Sarajevo	Plastics and Rubber
November 5-7	Zagreb	Textiles
November 5-8	Warsaw	Measurement and Control Technology

DATE	LOCATION	DESCRIPTION
November 5-8	Warsaw	Medicine
November 5-8	Warsaw	Pharmaceuticals
November 18-22	Sarajevo	Liquors, Beverages, and Food
November 19-22	Poznan	Ecology
November 19-23	Zagreb	Equipment for Catering, Hotel, and Tourism
November 26-28	Warsaw	Child Products
November 26-29	Vienna	MACWORLD Expo/Austria
November 28-December 2	Poznan	International Art Fair
December 14-29	Zagreb	New Year's Fair

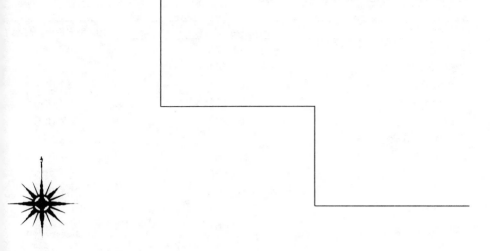

APPENDIX

Table A-1: Total Area of Europe

	Square Miles	Square Kilometers
Austria	32,375	83,851
Belgium	11,781	30,513
Denmark	16,631	43,075
Finland	130,119	337,009
France	211,208	547,026
Germany (West)		248,580
Greece	50,961	131,990
Ireland	27,136	70,282
Italy	116,500	301,278
Liechtenstein	61	157
Luxembourg	999	2,586
Monaco	0.739 (465 acres)	—
Netherlands	16,041	41,548
Norway	125,049	323,877
Portugal	35,550	92,075
Spain	194,884	504,750
Switzerland	15,941	41,288
United Kingdom	94,247	244,100

Source: Central Intelligence Agency. Directorate of Intelligence. 1991. *Handbook of Economic Statistics*, 1991. Washington, D.C.: Government Printing Office.

Table A-2: Total Area of Europe Ranked by Size

	Square Miles	Square Kilometers
France	211,208	547,026
Spain	194,884	504,750
Finland	130,119	337,009
Norway	125,049	323,877
Italy	116,500	301,278
Germany (West)	95,735	248,580
United Kingdom	94,247	244,100
Greece	50,961	131,990
Portugal	35,550	92,075
Austria	32,375	83,851
Ireland	27,136	70,282
Denmark	16,631	43,075
Netherlands	16,041	41,548
Switzerland	15,941	41,288
Belgium	11,781	30,513
Luxembourg	999	2,586
Liechtenstein	61	157
Monaco	0.739 (465 acres)	—

Source: Central Intelligence Agency. Directorate of Intelligence. 1991. *Handbook of Economic Statistics*, 1991. Washington, D.C.: Government Printing Office.

Table A-3: Total Areas of Eastern Europe Compared to the United States

	Square Kilometers	Comparable Area Europe	Comparable Area United States
Albania	28,750	Belgium	Maryland
Bulgaria	110,910	Portugal	Tennessee
Czechoslovakia	127,870	Greece	New York
Germany (East)	108,330	Portugal	Tennessee
Hungary	93,030	United Kingdom	Indiana
Poland	312,680	Italy	New Mexico
Romania	237,500	United Kingdom	Oregon
Yugoslavia	255,800	Germany-West	Wyoming

Source: Central Intelligency Agency. Directorate of Intelligence. 1991. *Handbook of Economic Statistics*, 1991. Washington, D.C.: Government Printing Office.

Table A-4: Total Areas of Eastern Europe Compared to the Unite States (Ranked by Size)

	Square Kilometers	Comparable Area Europe	Comparable Area United States
Poland	312,680	Italy	New Mexico
Yugoslavia	255,800	Germany-West	Wyoming
Romania	237,500	United Kingdom	Oregon
Czechoslovakia	127,870	Greece	New York
Bulgaria	110,910	Portugal	Tennessee
Germany (East)	108,330	Portugal	Tennessee
Hungary	93,030	United Kingdom	Indiana
Albania	28,750	Belgium	Maryland

Source: Central Intelligency Agency. Directorate of Intelligence. 1991. *Handbook of Economic Statistics*, 1991. Washington, D.C.: Government Printing Office.

Table A-5: World Population (In Thousands)

Region/Country/Area	1985	1990	1995	2000	2025
World total	4,851,433	5,292,195	5,770,286	6,260,800	8,504,223
More developed regions	1,174,365	1,206,556	1,236,045	1,264,078	1,353,936
Less developed regions	3,677,068	4,085,638	4,534,241	4,996,722	7,150,287
Africa	167,815	196,873	746,819	866,585	1,596,855
Caribbean	31,247	33,685	36,127	38,546	50,476
Central America	104,750	117,676	131,281	145,135	213,183
Mexico	79,376	88,598	97,967	107,233	150,062
South America	268,277	296,716	325,672	354,759	493,732
Argentina	30,331	32,322	34,264	36,238	45,505
Bolivia	6,371	7,314	8,422	9,724	18,294
Brazil	135,564	150,368	165,083	179,487	245,809
Chile	12,122	13,173	14,237	15,272	19,774
Colombia	29,879	32,978	36,182	39,397	54,196
Ecuador	9,317	10,587	11,934	13,319	19,923
Falkland Islands	2	2	2	2	2
French Guiana	83	98	114	130	188
Guyana	790	796	829	891	1,156
Paraguay	3,693	4,277	4,893	5,538	9,182
Peru	19,417	21,550	23,854	26,276	37,350
Suriname	383	422	460	497	664
Uruguay	3,008	3,094	3,186	3,274	3,691
Venezuela	17,317	19,735	22,212	24,715	37,999
Canada	25,379	26,521	27,557	28,488	31,923
United States of America	239,283	249,224	258,162	266,096	299,884
Asia	2,835,165	3,112,695	3,413,343	3,712,542	4,912,484
Eastern Asia	1,248,810	1,335,605	1,426,268	1,510,009	1,736,879
China	1,059,522	1,139,060	1,222,562	1,299,180	1,512,585
Hong Kong	5,456	5,851	6,108	6,336	6,456
Japan	120,837	123,460	125,904	128,470	127,496
Korea	60,694	64,566	68,620	72,520	84,694
Dem. Peo. Republic	19,888	21,773	23,966	26,117	33,063
Republic of Korea	40,806	42,793	44,655	46,403	51,631
Southeastern Asia	401,498	444,767	490,104	535,057	726,017
Indonesia	167,332	184,283	201,797	218,661	285,913
Malaysia	15,677	17,891	20,037	21,983	30,116
Philippines	55,121	62,413	69,935	77,473	111,509
Singapore	2,558	2,723	2,874	2,997	3,319
Thailand	51,604	55,702	59,605	63,670	80,911

Table A-5: World Population (In Thousands)(Continued)

Region/Country/Area	1985	1990	1995	2000	2025
Southern Asia	1,070,273	1,200,569	1,345,776	1,495,500	2,161,83
India	769,183	853,094	946,716	1,041,543	1,442,38
Western Asia	114,584	131,754	151,196	171,975	287,75
Europe	492,208	498,371	504,247	510,015	515,21
Eastern Europe	111,681	113,174	114,820	116,713	122,90
Albania	2,962	3,245	3,521	3,795	5,01
Bulgaria	8,960	9,010	9,036	9,071	8,94
Czechoslovakia	15,500	15,667	15,874	16,179	17,18
Hungary	10,649	10,552	10,509	10,531	10,19
Poland	37,203	38,423	39,365	40,366	45,06
Romania	22,725	23,272	23,816	24,346	25,74
Yugoslavia	23,124	23,807	24,389	24,900	25,99
Northern Europe	83,180	84,233	85,251	86,132	88,29
Denmark	5,122	5,143	5,158	5,153	4,88
Finland	4,902	4,975	5,031	5,077	5,11
Ireland	3,552	3,720	3,900	4,086	4,95
Norway	4,153	4,212	4,271	4,331	4,50
Sweden	8,350	8,444	8,509	8,560	8,584
United Kingdom	56,618	57,237	57,864	58,393	59,65
Southern Europe	142,362	144,087	145,956	147,811	147,75
Greece	9,934	10,047	10,124	10,193	10,08
Italy	57,141	57,061	57,114	57,195	52,964
Portugal	10,157	10,285	10,429	10,587	10,94
Spain	38,602	39,187	39,915	40,667	42,26
Western Europe	154,985	156,878	158,220	159,359	156,25
Austria	7,558	7,583	7,601	7,613	7,343
Belgium	9,858	9,845	9,845	9,832	9,37
France	55,170	56,138	57,138	58,145	60,372
Germany	77,668	77,573	77,330	76,962	70,90
Liechtenstein	27	28	28	28	28
Luxembourg	367	373	376	377	361
Monaco	27	28	29	30	30
Netherlands	14,484	14,951	15,409	15,829	16,819
Switzerland	6,470	6,609	6,682	6,762	6,79
Oceania	24,587	26,481	28,338	30,144	38,207
Australia	15,758	16,873	17,901	18,855	23,038
New Zealand	3,247	3,392	3,534	3,662	4,117
USSR	277,537	288,595	298,616	308,363	352,116

Source: Department of International Economic and Social Affairs. 1991. World Population Prospects 1990. New York, New York: United Nations.

Table A-6: Trends in Total Population of Europe (In Thousands)

	1988	1989	Percentage Growth 1977-89	Percentage Share 1977	Percentage Share 1989
Albania	3,130	3,177	26.67	0.32	0.38
Bulgaria	8,995	9,030	2.57	1.13	1.08
Czechoslovakia	15,600	15,627	3.97	1.93	1.87
East Germany	16,650	16,648	-0.70	2.15	1.99
Hungary	10,626	10,639	0.02	1.37	1.27
Poland	37,703	37,742	8.77	4.45	4.52
Romania	22,900	22,864	5.57	2.78	2.74
Yugoslavia	23,535	23,659	8.65	2.79	2.83
EC Members	324,613	326,054	3.71	40.35	39.01
EFTA Members	31,922	32,107	3.07	4.00	3.84
USSR	283,500	283,900	9.60	33.24	33.97
Others	53,377	54,294	20.95	5.49	6.50
Total	832,551	835,741	7.25	100.00	100.00

Source: Information was compiled from the National Statistical Offices of each respective country.

Table A-7: Population Projections for 1990-2020 (In Thousands)

	1990	1995	2000	2020	Percentage Increase 1990-2020
Albania	3,245	3,521	3,795	4,792	47.67
Bulgaria	9,010	90,366	9,071	8,985	-0.28
Czechoslovakia	15,667	15,874	16,179	17,061	8.90
East Germany	16,149	16,118	16,118	15,863	-1.77
Hungary	10,552	10,509	10,531	10,291	-2.47
Poland	38,423	39,365	40,366	44,333	15.38
Romania	23,272	23,816	24,346	25,521	9.66
Yugoslavia	23,849	24,471	25,026	26,211	9.90
EC Members	325,022	327,746	330,330	328,350	1.02
EFTA Members	31,792	31,922	32,017	31,563	-0.72
Others	56,670	62,245	67,753	86,612	34.60
Total	553,651	645,953	575,532	599,582	7.66

Source: Department of International Economic and Social Affairs. 1991. World Population Prospects 1990. New York, New York: United Nations.

Figure A-1: 1989 European Population (Total 551 Million)

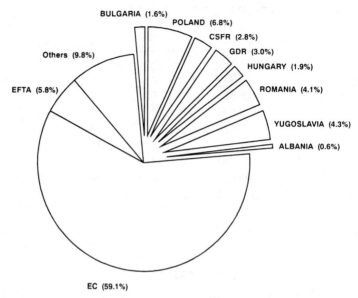

EC (59.1%)

Source: Department of International Economic and Social Affairs. 1991. *World Population Prospects 1990*. New York, New York: United Nations.

Figure A-2: Projected European Population for the Year 2000

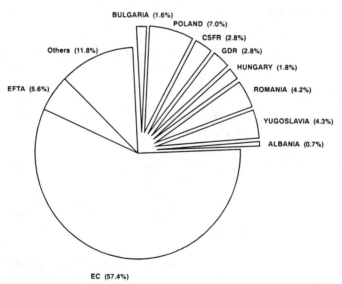

EC (57.4%)

Source: Department of International Economic and Social Affairs. 1991. *World Population Prospects 1990*. New York, New York: United Nations.

Figure A-3: Projected European Population for the Year 2020

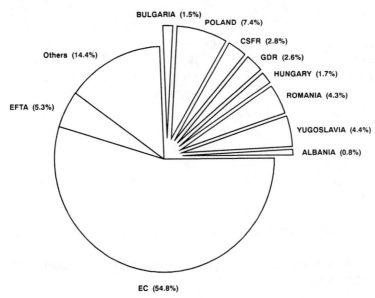

BULGARIA (1.5%)
POLAND (7.4%)
CSFR (2.8%)
GDR (2.6%)
HUNGARY (1.7%)
ROMANIA (4.3%)
YUGOSLAVIA (4.4%)
ALBANIA (0.8%)
Others (14.4%)
EFTA (5.3%)
EC (54.8%)

Source: Department of International Economic and Social Affairs. 1991. *World Population Prospects 1990*. New York, New York: United Nations.

Table A-8: 1989 Population Density (Persons per Square Kilometer)

Albania	113
Bulgaria	81.5
Czechoslovakia	123.1
East Germany	153.8
Hungary	114.7
Poland	121.8
Romania	97.1
Yugoslavia	93.3
EC Average	184.2
EFTA Average	63.3
Others	90.1
European Average	103.4

Source: Department of International Economic and Social Affairs. 1991. *World Population Prospects 1990*. New York, New York: United Nations.

Table A-9: Urban Population Statistics

	Urban Population ('000)	Percentage of Total Population	Percentage in Largest City	Percentage in Cities Over 500,000	Cities Over 500,000
Albania	1,038	34.0	26.0	0.0	0
Bulgaria	6,031	66.5	23.9	23.9	1
Czechoslovakia	10,180	65.3	11.3	11.3	1
East Germany	12,903	77.0	9.3	17.6	3
Hungary	6,017	56.2	34.2	34.2	1
Poland	22,686	61.0	7.3	19.6	5
Romania	11,289	49.0	19.7	19.7	1
Yugoslavia	10,714	46.3	10.2	16.7	2

Source: Information was compiled from the UN Prospects of World Urbanization/Demographic Yearbook/Statistical Offices.

Figure A-4: Percentage of East European Population in Cities of Ove 500,000 People

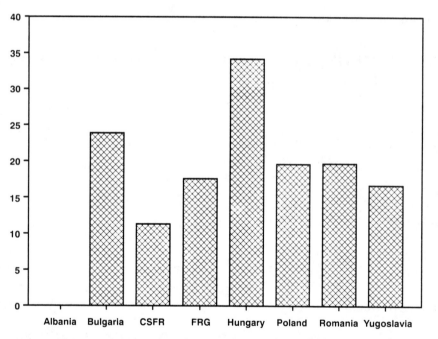

Source: Department of International Economic and Social Affairs. 1991. *World Populatiion Prospects 1990.* New York, New York: United Nations.

Table A-10: Number of Persons of Working Age (15-64) in 1989

Albania	N/R
Bulgaria	5,984
Czechoslovakia	10,063
East Germany	11,640
Hungary	7,002
Poland	24,542
Romania	15,100
Yugoslavia	N/R
EC Members	218,178
EFTA Members	21,283

Source: Information was compiled from the National Statistical Offices of each respective country.

Table A-11: Higher Education in Eastern Europe

	Establishments	Students ('000)	University Students ('000)	Percentage Students at University
Albania	8	23.8	23.8	100.0
Bulgaria	30	135.9	120.2	88.4
Czechoslovakia	36	170.6	170.6	100.0
East Germany	54	437.9	155.7	35.6[b]
Hungary	54	99.0	64.2	64.8
Poland	92	458.6	393.6	79.3[ab]
Romania	44	157.0	157.0	100.0
Yugoslavia	340	348.1	297.0	85.3
EC Members	2,956	7,051.8	5,312.2	75.3
EFTA Members	898	742.5	513.6	69.2
USSR	5,301	5,025.7	N/R	N/R
Others	327	540.2	343.4	63.6
Total	9,813	14,650.9	7,177.9	49.0

Source: Information was compiled from the UNESCO United Nations National Statistical Offices of each respective country.

Notes: a University teachers only.
b Establishments refers to universities only.

Table A-12: Largest National Economies
(Top 25 Compared with Washington, D.C.)

	GNP $ Billion
1. United States	4,881
2. Japan	2,856
3. Soviet Union	2,526
4. Germany	1,400
5. France	920
6. United Kingdom	802
7. Italy	797
8. People's Republic of China	546
9. Canada	472
10. Brazil	373
11. Spain	330
12. Iran	318
13. India	269
14. Australia	230
15. Netherlands	226
16. Switzerland	189
17. Poland	180
18. Sweden	175
19. South Korea	189
20. Belgium	149
21. Czechoslovakia	138
22. Austria	124
* Metropolitan Washington D.C.	120
23. Taiwan	119
24. Romania	118
25. Denmark	104

Source: Information was compiled from the Greater Washington Board of Trade in 1990.

Table A-13: National Economies of Eastern Europe

	GNP $ Billion	Per Capita GNP
Poland	172.4	4,565
Germany (East)	159.5	9,679
Yugoslavia	129.5	5,464
Czechoslovakia	123.2	7,878
Romania	79.8	3,445
Hungary	64.6	6,108
Bulgaria	51.2	5,710
Albania	3.8	1,200

Note: May 1990 estimates were used for 1989.
Source: Central Intelligency Agency. Directorate of Intelligence. September 1990. *Handbook of Economic Statistics, 1990*. Washignton, D.C.: Government Printing Office.

Table A-14: Western Aid to Eastern Europe

Country	Total Aid ($ Million)	Grant Aid ($ Million)
EC Members*		
Belgium	428.7	141.8
Denmark	605.0	355.4
France	2,417.2	851.5
Germany	6,669.6	1,921.2
Greece	85.3	46.5
Ireland	85.0	46.2
Italy	2,423.5	902.7
Luxembourg	43.1	9.8
Netherlands	353.1	215.7
Portugal	35.1	17.3
Spain	914.9	240.0
United Kingdom	1,426.8	913.2

Continued on following page.

Table A-14: Western Aid to Eastern Europe (Continued)

Country	Total Aid ($ Million)	Grant Aid ($ Million)
Other Countries in Europe		
Austria	880.7	646.4
Finland	319.5	87.0
Iceland	4.3	3.9
Norway	75.2	39.7
Sweden	285.8	72.9
Switzerland	538.3	117.9
Turkey	440.8	3.1
Other Industrialized Countries		
Australia	5.7	4.7
Canada	167.1	96.7
Japan	2,176.5	58.8
New Zealand	69.8	0.8
United States	1,325.0	1,053.0

* For EC countries the aid figures include a prorated share of the $6.5 billion pledged by the EC.

Source: Central Intelligency Agency. Directorate of Intelligence. September 1990. *Handbook of Economic Statistics, 1990.* Washington, D.C.: Government Printing Office.

Table A-15: Gross Hard Currency Debt of Eastern Europe (US$ Billion)

	1989	1990*
Poland	40.8	46.6
Hungary	20.3	21.0
Yugoslavia	15.7	15.2
Bulgaria	10.2	10.6
Czechoslovakia	7.9	8.1
Romania	0.0	2.2
Total Eastern Europe	94.9	103.7

* Year-end data was utilized for 1990.

Source: Central Intelligency Agency. Directorate of Intelligence. September 1990. *Handbook of Economic Statistics, 1990.* Washington, D.C.: Government Printing Office.

Table A-16: Trends in Total GNP 1977-1988 for Europe (Current U.S. Dollars in Billions)

	1987	1988	Percentage Growth 1977-88	Percentage Share 1977	Percentage Share 1988
Albania	N/R	N/R	N/R	N/R	N/R
Bulgaria	22.3	18.3	-0.9	0.7	0.3
Czechoslovakia	61.2	62.7	52.5	1.6	0.9
East Germany	149.4	139.6	13.5	4.9	2.0
Hungary	21.3	22.9	96.3	0.5	0.3
Poland	52.9	58.1	N/R	N/R	0.8
Romania	52.6	56.0	157.0	0.9	0.8
Yugoslavia	73.7	N/R	N/R	N/R	N/R
EC Members	4,298.9	4,715.8	234.2	56.6	69.1
EFTA Members	629.3	689.5	168.9	10.3	10.1
USSR	915.6	998.4	78.2	22.5	14.6
Others	75.0	77.3	57.4	2.0	1.1
Total	6,352.2	6,838.6	174.3	100	100

Source: Central Intelligence Agency. Directorate of Intelligence. September 1990. *Handbook of Economic Statistics, 1990*. Washington, D.C.: Government Printing Office.

Table A-17: Total Consumer Expenditure of Europe (National Currencies in Millions)

	1988	Percentage Share 1988	Total US$ (Million) 1988	Dollars Per Capita 1988
Albania	32,800	0.12	5,467	1,721
Bulgaria	21,094	0.28	12,408	1,374
Czechoslovakia	440,098	1.05	46,819	2,996
East Germany	206,303	2.47	110,322	6,627
Hungary	962,650	0.43	19,100	1,795
Poland	16,916,000	0.88	39,294	1,041
Romania	530,000	0.83	37,123	1,624
Yugoslavia	71,815,000	0.31	13,782	583
EC Members		64.38	2,876,763	8,823[a]
EFTA Members		8.40	375,392	11,692[a]
USSR	540,000	19.75	882,353	3,108
Others		1.10	49,765	851[a]
Total		100	4,468,588	

Source: Information was compiled from the National Statistical Offices of each respective country.
Notes: a Dollar total based on 1989 figures.

Table A-18: Annual Rates of Inflation 1985-1989 (Percentage Growth)

	1985	1986	1987	1988	1989
Albania	N/R	N/R	N/R	N/R	N/R
Bulgaria	1.7	3.4	0.0	1.3	9.2[a]
Czechoslovakia	1.7	0.4	0.1	0.2	1.5[a]
East Germany	-0.1	0.0	0.0	0.0	2.0[b]
Hungary	7.0	5.3	8.7	15.8	17.0
Poland	14.6	17.7	25.2	60.0	244.5
Romania	-0.4	-0.1	0.2	N/R	N/R
Yugoslavia	72.3	89.8	120.8	194.1	1,239.9

Source: Information was compiled from the International Monetary Fund, United Nations, and Organization for Economic Cooperation and Development.
Notes: a Calculated from state retail price index.
b Calculated from index of retail prices, service charges, and fares.

Table A-19: European Currency Unit (ECU)[1] (Composition in Percentage)

	Percentage
Deutsche Mark (Germany)	30.4
Franc (France)	19.3
Pound Sterling (United Kingdom)	12.6
Lira (Italy)	9.9
Guilder (Netherlands)	9.5
Franc (Belgium)	7.8
Peso (Spain)	5.2
Krone (Denmark)	2.5
Pound (Ireland)	1.1
Escudos (Portugal)	0.8
Drachma (Greece)	0.6
Franc (Luxembourg)	0.3
	100.0

[1] ECU = 2.05 Deutsche Mark, November 1991.
Source: Deutsche Bank (Frankfurt Germany) Annual Report 1991.

Table A-20: Weighted Ranking of U.S. Trade Partners by Opportunity (Listed Alphabetically Within Each Group)

Group 1

Belgium	Hong Kong	Netherlands
Brazil	India	Saudi Arabia
Canada	Italy	Spain
China	Japan	Taiwan
France	Korea	United Kingdom
Germany		

Group 2

Australia	Pakistan	Thailand
Austria	Singapore	Turkey
Chile	South Africa	Venezuela
Colombia	Sweden	United Arab Emirates
Indonesia	Switzerland	U.S.S.R.
Malaysia		

Group 3

Algeria	Greece	Panama
Argentina	Ireland	Philippines
Czechoslovakia	Israel	Poland
Denmark	Nigeria	Portugal
Egypt	Norway	Yugoslavia
Finland		

Group 4

Barbados	Honduras	Morocco
Cameroon	Hungary	New Zealand
Costa Rica	Ivory Coast	Peru
Dominican Republic	Jamaica	Romania
Ecuador	Kenya	Trinidad and Tobago
Guatamala		

Note: Iraq and Kuwait are not ranked due to economic conditions at time of assessment in October 1991.

Weighting factors include: GNP/GDP; imports of manufactured goods and U.S. exports of manufacturers; political, social. geographic, and strategic conditions; projected annual dollar gain through 1992 in import market, U.S. exports, and total consumption; projected change in U.S. share of import market; competition for U.S. exporters from local domestic suppliers and third-country suppliers; barriers to market access for U.S. exporters; and industry market priority. (Ranked on 1-5 scale.)

Source: U.S. Department of Commerce. International Trade Association. 1991. *Foreign Economic Trends and Their Implications for the United States*. Washington, D.C.: Government Printing Office.

Table A-21: Peace Dividend Potential: Military Expenditures (US$ Billion)

U.S.S.R.	303.0
United States	296.2
France	34.1
Germany (West)	31.6
United Kingdom	24.3
Japan	20.7
China	19.2
Iran	18.4
Italy	18.0
Germany (East)	14.4
Iraq	12.0
Saudi Arabia	10.5
Czechoslovakia	10.3
India	9.6
Canada	8.8
Romania	7.6
Spain	6.9
Bulgaria	6.7
Netherlands	6.3

Source: Information was compiled from the U.S. Arms Control & Disarmament Agency (March 1990).

Table A-22: Best Sites for European Headquarters and European Manufacturing Plants

European Headquarters
1. Berlin, Germany
2. Brussels, Belgium
3. Denmark, Denmark
4. Hamburg, Germany
5. Hessen (Frankfurt region), Germany
6. Ile de France (Paris region), France
7. Nordrhein-Westfalen (Dusseldorf), Germany
8. South East, United Kingdom
9. Vlassams Gewest (Antwerp region), Belgium
10. West Nederland, the Netherlands

European Manufacturing Plants
1. Abrusi-Molise (East of Rome), Italy
2. Cetro, Spain
3. Ireland, Ireland
4. Kentriki Ellada (Athens region), Greece
5. Norte do Continente, Portugal
6. Northern Ireland, United Kingdom
7. Sud-Ouest, France
8. Sul do Continente, Portugal
9. Sur, Spain
10. Voeia Ellada (Salonika region), Greece

Source: World Trade Magazine, October 1991, New York:

Figure A-5: Total Imports for East European Countries in 1988

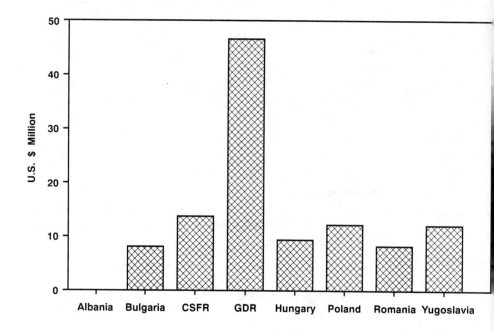

Source: U.S. Department of Commerce. International Trade Administration. 1991. *Foreign Economic Trends and Their Implications for the United States*. Washington, D.C.: Government Printing Office.

Table A-23: Total Imports for Europe (National Currencies in Billions)

	Percentage Growth 1988	Percentage Growth 1978-88	Percentage Share 1988	Total U.S.$ (Million) 1988	Dollars Per Capita 1988
Albania	N/R	N/R	N/R	N/R	N/R
Bulgaria	13.8	130	0.6	8.1	902.5 [b]
Czechoslovakia	129.1	104.3	1	13.7	880.4 [a,b]
East Germany	87.1	74.5	3.2	46.6	2,797.4 [a]
Hungary	472.5	79.7	0.7	9.4	882.3 [a]
Poland	5,252.1	838	0.8	12.2	323.6 [a,c]
Romania	118.5	-15.6	0.6	8.3	362.4 [a,c]
Yugoslavia	63,050.7	38,916.5	0.8	12.1	514.1 [b]
EC Members			71.3	1,026.7	N/R
EFTA Members			12.3	179.1	N/R
USSR	65	115.9	7.4	106.2	374.6
Others			1.3	17.7	N/R
Total			100	1,440.1	

Notes: a Foreign-exchange currency.
  b Imports (cif).
  c 1987 and 1988 figures calculated, in the absence of national data, from external dollar amounts.
Source: The information was compiled from the IMF International Financial Statistics/Common Foreign Trade Data/National trade statistics.

Table A-24: Eastern Europe Imports by Country of Origin 1988 (US$ Millions)

	EEC	EFTA	CMEA[a]	USA	Total
Albania	87.0	N/R	N/R	N/R	232.0
Bulgaria	1,844.6	452.6	N/R	140.0	4,460.1
Czechoslovakia	2,813.0	953.8	N/R	60.6	7,862.0
East Germany	1,624.1	1,211.2	N/R	120.0	7,060.4
Hungary	2,355.6	1,136.8	4,096.6	210.0	9,340.3
Poland	32.7	887.0	9,470.0	304.0	16,773.0
Romania	747.0	75.0	5,408.0	203.0	9,285.0
Yugoslavia	5,091.0	1,147.0	3,584.0	725.0	13,155.0

Notes: a CMEA figures do not include USSR.

Source: Information was compiled from the OECD Foreign Trade Statistics/IMF Direction of Trade Statistics.

Table A-25: Eastern Europe Imports by Country of Origin (1988 Percentage by Total of Country)

	EEC	EFTA	CMEA[a]	USA	Japan
Albania	37.5	N/R	N/R	N/R	N/R
Bulgaria	41.4	10.1	N/R	3.1	3.9
Czechoslovakia	35.8	12.1	N/R	0.8	0.7
East Germany	23.0	17.2	N/R	1.7	2.4
Hungary	25.2	12.2	43.9	2.2	1.4
Polan	19.5	5.3	56.5	1.8	1.5
Romania	8.0	0.8	58.2	2.2	0.6
Yugoslavia	38.7	8.7	27.2	5.5	1.3

Notes: [a] CMEA figures do not include USSR.

Source: Information was compiled from the OECD Foreign Trade Statistics/IMF Direction of Trade Statistics.

Figure A-6: Total Exports for East European Countries in 1988

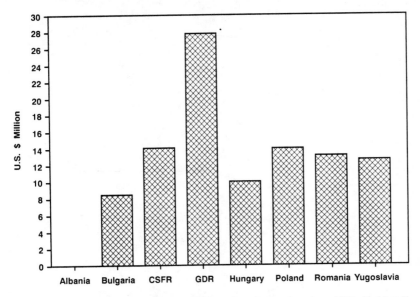

Source: U.S. Department of Commerce. International Trade Administration. 1991. *Foreign Economic Trends and Their Implications for the United States*. Washington, D.C.: Government Printing Office.

Table A-26: Total Exports for Europe (National Currencies in Billions)

	1988	Percentage Growth 1978-88	Percentage Share 1989	Total U.S. $ (Millions) 1988	Dollars Per Capita 1989
Albania	N/R	N/R	N/R	N/R	N/R
Bulgaria	14.4	140.0	0.6	8.5	941.7[a]
Czechoslovakia	132.8	128.2	1.0	14.1	905.6[a]
East Germany	52.0	24.4	1.9	27.8	1,669.7[a]
Hungary	504.1	111.3	0.7	10.0	941.3
Poland	6,027.0	1,300.7	1.0	14.0	371.3
Romania	187.0	52.3	0.9	13.1	572.1[b]
Yugoslavia	65,656.1	68,220.6	0.9	12.6	535.4
EC Members			72.7	1,056.1	3,253.5
EFTA Members			12.2	176.6	5,532.6
USSR	67.1	101.5	7.5	109.6	386.7
Others			0.6	9.8	203.8
Total			100.0	1,452.2	1,744.3

Notes: a Billion units foreign-exchange currency.
 b Calculated, in the absence of national data, from external dollar estimates.
Source: Information was compiled from the IMF International Financial Statistics/Comecon Foreign Trade Data/National Trade Statistics of each respective country.

Figure A-7: Total Generation of Electricity for 1988

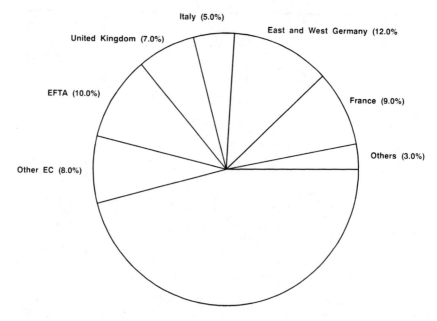

Italy (5.0%)

East and West Germany (12.0%

United Kingdom (7.0%)

EFTA (10.0%)

France (9.0%)

Others (3.0%)

Other EC (8.0%)

CMEA excluding East Germany (46.0%)

Source: Central Intelligence Agency. Directorate of Intelligence. 1991. *Handbook of Economic Statistics, 1991*. Washington, D.C.: Government Printing Office.

Table A-27: Eastern Europe Electrical Energy Statistics (GWh)

	Public Supply	Self-Producer Supply	Net Total Production	Per Capita Consumption Per Annum
Albania	N/R	N/R	N/R	N/R
Bulgaria	40,682	4,388	43,240	4,767
Czechoslovakia	77,091	10,283	81,299	4,891[a]
East Germany	110,538	7,790	106,388	5,782
Hungary	28,228	988	26,642	3,180
Poland	135,933	8,407	134,345	3,205
Romania	70,150	3,929	69,060	3,060[b]
Yugoslavia	N/R	N/R	78,452	2,959

Notes: a 1987
   b Per capita consumption 1987.
Source: UN ECE Annual Bulletin of Electrical Energy Statistics for Europe.

Table A-28: Consumption of Refined Products in 1988 for Eastern Europe

	Motor Gasoline	Diesel/ Gasoil	Aviation Fuels	Liquified Gases
Albania	210	325	70	N/R
Bulgaria	1,750	400	220	73
Czechoslovakia	1,500	1,091	415	135
East Germany	4,680	5,765	13	220
Hungary	1,290	3,468	224	314
Poland	3,534	6,189	270	171
Romania	1,700	4,090	470	250
Yugoslavia	1,954	4,113	369	417

Source: Organization for Economic Cooperation and Development (OECD) Quarterly Oil and Gas Statistics/CMEA Handbook.

Figure A-8: Gasoline Consumption for 1988

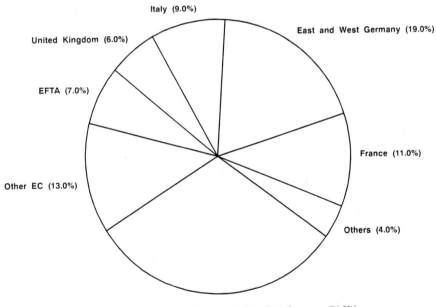

Italy (9.0%)

United Kingdom (6.0%)

East and West Germany (19.0%)

EFTA (7.0%)

France (11.0%)

Other EC (13.0%)

Others (4.0%)

CMEA excluding East Germany (31.0%)

Source: Central Intelligency Agency. Directorate of Intelligence. 1991. Handbook of Economic Statistics, 1991. Washington, D.C.: Government Printing Office.

Table A-29: Distance in Kilometers Between Major Cities in Eastern and Western Europe*

	Berlin	Prague	Sofia	Belgrade	Warsaw	Budapest	Bucarest
London	996	1,285	2,542	2,160	1,586	1,771	2,657
Paris	1,100	1,075	2,201	1,819	1,690	1,561	2,447
Frankfurt	555	502	1,759	1,377	1,145	988	1,874
Brussels	789	911	2,168	1,786	1,379	1,397	2,283
Vienna	657	309	1,042	660	679	265	1,151
Amsterdam	685	956	2,213	1,831	1,275	1,442	2,328
Athens	2,556	2,208	872	1,239	2,308	1,634	1,299
Dubrovnik	1,795	1,447	1,010	617	1,686	1,012	1,330
Geneva	1,139	948	1,841	1,459	1,729	1,294	2,172
Kiev	1,385	1,401	1,529	1,331	795	1,137	1,102
Luxembourg	768	743	1,942	1,560	1,358	1,229	2,115
Moscow	1,856	1,897	2,345	2,147	1,266	1,953	1,918
Rome	1,529	1,290	1,703	1,321	1,921	1,349	2,034

* August 12, 1991

Table A-30: European per Diem Rates*

	U.S. Dollars
London	364
Paris	332
Stockholm	313
Copenhagen	302
Milan	287
Frankfurt	276
Rome	271
Geneva	270
Oslo	267
Brussels	257
Istanbul	230
Berlin	229
Zurich	213
Prague, Czechoslovakia	210
Lisbon	191
Sofia, Bulgaria	187
Belgrade, Yugoslavia	174
Bucarest, Romania	168
Warsaw, Poland	135
CZECHOSLOVAKIA (Other)	130
Budapest, Hungary	124
Dubrovnik, Yugoslavia	117
Krakow, Poland	114
Zagreb, Yugoslavia	106
Ljubljana, Yugoslavia	100
Pecs, Hungary	96
Bled, Yugoslavia	96
Sarejevo, Yugoslavia	91
Otocec, Yugoslavia	88
ROMANIA (Other)	87
Skopje, Yugoslavia	86
Cavtat, Yugoslavia	85
Brela, Yugoslavia	82
POLAND (Other)	77
YUGOSLAVIA (Other)	77
Szeged, Hungary	74
HUNGARY (Other)	53

* October 1991

Table A-31: Typical Expenses in Europe in 1991

	Hotel (Double)		Dinner for Two		Gallon	Taxi	Aspirin	Movie	Color Film
	Deluxe	Moderate	Deluxe	Moderate	of Gas	1st km	(100)	Ticket	35mm,24 exp.
Amsterdam	$340	$190	$120	$58	$3.65	$3.95	$2.66	$7.47	$7.70
Berlin	310	148	130	53	2.90	3.43	11.92	6.74	5.02
Budapest	200	103	60	33	2.81	0.49	0.74	0.88	4.28
Brussels	233	198	150	63	3.72	4.09	5.53	6.54	6.58
Copenhagen	275	156	130	71	3.66	4.03	8.22	8.17	8.34
Geneva	276	180	192	67	3.07	5.66	13.51	9.42	5.10
Lisbon	204	152	115	52	3.98	1.03	9.54	2.89	5.17
London	350	233	180	86	3.11	1.61	9.55	7.84	5.86
Madrid	250	172	140	60	3.24	1.62	10.54	5.22	5.63
Milan	385	218	168	61	4.86	3.96	5.93	7.32	6.84
Paris	400	163	195	77	4.02	2.50	12.98	6.88	5.83
Stockholm	264	169	170	71	4.45	7.21	4.96	8.71	7.21
Vienna	370	174	150	63	3.34	3.36	8.80	7.68	6.94

Source: Runzheimer International, *Reports on Travel Management* (monthly), Northbrook, Illinois (414) 534-3121.

Table A-32: Typical Travel Expenses in Europe in 1991

City	Airport	Taxi to Downtown U.S. Dollars	Taxi to Downtown Local Currency	Bus to Downtown U.S. Dollars	Bus to Downtown Local Currency
Amsterdam	Schiphol	$30-$40	51-68 guilders	$5	9
Bangkok	Don Muang	$10-$15	252-323 baht	*	—
Berlin	Tegel	$20	30 deutsche marks	$2	2.7
Brussels	National	$30-$40	960-1,280 Belgian francs	$3	96
Copenhagen	Kastrup	$15-$25	86-143 kroner	$5	29
Frankfurt	Frankfurt	$20-$30	30-45 deutsche marks	$3	5
Hong Kong	Hong Kong	$6.70-$7	52-55 Hong Kong dollars	$1	8
London	Gatwick	$10(train)	5 pounds	$12	6
London	Heathrow	$40-$50	21-27 pounds	$8	4
Madrid	Barajas	$12-$15	1,176-1,470 pesetas	$2	200
Mexico City	Benito Juarez	$20	58,800 pesos	*	—
Milan	Malpensa	$30-$40	34,800-46,400 lire	$10	11,600
Oslo	Forenbu	$15-$25	90-150 kroner	$7	40
Paris	Charles de Gaulle	$30-$40	150-200 francs	$7	35
Paris	Orly	$25-$30	125-150 francs	$6	30
Rome	Leonardo da Vinci	$50-$60	58,000-69,600 lire	$4.50-$5.50	5,220-6,380
Singapore	Changi	$15-$20	26-34 Singapore dollars	$1-$2	2-4
Stockholm	Arlanda	$70	399 kroner	$10	57
Sydney	Kingsford Smith	$12-$15	16-20 Austrailian dollars	$2.50	3
Tokyo	Narita	$110	15,000 yen	$18.50	2,500

Source: Runzheimer International, *Reports on Travel Management* (monthly), Northbrook, Illinois (414) 534-3121.

Table A-33:Comparison of Typical Expenses

	Exchange US$ =	Yogurt (8 oz.)	Breakfast (1)	Cigarettes (1 carton)	Wine (750 ml)	Woman's Haircut	Man' Haircut	Single Lodging
Belfast	0.61	0.56	10.87	27.49	5.52	15.92	10.65	107.00
Bombay	17.37	0.55	5.01	13.50	1.81	5.09	2.77	98.00
Budapest	64.05	0.12	6.02	9.14	1.24	5.11	2.69	94.00
Buenos Aires	5,275.10	0.32	6.86	10.40	2.71	8.13	4.59	135.00
Cairo	2.70	0.24	5.38	8.13	1.75	11.68	3.13	93.00
Guangzhou	4.72	0.81	6.55	9.82	5.14	7.43	6.56	78.00
Jakarta	1,848.02	1.09	8.09	4.84	18.00	12.56	7.09	125.00
Karachi	21.67	0.31	4.66	9.05	3.47	10.86	1.79	92.00
Lisbon	144.60	0.50	12.03	14.97	2.26	12.48	6.65	140.00
London	0.55	0.71	18.30	27.44	4.95	34.85	21.29	254.00
Manama	0.38	0.74	10.87	9.80	8.96	26.71	13.90	105.00
Memphis	1.00	0.77	7.94	12.99	2.62	16.24	9.15	73.00
New York City	1.00	0.79	9.53	16.79	2.25	18.00	13.50	214.00
Oslo	6.30	0.82	12.38	49.29	7.85	43.43	20.94	210.00
Phoenix	1.00	0.71	7.77	12.44	2.41	20.80	13.16	75.00
Sydney	1.28	0.42	12.67	18.99	6.14	30.65	21.12	213.00
Taipei	26.72	1.05	14.37	12.26	9.20	16.19	11.92	189.00

Source: Runzheimer International, *Reports on Travel Management* (monthly), Northbrook, Illinois (414) 534-3121.

Table A-34: Hotel Rates in Budapest

Hotel	Category	April 1 - October 31				Peak Periods			
		Single	Double	Ext. Bed	Suite	Single	Double	Ext. Bed	Suite
Atrium Hyatt	***** Deluxe Regency	162 194	206 241	55 55	295 440	162 194	206 241	55 55	295 440
Duna Inter-Cont.	****	150	191	45	340	150	191	45	340
Budapest Hilton	***** Executive	179 206	226 253	47 47	359 394	179 206	226 253	47 47	359 394
Thermal	*****	111	153	42	222	111	153	42	222
Béke Radisson ◆	****	135	165	30	290	135	165	30	290
Buda Penta ◆	****	94	121	30	–	111	153	30	–
Flamenco ◆	****	100	120	35	260	112	135	35	260
Forum	**** Danube-view	165 188	200 224	35 35	380 380	165 188	200 244	35 35	380 380
Gellért ⊗	****	99	158	35	235	119	190	42	282
Grand Hotel Hungaria ◆	****	79	106	35	153	106	129	47	188
Korona ◆	****	103	132	32	–	123	162	32	–
Nemzeti ◆	****	86	91	21	–	111	116	21	–
Novotel ◆	****	94	121	30	–	111	145	30	–
Olympia ◆	****	51	74	18	100	65	85	18	118
Ramada Grand ◆	****	117	156	33	233	117	156	33	233
Royal ◆	***	62	101	26	139	75	114	28	156
Astoria ◆	***	95	98	28	147	105	108	28	162
Budapest ◆	***	76	91	26	–	82	100	26	–
Emke ◆	***	53	75	18	94	61	81	18	103
Erzsébet ◆	***	92	97	32	–	113	118	41	–
Stadion ◆	***	71	89	25	–	74	95	25	–
Tavena	***	88	112	24	194	88	112	24	194
Volga ◆		61	81	23	–	66	88	23	–

Rates include breakfast except Hilton.
Peak Periods ◆ April 25-June 27, August 2-October 13, December 28, '91-January 1, '92.
Peak Periods ⊗ May 9-11, May 17-19, May 30-June 1, June 14-16, August 9-11. Dates indicate first and last night of peak periods.
All U.S. Dollar rates are subject to change without notice.

Source: Tourism Office in Budapest.

Table A-35: Eastern European Media Estimates

COUNTRY	TV Households	Cable TV Percentage	Satellite Dishes	VCRs	Sources of Foreign Programming Over the Air TV
Bulgaria	3.9 million	none known	1,000	550,000	Bulgaria TV 1 (Sofia) Bulgaria TV 2 (Sofia) Gopsteleradio 1 (Moscow)
Czechoslovakia	4.3 million	Bratislawa to begin with Videoton	30,000	800,000	Czech TV (Prague) Slovak TV (Bratislawa) Gosteleradio 1
Hungary	2.6 million	18% (30+ systems, inc. Budapest Szekesfehervr	15,000	860,000	MTV 1 (Budapest) MTV 2 (Budapest) Gosteleradio 1 Private: Nap TV (Budapest) Balaton Ch. (Siofok)
Poland	9.8 million	Chase Cable to begin wiring Warsaw and Krakow 6/90	18,000	1.1 million	PRTV 1 (Warsaw) PRTV 2 (Warsaw) Gosteleradio 1 (nationwide except Krakow with RAI 1) Private: I.T.I. (Warsaw)
Romania	3.8 million	none known	less than 100	460,000	Free Romanian TV
USSR	86.0 million	Manex Cable to begin in Moscow 7/90	15,000	2.2 million	Gosteleradio 1 (Moscow) Gosteleradio 2 (Moscow) Leningrad 1 (Leningrad) Regional: each republic Private: Nika TV (Moscow)
Yugoslavia	5.5 million	200,00 apts. by master antenna	30,000+	2 million	JRTV 1 (Belgrade) JRTV 2 (Belgrade) Regional: each republic

Table A-36: Ranking of Level of Interest to Establish or Increase Business Activities in Eastern Europe[*]

	Preference
Former East Germany	48%
Poland	32%
U.S.S.R.	32%
Hungary	27%
Czechoslovakia	26%
Yugoslavia	23%
Romania	14%
Bulgaria	11%
Albania	9%

* Survey of 1,400 U.S. business executives in April 1990.
Source: Opinion Research Corporation (Princeton, New Jersey).

Table A-37: Europe Telecom Infrastructure 1989

	Total Exchange Access Lines	Percentage Business Lines	Percentage Residential Lines	Lines per 100 Population
Albania	N/R	N/R	N/R	N/R
Bulgaria	1,900,000	N/R	N/R	1.0
Czechlosovakia	2,006,980	31.8	68.2	12.8
East Germany	3,944,609	N/R	N/R	23.7
Hungary	1,200,000	N/R	N/R	10.0
Poland	3,000,000	N/R	N/R	7.0
Romania	2,000,000	N/R	N/R	6.7
Yugoslavia	3,304,735	17.0	83.0	14.0
Austria	3,039,640	N/R	N/R	40.0
Belgium	3,955,387	N/R	N/R	40.1
Finland	2,470,038	19.6	80.4	49.9
France	25,827,282	16.5	83.5	45.2
West Germany	28,377,000	N/R	N/R	46.3
Greece	3,618,065	30.7	69.3	36.2
Italy	20,091,533	20.9	79.1	34.9
Netherlands	6,466,000	24.0	76.0	43.7
Norway	2,016,213	18.9	81.1	47.8
Portugal	1,849,247	27.1	72.9	17.8
Spain	10,972,000	26.5	73.5	28.1
Sweden	5,600,000	21.4	78.6	66.7
Switzerland	3,632,765	24.3	75.7	54.1
United Kingdom	23,492,000	22.3	77.7	41.1

Source: International Telecommunications Union. October 1991. World of Nations: Country Data. Geneva, Switzerland.

Table A-38: Telephone Traffic with the United States* (Selected Countries from the Top 50 by Revenues)

	US$ Billion
Mexico	533.9
West Germany	167.2
Philippines	114.8
South Korea	111.6
Japan	78.5
United Kingdom	46.2
Taiwan	45.0
POLAND	36.2
France	32.9
Thailand	30.2
People's Republic of China	26.4
Indonesia	14.7
Hong Kong	14.1
YUGOSLAVIA	12.5
Malaysia	12.1
ROMANIA	8.4
Jordan	7.9

* Includes voice telephony, datacom, telex, and telegraph traffic.
Source: U.S. Federal Communications Commission, September 1991.

Table A-39: Telecom Infrastructure Investments—Projected Expenditures to Reach 30% Telephone Penetration

	US$ Billion	Percentage of Total
Poland	18.54	36%
Romania	10.82	21%
Yugoslavia	8.86	17%
Czechoslovakia	6.18	12%
Hungary	5.15	10%
Bulgaria	2.06	4%
Total	51.61	100%

Source: NYNEX/BIS, October 1991.

Index

labor force, 169
licensing, 165
living conditions, 165-168
market research, 161
patents, 165
political organization, 155
privatization, 154, 160, 162
securities, 164-165
taxation, 159, 162-163
tourist information, 168
trademarks, 165
transportation, 162, 165, 168
visas, 165
wages, 169

International Bank for Reconstruction and Development (IBRD), 41, 47, 106, 217, 268
International Finance Corporation (IFC), 107
International Monetary Fund (IMF), 16, 41, 47, 73, 106, 217, 268

Poland
accommodations, 220
banks and banking, 216-217, 218
business contacts, 223-249
business operations, setting up, 213
climate, 203
commodities, import/export, 207-208
communications, 221
copyright protection, 219
currency, 217, 219
demographics, 205
economic conditions, 204-205, 206
feasibility studies, 212
financing, 209, 216-218
foreign investment policies, 209-211, 212, 213
government, 204, 205-206
history, 203-204
import/export trade partners, 207
insurance, 216
investment climate, 214
joint ventures, 215

ABOUT THE AUTHORS

OLIVER C. DZIGGEL

Oliver C. Dziggel is President of Enterprise Development International, Inc. (EDI), a high technology firm based in Washington, D.C. specializing in international business development and technology transfer in Eastern and Western Europe, Latin America, the Pacific Rim, and Africa. Prior to founding EDI, Mr. Dziggel managed MCI's antitrust litigations in the precedent-setting actions which resulted in the total restructuring of the U.S. telecom industry. He also achieved significant accomplishments with ITT WorldCom, International Data Corporation, and Booz-Allen & Hamilton. Mr. Dziggel earned his Masters degree in International Affairs from The George Washington University in Washington, D.C., and a Masters-equivalent in European integration from the Friedrich-Wilhelm Universitat in Bonn, Germany.

ALLYN ENDERLYN

Allyn Enderlyn is Senior Vice President and co-founder of Enterprise Development International, Inc. (EDI). She is Project Manager for the Telecommunications and Electronics Consortium in Eastern Europe (one of the five consortia of American businesses in Eastern Europe — CABEE — a component of the American Business and Private Sector Development Initiative, a joint effort of the Commerce Department and the Agency for International Development). The Telecommunications Industry Association is the recipient of that grant.

Ms. Enderlyn is the Executive Vice President of the National Association of Women Business Owners (NAWBO). She has also held leadership positions for the past fifteen years in other organizations. Ms. Enderlyn has co-authored numerous trade volumes for other regions of the world. She and Mr. Dziggel are currently writing a book on *Cracking Latin America*. She has a B.A. from The American University and an M.B.A. in Finance and Investments from The George Washington University.